SET...

*Journeys Through the Food,
Faith and Culture of Black
African London*

Jimi Famurewa

BLOOMSBURY CONTINUUM
LONDON · OXFORD · NEW YORK · NEW DELHI · SYDNEY

BLOOMSBURY CONTINUUM
Bloomsbury Publishing Plc
50 Bedford Square, London, WC1B 3DP, UK
29 Earlsfort Terrace, Dublin 2, Ireland

BLOOMSBURY, BLOOMSBURY CONTINUUM and the Diana logo are
trademarks of Bloomsbury Publishing Plc

First published in Great Britain 2022
Paperback 2023

A catalogue record for this book is available from the British Library

Library of Congress Cataloguing-in-Publication data has been applied for

ISBN: PB: 978-1-4729-9156-0; eBook: 978-1-4729-9152-2; ePDF: 978-1-4729-9154-6

2 4 6 8 10 9 7 5 3 1

Typeset by Deanta Global Publishing Services, Chennai, India
Printed and bound in Great Britain by CPI Group (UK) Ltd, Croydon CR0 4YY

To find out more about our authors and books visit www.bloomsbury.com
and sign up for our newsletters

For Madeleine, Dylan and Remi. And for my late, beloved uncle, Jibola Oyeyinka – a man who opened up our city and our world.

Praise for *Settlers*

'As thrilling as it is touching and revealing – this book is an indispensable map to London today.'

Ben Judah, journalist and author of *This is London:*
Life and Death in the World City

'Illuminating and fascinating, with humour and some surprises, Jimi Famurewa examines Britain's African communities, past and present.'

Stephen Bourne, author of *Black Poppies:*
Britain's Black Community and the Great War

'Jimi brings modern black London alive like no other author. This feels like an important book that is also a total pleasure to read.'

Sathnam Sanghera, author of *Empireland:*
How Modern Britain is Shaped by its Imperial Past

'*Settlers* is the book I didn't know I was waiting for. Jimi Famurewa approaches an incredibly complicated topic with a steady hand and fine precision that results in a book that is well researched, rich in nuance and handled with care. It was as enjoyable to read as it was enlightening.'

Jendella Benson, author of *Hope & Glory*

'[Jimi's] voice and the way he writes I just love.'

Jamie Oliver

'Settlers is a testament to Jimi Famurewa's love not just for his lineage, but for the culture. An incisive, intimate and profound work.'

Candice Carty-Williams, author of *Queenie* and *People Person*

'This is an extraordinary and beautifully written piece of work that deals with a deeply complex and rich history with a remarkable lightness of touch, sensitivity, warmth and insight. It is depressing to reflect on the reality that all too many people continue to question the benefits of immigration. This fine book shows beyond any doubt that London, and this country, is all the better for its Black African population.'

James Ramsden

'A spellbinding portrait of culture, talent, food and activism.'

Stylist Magazine

'*Settlers* is replete with revealing anecdotes… Famurewa's writing is thoughtful, cogent and admirably even-handed.'

theguardian.com

'Dazzling.'

Waitrose Food Magazine

'*Settlers* is a pleasure to read, by turns lyrical, approachable, funny, sensitive and always well-researched… [Famurewa] sweeps you along so thoroughly that you don't realise until you close the book quite how much you have enjoyed it, how much you have learnt and how much it will stay with you.'

The Spectator

Contents

But how could I, tropical African,
Who claim the sun as my authentic sire,
Find beauty in that chilling atmosphere?
Ancestral intellect could help me bear
A little while, but surely not admire
The civilisation of the Englishman.

Claude McKay, *London*

Prologue

The Second Great Wave

Where is Black African life in London?

If you know the modern city then you will know that it is at once everywhere and nowhere; both an undeniable fact of the landscape and something unlikely to be set down on an Underground map or marked by official signage. Head north and you can find it in the strip-lit glare of tutoring businesses on Tottenham High Road, or out in Hayes, heralded by green Dahabshiil signs advertising money transfer to Somalia. In the south, it is the woman clicking her way to a Thamesmead community hall, in party heels and sparkling Nigerian native wear. Or the Brixton street preacher, imploring an ambivalent passing crowd to repent through a speaker intended for karaoke.

Black African presence can be glimpsed in the whir of seamstresses at work in tiny doorway operations off Dalston's Ridley Road Market, smelled in the spice-prickled puff of barbecued croaker fish drifting on the Old Kent Road air and heard in the eavesdropped snippets of Nigerian Yoruba, Ghanaian Twi, Ugandan-accented

Swahili and Sierra Leonean Krio ricocheting on the street. Once, this life would have been tucked away and out of sight. Hidden in the form of private card games among turn-of-the-century Somali seamen, interwar hostels established for West African students and prayer meetings in the council flat front rooms of the 1970s. But now, it spills out and bursts forth. Now, this African London is kinetic and ever-expanding, stretching out and beyond the city's hazy border like something that cannot be wholly contained. Not just as people but as architecture. As listed former cinemas, bingo halls, pubs and banks that now bear the names of newly planted Pentecostal churches and stand as looming monuments to a quiet sort of urban conquest.

Yes, if you know the city then you will know that modern Black African presence is an inescapable reality, strewn in every corner. But look for scholarship, exploration or historical record of this life and things become a little less clear. History books about Black British settlement – whether they are the scattering of publications released throughout the latter half of the twentieth century or the swelling post-2010s wave that coincided with a broader period of reappraisal and re-education with regard to race – tend to focus on modern Africans as a subcategory of a larger Black whole; one thread woven into a predominantly Caribbean social tapestry.

In fact, Black UK residents directly drawn from Africa have only existed in an official sense for just over 30 years. Until the 1991 census introduced 'Black African' as an option on its identity menu, we were not considered worthy of specific categorization. One reason for this is the simple fact of numbers: Black

Africans, at that particular point in British history, did not have the same immigrant population size or cultural presence as Afro-Caribbeans. But another is that – given the nascent Black British community was generally forged in the fires of a hostile, structurally racist post-war society – political solidarity was more important than quibbling over the specific source of your Blackness. It is only in the last 40 years that 'Black', both as a term and a political idea, has fully ceased to apply to South Asian Brits. The thinking that created this glomming together of ethnicities is obvious enough: in the face of landlords, employers and police whose bigotry didn't specify, a certain monolithic solidarity was vital.

But I think this phenomenon as it applies to Black Africans – namely, the surprising absence of modern Africans in many of the official chronicles of Black British life – is a by-product of something else: the wider collective attempt to move the conversation about Black settlement and presence in the UK away from the symbolic enormity of the *Empire Windrush*. Because, of course, beyond its status as the undoubted creation myth of Black life in the UK, this ship's 1948 arrival was the continuation rather than the beginning of Britain's Black immigrant narrative.

Peter Fryer's seminal 1984 book *Staying Power* opens with the arresting statement that 'There were Africans in Britain before the English came here'. The fact is that whether it was the North African soldiers who established a third-century Roman settlement near Hadrian's Wall, the African merchants who were fixtures in Georgian London, or the Black political agitators and intellectuals who turned the metropole into their home, pulpit and playground in the 1930s,

Blackness in Britain has a history and a lineage beyond the mythic mid-century arrivals that followed 1948's British Nationality Act.

Fryer and the other historians who have stood on his shoulders — not just *Staying Power* but the likes of *Black Tudors* by Miranda Kauffman, *Black Poppies* by Stephen Bourne and, perhaps most impactfully, *Black and British* by David Olusoga — have given us an important rebuke to the postcolonial view that Black Britons are recent arrivals with no significant claim on the land. Or that they are interlopers who can simply be told to go back where they came from. 'We are here, because you were there,' as the British-Sri Lankan novelist A. Sivanandan put it, with enviable economy.

Yet, to my mind, this noble effort to excavate the pre-*Windrush* history of Black Britishness has, however inadvertently, somewhat diminished the attention paid to more recent stories. In looking further back, we perhaps miss the social shifts happening right under our noses. This is not to suggest that significant moments from the last 50 years of Black history in this country — from the trial of the Mangrove Nine and the tragic death of Stephen Lawrence to the Covid-masked social uprising of 2020 — have gone unexamined. It is rather that the breadth of Black experience, and the increasingly dominant presence of Black Africans, hasn't always been reflected in how we look at race and Britishness today. Even Olusoga himself, right near the close of *Black and British*, acknowledges this point — that there has been a shift in the demography of Britain's Black population that has not been fully recognized. The Black Africans who have come to Britain since the 1980s are, in Olusoga's words, part of 'a second great wave of Black migration . . . that has largely gone unnoticed'.

It's an observation borne out by the updated immigration statistics: 2011 census figures revealed that Black Africans had officially become the UK's dominant Black group, doubling in number during the preceding decade as growth within the longer-established Caribbean community steadied. Projections for the 2022 census show that, in London alone, Black Africans now represent the third largest ethnic group (after White British and White Other). This, of course, was the kind of thing that anyone who had actually spent time in a city like London – who had walked down streets that have been subtly and steadily transformed by African presence in recent years – could have told you for free. And yet there seems, to my mind, to have been a lack of specific curiosity about the UK's largest Black group; about the circumstances that precipitated their arrival, their growing influence on the country, and how they have both fundamentally altered and been altered by their surroundings.

This book was born from that unscratched itch of curiosity. Not to diminish the importance of the collective Black British story but to enhance it through a sharper focus and subtle disaggregation; to look at how the early-1980s arrival of my own parents here, and its place among countless airport arrivals during that decade and beyond, slots into a broader jigsaw puzzle of Black settlement in the UK. And, with that, to learn what it says about where we've been, where we are now, and where we might be going.

Because the story of Black African life in this country, and in this city, has a ripple effect far beyond the visible reality of a few businesses on a high street. And as I'm moved to remind myself – as I drink in the intensely African sensory overload of Peckham High Street or Seven Sisters or Walworth Road – there's a vast chasm between seeing something and actually understanding it.

I owe the fact that I grew up in Britain to the twin brother and sister I never got to meet. In 1982, my mum – living in Nigeria and already a mother of two – was six months pregnant when she prematurely went into labour and was informed, after two days in the relative chaos of a Lagos maternity ward, that her babies had not survived. Psychologically scarred by the experience (and what she saw as medical negligence on the part of her Nigerian doctors), she resolved never to give birth – or attempt to – in the country again.

And so, when she fell pregnant with me, early the following year, it would be London that she would travel to. It had always been a place she would visit frequently, like many other Nigerians of her generation and class. At a time when the Nigerian economy was cratering, London signified escape and attainable glamour; time spent with London-based relatives, shopping trips and suitcases filled to bursting with things that couldn't be found at home. In October 1983, I was born here – without incident – in Edgware General Hospital. And, thanks to my older brother's need for a hip operation a few years later – coupled with the high esteem my parents' generation always had for the British schooling system – London began to present itself by default as a kind of home.

Though this origin story is mine and mine alone, the broad strokes of it are not rare. Access to more reliable healthcare, better education, societal stability and greater opportunities for your offspring: these were the prime motivators prompting many West Africans to make the move to the UK in the post-war era. First, the mid-century trickle that followed the independence of West African countries (notably, Ghana's pioneering break from Empire rule in 1957). And then, as the 1980s and 1990s arrived, as a burst-dam deluge that saw a class of Nigerians, Ghanaians and Sierra Leoneans especially establish themselves here. In turn, they were followed by Ugandans, Somalis, Zimbabweans and others who came to alter the cultural framework of African London.

But less important than the arrival of people like my parents was the context of how they ended up here. And in this sense, our journey and eventual settlement are part of a broader narrative stretching back centuries. Though I never questioned why my Nigerian family – and other Black Africans just like us – had ended up in the cold, dense sprawl of a Western European city, I now know we had been shepherded there by the centuries-long domino trail of circumstance. First, by the scramble for Africa and years of colonial rule, then by the post-war civil training vacuum in newly independent countries, and the volatile geopolitics that burned across various patches of the continent from the 1960s onwards (in itself a symptom of African nations' struggle to assert themselves in a postcolonial world). All these forces had worked to put me where I ended up, growing up in a suburban house on the south-eastern outer rim of London, far away from the land and reality of my ancestors. Diaspora is a word we use to denote an immigrant population away from its traditional homeland. But that it also suggests dispersal, displacement and exile is instructive. There is no untainted and uncolonized version of the mother country to return to. I am here because they were there.

And I began to notice that I was not the only one. Both in the micro of my personal life and the highly visible macro of wider society, there were, all at once it seemed, prominent Black figures who shared this broad, African prehistory. Anthony Joshua and Bukayo Saka in the world of sport; David Adjaye and Edward Enninful in the sphere of design and fashion; Michaela Coel and Daniel Kaluuya from acting, plus Stormzy and Dave and Little Simz (and innumerable other acclaimed musicians) from a British music scene that, though it drew strongly from Afro-Caribbean traditions, felt suddenly tuned to the specific frequencies and argot of Black African culture at its loudest and proudest. That beaming West African mothers are now such a regular fixture on award show red carpets and stages tells its own story.

Even taking into account the Afrocentric blinkers that tend to be the birthright of all Nigerians in particular, something significant and undeniable was happening; a widespread social uprising of sorts that didn't appear to have a parallel. And over the past half decade or so, from my unique vantage point as a Black features journalist – which is to say, the person that well-intentioned White magazine editors would increasingly send along to interview practically anyone Black – I began to shape an accidental chronicle of this specifically African renaissance.

Or, to put it another way, I compared notes. And through that comparison – with chefs and writers, artists and actors – a shared picture began to coalesce.

This meant the small incidental ways in which the great migratory wave of Black Africans built their lives and homes; the formative domestic world of unofficial 'cousins', blipping cauldrons of stew, bucket baths and floors swept with traditional African, palm-frond brooms. But it also meant discussing the larger, ineffable things that had shaped us: the focus on education as a means to prosper within a rigged system; the fact that faith formed a central pillar of our lives; the ragtag family units – occasionally supplemented by additional visiting relatives and generally ruled by overworked, lone matriarchs.

It would be folly to try to cast individual families from distinct countries, ethnic groups and regions across a vast, wildly diverse 54-nation continent as in any way homogeneous. But through conducting this unofficial conversational census with other members of my own broad diaspora, I found that there were central principles drawing us together. And that the ways in which our Britishness and Africanness sat side by side formed a distinct history that was casting a longer and longer cultural shadow. Yes, two long decades after Black Africans had become an official descriptive category in the UK, they had implanted themselves on the consciousness in all sorts of different, fascinating ways. And there was something there to explore. But first, I would have to make my own peace with a heritage that I hadn't always gripped quite so tightly.

So, where is Black African life in London? Well, if you go solely by people's Christian names, then it can be hard to spot it. Just as the West Indian passengers on the *Windrush* and subsequent settler vessels proudly cloaked themselves in the styles of the English motherland – wearing sharp suits on their frames and even sharper side-partings in their neatly trimmed Afros – so too did the first middle-class arrivals from independent African countries adopt the social costume of their new post-colonial home. They gave themselves Western names that could be more easily pronounced by their White countrymen. If they had the means, they sent their children to the same respectable, fee-paying schools as the English aristocracy. And, in some cases, they even privately fostered their offspring with White families that could, in theory, provide an invaluable societal education alongside long-term childcare in an unfamiliar land.

But the crucial factor in all this is that, in my experience, this Englishness was very much a superficial means to an end; an evolved way to prosper in a society that the first generation of Black African immigrants (in the same manner as those smiling, hope-filled passengers on the *Windrush*) very quickly understood to be systemically racist. Our social costume was just that – costume, to be thrown on and shrugged off depending on the demands of the spaces we occupied.

Because where it counted – in our values, our sense of self, our food, our culture and the standards of betterment we had to uphold – we were never allowed to forget that we were Africans first. Not Brits. Not even merely Black. But Africans, who had access to traditions, heritage, names and language that formed an unbroken link back to something important.

Still, to my mind, this attitude of African exceptionalism throws up its own challenges and a complicated legacy that comes from attempting to transfer an at times rigid way of living to a new land. There is a cultural dissonance at the heart of the British Black African experience; a tension that touches on everything from the feelings of abandonment felt by those Black children who were privately fostered with White families to a struggle to push difficult family issues – of mental ill health, marriage breakdown, incarceration, sex, gender and sexuality – through the prism of unbending traditional African values.

Throw in the fact of a 1980s and 1990s era where the dominant pop cultural depictions of Blackness were either Afro-Caribbean (meaning African-heritage Caribbeans) or African American, and you start to get a sense of the strange dichotomy at the heart of an entire generation's relationship to their African heritage. On the one hand, it was a source of bulletproof pride and security; the anchoring ballast of knowing yourself, your community, your place in the world and the sacrifices your parents had made to set you on this path of opportunity. On the other – when bundled together with cartoonish African stereotypes in popular culture – this part of your identity could make you a moving target in the playground. Or it could simply be something you viewed with ambivalence, tipping over, perhaps, into shame, embarrassment and secrecy. For a long time, to be 'African' was many things. But – set against the culturally defining Blackness of, say, Bob Marley – it was never, ever cool.

It is a sentiment I'm sure many Black African Londoners who were the first generation born in the UK were acquainted with. And, again, you only need to look at the mini biographies encoded in what we call ourselves. My full name is Olufolajimi Oluwadamilola

Famurewa – an almost overwhelmingly Nigerian collision of syllables, rich with meaning and significance in relation to my Yoruba heritage. But around the time of my birth in that North London hospital, my mother and father had decreed that my English name would be 'Roger'. This was the case throughout primary school until I decided, at the age of around 11, to adopt the lightly Anglicized pet form of my first name and relegate 'Roger' to a middle name. It is nowhere near my birth certificate, but it still appears on official pieces of NHS correspondence like a ghost of some former life; 'Jimi Roger Famurewa' – a strange cut-and-shut, reflecting the jamming together of different consciousnesses and cultures. And perhaps the fact that, thanks to the butterfly-wing flap of the time and place I was born, my African ancestry was something I felt the need to at least partially conceal or soften; a part of myself I had to gradually find my way back to.

Duly, the more I started to reflect on this journey – namely, the shift from my African heritage being an occasional social embarrassment to something I wanted to celebrate and proclaim from the proverbial rooftops – the more I recognized prominent British Africans, those heralds of a diasporic cultural revolution, ruminating on their own paths. The Nigerian-born playwright Inua Ellams set the darkness, light and crackling wit of the Black African barbershop before packed crowds at the National Theatre. Michaela Coel used an episode of *I May Destroy You*, her auteurist, BAFTA-winning BBC One series, to probe the intricacies of a non-conventional, British–Ghanaian family set-up. The innovative podcaster George The Poet won listeners (plus a Peabody Award and a spurned MBE) for, among other things, throwing a spotlight on the supportive toughness of his Ugandan mother's parental approach.

Again, I could go on. Search practically every corner of modern life in Britain over the past five years and you will find the descendants of that second great wave of Black African migration weighing their distinct history – its glories, its gifts, its limits – and excavating the results. Viewed from a certain angle, all of this art, these books and albums and films and TV shows, resembles one long process of both personal and public cultural reclamation.

And as I watched this sample size grow, and saw the entire notion of Black African British history gain a visibility and prominence that wasn't matched by many serious attempts to unpack it, my mind swarmed with questions I did not have easily available answers to. What, if anything, unites the diverse cohort of Black Africans who have settled in London and other parts of the UK? Do the African families that have recently followed their White forbears by drifting to London's leafy orbital suburbs feel fully part of those communities? And to what extent – more than 2,000 years after those African Roman soldiers were temporarily garrisoned in a spot near Cumbria – do we think of this place as a permanent home?

The book you hold in your hands formed as a response to those questions and many more like them. It is my attempt to venture both outside and within to sketch a living map of a cultural terrain that has remained stubbornly uncharted. Its name, *Settlers,* emerged naturally, as I kept seeing that word used in literature about immigrant communities in the UK. The notion of settling denotes a sense of steadfastness, of compromise, and of claiming something as your own. It has a certain quiet defiance and reversal of colonial occupation that feels appropriate. I can think of no better word or way to describe the people that inspire the stories and contemplations that you're about to read.

But before we fully embark, I suppose one of the more important things I need to do is to deal with the questions that a reader may reasonably be muttering aloud right now; to get my caveats, qualifying statements and excuses in early. The first thing to acknowledge is that 'Black African London', in this context and any, is an elastic concept. Black African is a census term but I generally prefer its directness to the euphemism of, say, 'Sub-Saharan'. But Africa, as you may have heard, is quite big. And so attempting to fully reflect the British diaspora experience of every majority Black nation in the second biggest and most populous continent in the world – never mind the nuances of different cultures, tribes and colonial influences within each country and region – is an impossible task.

But, equally, to limit my gaze to the social impact of, say, just Ghanaians or Nigerians seems wrong; a fast route to erasing the significance, just for example, of Londoners drawn from East Africa, the unique plight and stigma faced by Africans who came to the UK as political refugees from Central Africa, and glossing over the profound, Pan-African cultural links that go beyond lines drawn on a map. There are perhaps other broad groups I could have limited my focus to – Nigerian London? West African London? – but I find that each one doesn't quite feel like a satisfactory reflection of the Black African crossover, solidarity and interaction evident throughout London's history or my own personal experience of the community. I grew up in a house where my mother's friends were Ghanaians and Tanzanians as well as Nigerians, and for a brief period we had a Gambian lodger. To be both Black and African is, in my experience, to be part of an important, long-lasting and ever-evolving form of kinship.

My aim, then, will be to attempt this daunting task unburdened by any notion that I could ever truly succeed; to convey a Black African London that feels like an emotionally accurate portrait rather than a fastidious census. Yes, my personal heritage has undoubtedly given things a West African emphasis; I am a Yoruba Nigerian and my views inevitably reflect this. But, given much of Britain's most sustained immigration from Africa has come from its former colonies in West Africa (namely Ghana, Nigeria and Sierra Leone), my hope is that this will ultimately feel true to the spirit of the city.

The other thing to mention is where Afro-Caribbean culture sits alongside all this. Though one aim of this book is to carve out a distinct space for the African experience amid a Black Britishness that can often default to a *Windrush*-adjacent, West Indian story, it is about unity rather than any sort of unhelpful division of a Black community with far more deep similarities than superficial differences. The triumph of the ascendent class of Black Brits currently on billboards, TVs and multiplex screens – most clearly expressed in the form of grime, drill, rap, Afrobeats and its surrounding creative ecosystems – is, in many ways, a story of African and Caribbean cultural cross-pollination; a mutual melding that, in everything from food to fashion, is yielding a new, strikingly confident and proud form of hybrid Black identity. I intend to honour this culture and show, where relevant, the rocky historical path of wariness, misunderstanding and occasional infighting that Black Brits had to navigate to get to this position of galvanized strength. Ultimately, this is a book about Black British history as a whole, with Afro-Caribbean influence right at the forefront of that. At each juncture, I have merely applied a specifically Black African lens and examined what it shows us.

Naturally, my version of Black African London will differ vastly from that of someone born in an even slightly different postcode, time or social circumstance. I am, in many ways, a product of the majority-White environment and implicitly White culture that I grew up in: outwardly English enough to be a figure of lightly amused fascination among the Nigerian-born members of my family but conspicuously African in the eyes of the rest of the world. In this sense, I journey through the history of Black African London as both native and tourist.

But I do so with the faith that the only way to tell this story is by putting the personal in a political context. I do so with the knowledge that my shifting sense of what it has meant to be a Black African over the past 30 years chimes with a broader, collective evolution in how we all parse – and, generally, celebrate – our individual immigrant or cultural identities. And I do so with the sense that there has never been a more urgent or pressing need to better understand what it is to be Black in the UK.

And so, where is Black African life in London? I caught an unexpected glimpse of it, in early 2018, when I attended a few sessions of a Yoruba language class, run out of a drab community centre, hidden amid the surrounding grandeur of London's Covent Garden.

I had signed up for the classes because I wanted to refresh my dwindling knowledge of what is my ancestral tongue, while also writing about the experience.

Those sessions – led by an exacting, infectiously passionate Yoruba man who asked that we call him 'Chief K' – soon took the form of a kind of support group for lapsed Nigerians. The half a dozen or so of us who meekly shuffled in on a Saturday afternoon would spout our mangled Yoruba phrases, read from textbooks and engage in halting conversations. We would reveal the circumstances that had brought us there to relocate this mislaid part of ourselves. And we would talk philosophically about Nigeria and about the UK, about bad service in West African restaurants and whether the language we had ostensibly come there to learn was truly endangered. We would, in other words, talk about that city-within-a-city; the one we saw flashes of where others didn't know to look.

I perhaps did not attend those lessons for as long as I should have but, nonetheless, I got what I needed from them. I realized that Black African London can be accessed through the people who have passed through it and are, even now, stretching the concept of what it can be. I also sensed that greater understanding of some of the challenges still facing Britain's Black population – structural racism, the legacy of empire, social inequality and the disproportionate impact of the coronavirus pandemic – could come through this unwritten history; through looking beyond the simple markers of Black African settlement and paying more attention to the forces that actually put them there.

My intention in the first throes of writing this book had been to accentuate the positive; to compose a purposefully celebratory and joyous snapshot of Black African diaspora culture. And it is indeed that. But, of course, you cannot spend much time delving into Black British history without encountering the continuing horrors, indignities and challenges that still, lamentably, are the backbeat of so much of Black life in this country and around the world. Racism and socioeconomic disadvantage can feel like an inescapable gravitational pull. But what you learn is that the Black British – and the Black African – story is one of finding ways to creatively defy that gravity time and time again.

So, come, let us go. Let us walk with unwrinkled noses past the market stalls piled high with plantain, cassava, cow foot and strung garlands of stockfish, through restaurants, Congolese pubs and Hennessy-soaked South African *amapiano* clubs, past those tutoring businesses and into the congregation of those megachurches; let us brush our fingers across those Yoruba surnames etched on the honour roll lists of illustrious fee-paying schools, track the dark-skinned women going from a nocturnal cleaning job to a daytime desk, and venture out to the perimeter of the city, where pie-and-mash parlours now sit next to suya spots and *waakye* joints. The city surrenders its secrets if you delve deep enough. And this one has more than most.

Farm

'Pretty baby girl needs a new home.'

Nursery World (1971)

Kemi Martins' foster mother used to tell her a story about her childhood; a story that helped explain what it was like to be the White English parent of a Black African child. Martins was a baby when it happened, so it would have been the early 1970s. Her foster mum was pushing her in a pram through Canvey Island, the blustery seaside settlement where she lived with her foster siblings, when she spotted a mirrored version of herself approaching from the other direction. Another White woman; another gurgling, conspicuously fostered Black baby in a pushchair.

There was a nervous, excited flash of recognition, like two VW Campervan drivers waggling awkward hand signals at each other on the motorway. 'This other woman apparently went, "Ooh, you've got one as well",' says Martins, with a laugh, telling me the story half a century later. 'And then she said, "What do you feed yours?"' Martins leaves a beat, raises an eyebrow. 'And my foster mum said, "Well, they just have the same food that we have." To which this woman said, "Oh, I just cook boiled rice for mine. That's all they have."' There is another careful pause, a disbelieving chuckle. 'Needless to say my foster mum was incredulous. And she sent this woman off with a bit of a flea in her ear about how disgusting it was – [that] you could just give your kids boiled rice all the time. But it was quite interesting to hear that story, given that my fostering experience was so positive.'

It feels, on the face of it, like a particularly strange and unsettling vignette. A baroque instance of ill-informed prejudice and unexpected cultural collision distinctive enough to stick out even amid the notoriously intolerant landscape of 1970s Britain (in 1974, the National Front – who called for the compulsory deportation of non-White settlers and their descendants – fielded a then record 90 candidates in local elections). But perhaps the most striking thing about the story that Martins (not her real name) was told by her foster mother is that it is not unusual at all. In the wake of the Second World War, thanks to a perfect storm of societal factors, it became commonplace for African immigrants establishing themselves in the UK to privately foster their children with White families. Martins' account as a British–Nigerian woman whose formative years were spent with beloved, White English carers paid for by her birth parents, is just one example among many.

In fact, to merely call it commonplace is perhaps to undersell it. From the moment of a first 1955 advert placed by a Nigerian family in the childcare journal *Nursery World*, there was an explosion in demand. As a later listing in 1971 read: 'Pretty baby girl needs a new home.' By 1956 the magazine had introduced a regular Homes Wanted section in the classified ads, and in the period between 1966 and 1970, 6,700 adverts were placed by West African parents seeking carers for their children. Though official figures on the number of approved agreements are hazy, a 1968 story in *The Times* reported that up to 5,000 children from West Africa were being fostered – or 'farmed', as it came to be informally known – in this way every year. By 1974 it was claimed that 60 per cent of the 10,000 privately fostered children in Britain were the offspring of African students. The British–Nigerian actor and director Adewale Akinnuoye-Agbaje, whose personal and professional life has been decisively shaped by the experience, and ensuing trauma, of being farmed to a White family in 1970s Tilbury, put it in even starker terms: in a 2019 interview, he speculated that well over half of all British-born Nigerian children would have been temporarily sent away from their families to be cared for by English foster parents.

And so, set against this backdrop, Kemi Martins' story feels less like an outlier and more like one thread in a vast, multifaceted tapestry; another tale to add to hundreds and hundreds of others that, collectively, form a powerful shared testimony about what it was – and is – to be both Black African and British. In the public sphere, that interlude between Martins' foster mother and the woman who fed her child only rice can be bracketed alongside countless other stories that have been shared, slowly but surely, in recent years.

Not unexpectedly, some of these stories are of unthinkable prejudice, abuse and a kind of traumatizing cultural disorientation; of Afro-textured hair left to grow unkempt and knotted because White foster parents didn't know what to do with it; of Black children forced to eat their meals off the floor like domesticated animals; of being singled out, demeaned and – in the case of Akinnuoye – spat at by a racist policeman when you were just five years old. These horrifying accounts perhaps reach their nadir in the real-life case of a child like Tower Ibikunle: a five-year-old West African boy whose White carers were charged with abuse in 1965 after he was discovered locked in a cellar, missing part of his toes from frostbite.

That such suffering would be so widespread is unthinkable. And yet, it was not always negative. For some, being farmed to a White foster family was a short-lived, benign experience; an unusual, temporary engagement to be filed away deep in the memory, and only jogged loose years later. In this sense, private foster parents were just one presence on the long production line of a child's early life.

And it is this point that brings us to the nub of what those generations of post-war African parents were thinking – and helps us, perhaps, to make more sense of an act (the giving away of your children to paid strangers in a foreign land) that is hard to justify when viewed through a modern, Western lens. Or as Joy Okoye, a barrister and transracial adoption specialist, put it in a 2001 *Guardian* interview:

> West African children, unlike their European counterparts, are not seen as possessions of a nuclear family. In Africa, it takes a village to raise a child – and very often a village miles away from the family home. It is normal, extended family kinship and the children placed away from home accepted it as such.

And yet, as we know, replicating this communal, rural form of child rearing in an unfamiliar metropolis came with its own unexpected difficulties and psychological reverberations. Not just in the chilling instances of abuse that we have heard about. But, often, through fostering stories that, like Kemi Martins', were the precise opposite: unambiguously positive experiences in which children's lives were enriched by caregivers who adored them as though they were their own and felt the same love flow back. 'My brother and I called [our foster parents] Mummy and Daddy, with their surnames to differentiate from our birth parents,' says Martins, by way of explanation. 'And they treated us as though we were their own kids. There was no element of, "You're the foster kids, you get second best."'

Naturally, this level of closeness posed a problem for what was supposed to be merely a transactional, temporary arrangement. Having been sent away while their parents finished their studies, saved money, found appropriate housing or, more broadly, got themselves situated, farmed children were mostly meant to return to their birth parents. But the emotional toll of being raised by someone else rarely made it that simple. The bonds forged between some of these children and their supposed foster parents were hard to break. And so when it came time to leave the figurative village of their fostering experience – to go and join their birth family in some other part of the UK or, on plenty of occasions, back in Nigeria or Ghana – understandably, many of them didn't want to go. Or, at the very least, they regarded what should have been a happy reunion, a restoring of the natural order, with pure dread.

'I had a really happy upbringing with my foster parents,' continues Martins. 'So the thought of going to live with my other mum and dad was almost like a shadow. A foreboding feeling. I knew it was coming and, if I'm honest, it was never something I was looking forward to at all. It was a pivotal moment in my life – to have to go back having had this happy time.'

When it is put in these terms, it's easy to see why there are multiple reports of African children who simply refused to leave the life and culture they knew in order to join biological parents who – despite regular visits – would often be relative strangers. Or that a mid-1970s expansion of the custody rights afforded to foster parents (specifically an amendment made to the Children Act 1975) precipitated numerous legal battles over the rights to raise privately fostered African children. And that this change, in turn, bred a climate of fear and paranoia that prompted newly arrived Black African parents to hurriedly claim their offspring, lest they lose them forever to these idolized White caregivers.

So let us count it up. Children cruelly locked in basements and losing appendages to the biting cold; Black kids so accustomed to their White stand-in parents that the thought of returning to their own birth families prompted fear and trauma; byzantine custody battles that sound like the manifestation of every parent's worst nightmare. And, of course, all these unresolved issues of abandonment within so many British-Africans themselves, smouldering away for years like unextinguished embers. It goes without saying that the farming experiment, even at its mildest, was not the frictionless, emotionally detached arrangement that some envisioned. It was messy. And confusing. And its legacy is a long shadow that has loomed over a vast proportion of the UK's Black African diaspora for almost 70 years. By that token, and at the most basic level, there is much to be sifted from the experiences of people like Kemi Martins; much to be learned from those who lived these stories and now, after decades of near silence, are ready to share them.

But beyond the specific testimonies of those who were farmed there is, I think, something universal to be explored. Those of us raised with even one of our birth parents – or in what you could probably generously term a traditional family unit – cannot possibly speak to the unique strangeness of being raised in such an obviously fractured way. But the cultural dissonance felt so keenly by lots of privately fostered Black African children will chime with other second-generation kids who feel caught between identities; to be shaped by both African and English parents feels almost like a literalized version of an intangible sensation shared by millions of British-born Africans. And it is a feeling that is eloquently expressed in a Buzzfeed article by Tobi Oredein, a journalist who was farmed at ten days old and remained with her White foster parents for the bulk of her life. It is during a first trip to Nigeria – in the company of both her mothers – that Oredein has this wide-ranging epiphany about what it is to be not just a child of private fostering, but a hyphenated British-Nigerian: 'Why had I thought my "motherland" would fill the void of unfamiliarity, when I struggled to achieve the comfort I sought in

Nigerian communities in London? I knew England would never quite accept me as one of her own, but Nigeria couldn't either.'

In this reading, the grand, dysfunctional experiment of African private fostering is a lived metaphor; a means to better understand issues of belonging that are at the very heart of Black settlement in the UK. Looking at Kemi Martins or Tobi Oredein's experience – or that of the many, many other children who were pushed through this process and just about lived to tell the tale – reveals a reflected truth about life and identity in Britain to all of us. The extreme pragmatism of those African parents who arrived amid the rubble of war and empire left us with something absolutely no one banked on – a shared psychological scar that is only in recent years being prodded and examined.

For so many farmed kids, there was the simple fact of two families, two lives, two selves. And the convulsing, life-altering reality of what it was to be dragged from one into the other. Because for all these children who actually survived these experiences – the boy who grew up amid landed White English bohemians, the woman taken from her loving White foster parents by overzealous social workers, the shy young man so bludgeoned by small-town prejudice that in the 1980s he became a self-hating racist skinhead, and all the others – there has only ever been one question. And that question, of course, is: why?

To truly understand private fostering you must first understand the ebb and flow of West African settlement in the UK. And also, the evolving way that some of the twentieth century's first Black African Londoners were regarded by the country they wished to call home. Let us start with how the temporary status they were handed on arrival proved to be defining. We know now, of course, that Black presence in the UK has a variety and a lineage that stretches back well beyond the relative modernity of the twentieth century. It encompasses eighteenth-century sailors and merchants, Regency-era domestic servants and, in the case of the part-Moorish Queen Charlotte, an actual reigning monarch. But the prototypical image of the African in Britain – be it in seminal Black works like Sam Selvon's 1956 novel *The Lonely Londoners* or the Channel 4 sitcom *Desmond's* – is invariably of the perennial adult student, drawn to the heart of empire for the purposes of further education. And there is historical precedent for this abiding caricature.

As early as 1788, Liverpool was host to more than 50 African students. More visiting West African scholars arrived in the mid-nineteenth century; drawn to the metropole of the British Empire to train as lawyers, doctors and civil servants before, it was hoped, returning to take on key governmental roles in their native territories, having been civilized and coddled by their time in a supposedly modernizing Western society. By the 1920s, significant organizations like WASU – the West African Students' Union that established a 'home from home' hostel in North London and soon became a hugely influential political pressure group that made the case for racial equality and self-governance – had sprung up.

And then, come the post-Second World War wave of West African nations nudging towards independence, there was an even greater drive (given the relative non-existence of higher education in Africa) to invite African students to the UK to arm themselves with not just an education, but the vocational skills to run these fledgling countries. In this reading, Britain became a sort of colonial finishing school; a place where the heirs of ruling families would come for a brief period, often heavily assisted by the government's Colonial Office, before happily returning to their corner of the nascent commonwealth to assume power. By 1945, the trend had accelerated so much that the *West African Review* newspaper was moved to note that 'never have there been so many sons of Chiefs in Great Britain'. It was to be a mutually beneficial arrangement for both African rulers looking to accrue skills and British policymakers hoping to maintain political control in the colonies. There seemed, on the face of it, to be no downside.

But, of course, things didn't go completely to plan. Just like the post-*Windrush* Caribbeans who were stung by the harsh reality of their arrival in the gold-paved streets of their supposed 'Mother Country', many early Black African settlers were subject to a sudden, jerking reality check; profoundly changed and – more often than not – deeply traumatized by what they faced in the UK. On Britain's shores there was a sense of isolation and cultural dislocation. There were temptations to transgress with alcohol or illicit sexual relationships. There was the tightening vice of financial pressure. And there was, above it all, British society's bone-deep, unwavering racism: a wearying constant that manifested through the threat of physical violence, demoralizing depictions in the press, or widespread 'colour bar' policies that made everything from accommodation to basic socializing a challenge.

The daily indignities of this anti–Black sentiment carried a heavy emotional toll. Which meant that, by the 1950s and 1960s, it was commonplace for African students in London to experience real psychological distress, symptomized by mental exhaustion, psychosis and a form of specific breakdown (localized in Nigerian students in 1960) that came to be known as 'brain fag'. Stories like that of John Mensah Sarbah, the son of a Gold Coast political activist and barrister who suffered a mental breakdown as a student in 1940s London and was eventually repatriated to a psychiatric hospital in 1958, were picked over by psychiatrists and government officials in both Britain and West African countries. Broadly speaking, explanations ranged from the feeling that African overseas students were ill-equipped for the rigours of study to the stark differences of British culture (in the 1960s, a study by the Nigerian psychiatrist Amechi Anumonye theorized that African students were especially disturbed by exposure to sexual activity and alcohol). In some cases, especially as far as British authority figures were concerned, there was perhaps an element of medical over-diagnosis – one Nigerian student in this era was listed as mentally ill, in part because 'he appeared to have no money sense'. But the core truth remains. Too many West African students were emerging from the mincer of the metropole either permanently scarred, distressed and politically radicalized or unmoored and resentful of the Empire. This fed anxieties about the growing issue of student well-being, both in Africa and within the British government agencies tasked with managing the transition of an empire to the process of decolonization.

And so, in early 1955, when the Colonial Office announced that married overseas students staying for longer than nine months – at that point, overwhelmingly male – could bring their wives with them to Britain, there was a traceable line of logic to it. It wasn't just that the presence of these African wives would help allay societal jitters about interracial marriages between White British women and Black African men – long-standing fuel for race hate that had spiked with the arrival of African American GIs during the war years. It was also that, so the Colonial Office hoped, the presence of these wives would offer a useful link to home for the students. It was a doubling-down on the British state's intention to offer moral education to its colonial subjects, and it was hoped it would also have a pacifying effect on the Communist politics gaining traction among some West African student groups. As the historian Jordanna Bailkin notes in her vital chronicle of this period, *The Afterlife of Empire*, the aim of this new policy was to keep African male students 'sexually and politically quiescent'.

So then, naturally, when the inevitable by-product of reunited husbands and wives occurred – which is to say, babies were born in Britain to Africans whose stay was always supposed to be temporary, and whose focus was training and study – it was a problem that needed solving. That same year, 1955, in what can be read as the Big Bang of the modern farming movement, that fateful issue of *Nursery World* published the first advert seeking private foster care for an African baby. And so it proved that a government-backed means to both support and control overseas students – to manage the extent to which these temporary guests would be impacted by their time in the metropole – precipitated an arrangement that would bind African and English, Black and White, together for decades to come.

But having a deeper understanding of the how of private fostering does not necessarily bring us any closer to making sense of the why. What caused it to persist as an arrangement? And what were those on either side of the transaction really getting out of it? Let us start with the White, often working-class, families that answered the adverts like that first one in *Nursery World*. Obviously, the financial benefits of paid wardship were a huge lure. Records show that families in the 1960s could make as much as £3 a week for taking in fostered children (the equivalent of around £60 today). In fact, public discourse at the time characterized it as a kind of sinister racket among White working-class women, with pearl-clutching press headlines fretting about 'Babies for Hire' and shiftless young women 'Squeezing Gold from Babies'.

True, money was almost certainly a prime motivator for a lot of the women. Especially when you factor in the potential ostracization and prejudice they would have faced for taking in Black children at a time when racial tensions were so high. This, after all, was an era where the summer of 1958 had brought anti-Black rioting in Notting Hill and, by 1964, Conservative MP Peter Griffiths won the Smethwick seat at the general election while promising to lobby for the repatriation of 'the coloureds'. But there is evidence that many of these White foster parents – occasionally childless or with grown-up children of their own and an appreciable paternal or maternal void – took these children in for reasons that weren't related to finances. Or rather, guided either by faith or simply their principles, they did it because of a sense that it was the right thing to do. That certainly describes the situation of Lola Jaye, who was taken in, as a six-week-old baby, in the mid-1970s by London-based pensioners with a long-standing history of privately fostering West African children.

'My nan had been fostering since the 1960s, so long before my time,' explains Jaye, a British-Nigerian author and therapist who, bar a brief, tumultuous return to her birth family as an adolescent, spent all of her childhood being raised by 'Nan and Ted' in Blackfriars. 'Her first foster children were children that had to move here because of the Biafran War. So that's when she started and, from then, it was just word of mouth in a small community of Nigerians who came here to work and study. Nan actually ended up looking after my cousins, who are ten years older than me, so she was looking after people in my family long before I was born.'

This kind of long-lasting relationship can't be explained away as merely an emotionless transaction between two disenfranchised groups. And that's doubly true when you note that, in Jaye's telling, the money her nan received was 'paltry'. Similarly, in a 1965 newsreel probing the phenomenon of private fostering, a Devon-based woman called Mrs Arnett explains her devotion to her many Nigerian foster children despite the fact that taking them in has meant sacrifice and financial constraints. 'So far I've used up all my husband's bank money,' says Mrs Arnett, with a slight, crooked-toothed smile in the black-and-white clip, flanked by half a dozen adorable Nigerian toddlers and perched before a crackling fire. 'I've had to give up things like [the] pictures, and hairdos, and cigarettes and anything for myself.'

What's striking is that this isn't said with any discernible resentment or anger. Rather, it carries the sleeves-up stolidness and pragmatism exhibited by the cash-strapped matriarchs of other, far more conventional large families. Mrs Arnett may be an anomaly in terms of the sheer depth of her desire to offer a home to the children of African strangers. (It is notable that, during the film, she mentions that it is only recent intervention from the welfare authorities that has prevented her from taking on even more than the 11 wards she has.) But her story and attitude show that, amid the tales of abuse and the unprepared White families upholding this odd, shadowy legacy for £3 a week, there were perhaps just as many White foster families whose motives were nothing more than straightforward compassion, and a lovestruck feeling that wasn't easily rationalized. Or as Mrs Arnett herself finally explains, as the newsreel presenter tries one last time to understand her strange compulsion for providing temporary, transracial foster care while practically beggaring herself in the process: 'It's my life. It's hard, but it's what I want in life.'

But what of the West Africans who entrusted their children, often when they were merely a few weeks old, to these people? What was there to be gained from the arrangement, beyond the initial desperate need for childcare? And why did farming continue well into the 1980s and 1990s, even after West Africans had presumably established some of the family networks they had lacked in the previous decades? Truthfully, it was an equally complicated transaction on the African side. On the one hand, there is evidence that aspirational, upper-middle-class West Africans quite liked the idea of having paid help, and English paid help at that. Nigerians especially were coming from a society where domestic servants, in the form of the live-in 'house boys' and 'house girls' who cook, clean and perform other menial tasks of the home, were and are commonplace. As Joanna Traynor, author of the transracial fostering novel *Sister Josephine*, theorized in a 2001 *Guardian* article on the subject of farming, 'for some, it was a status symbol to have a White nanny in the country [meaning Britain]'. It is hard to weigh the precise rationale of all those early West African students forced to think on their feet while temporarily displaced, starting families and trying to better themselves and their countries. But it is not wide of the mark to suggest that having the ability to outsource the most demanding aspects of early parenthood and focus entirely on the work that would improve your future prospects would have been viewed by some as an immense privilege rather than a particularly wrenching emotional decision.

'I've never really gotten to the bottom of why we were fostered,' says Kemi Martins of her and her brother's separate stints with their White proxy parents in Canvey Island. 'I don't think [my birth father] was doing any sort of formal qualifications. It was more just so he could apply himself more to his work as an engineer. And my mum was working as well, doing some clerical work. That was the impression I got. And when they have been cornered on it a bit more they've said, "Well, we wanted you to have a good start with British people." They didn't use the word assimilate. But I guess there was something around that.'

This notion of private fostering conferring the useful by-product of assimilation is also worth zeroing in on. West African parents knew enough about the hostilities of post-war society to realize that facility with English language and culture, a seamless ability to 'pass', had real value. Never mind that these bonus elocution lessons often didn't go quite to plan (in her book, the historian Jordanna Bailkin highlights a tale of 'Nigerian parents who required an interpreter to understand children raised by Cockney foster mothers'), they perhaps formed a powerful part of why farming endured across the decades. Giving your children an immersive education in Britishness could only be a positive thing – not just as a means to better embed them within postcolonial society, but to bestow greater advantages when you ultimately returned back home. Surely the ability to move seamlessly between spheres and cultures, between the Western and the indigenously African, was an added benefit to be welcomed?

It was, like so much related to the whole enterprise of farming, a well-meaning idea that did not have the desired result. Shuttling between two cultures – two homes, two parenting styles, two worlds – proved disorienting. As Martins remembers: 'I would have to adjust to different rules, different parents and different priorities.' What's more, sending African children to White families in supposedly quieter areas did not shield them from prejudice or abuse. The whole enterprise of private fostering, which had bloomed from the Colonial Office's attempt to soothe the emotional struggles of West African students, had succeeded in intensifying those issues and passing them on to another generation. And then, 60 or so mostly silent years after that first advert in *Nursery World*, these farmed children began to use their voices, and tally the psychological cost that came from private fostering's extreme pragmatism.

For Shola Amoo, a London-raised, British-Nigerian director who was privately fostered as a child, the decision to commit his personal experience to film was not an easy one. 'It took a while to find a way to tell the story,' says Amoo. Tall, solidly built and with close-shaven hair, Amoo selects his words with care and soft-spoken precision. Despite the casual nature of our meeting place – outside a North London pub, occasionally drowned out by the growl of a nearby motorbike – he is all business. Part of Amoo's realization was that the best way to do justice to this part of his history was to make sure that it wasn't solely about him. 'I was fostered from a racially chromatic [White] space to a more diverse, inner city one,' he says. '[So] I'm lifting from certain personal experiences. But I was talking to other people who were fostered, other Nigerians, and getting their stories. The film became a synthesis between these different people and myself to create a new narrative.'

Coupled with this choice, which made the story more universal while also affording some protective emotional distance, Amoo decided to nudge things beyond the literal in terms of style; to aim for something sweeping and majestic rather than straightforwardly gritty. 'That was [another] key thing,' he continues. 'Once I settled on the concept of a single perspective through the landscapes, that's when I had a real breakthrough. Myself and my DP [director of photography] really worked out the language and looked at it as this immersive first-person experience.'

What this thoughtful, counter-intuitive approach to a farming story yielded was *The Last Tree*: a sumptuously shot, lyrical triptych that follows a young boy called Femi as he comes of age in rural Lincolnshire, multicultural South-East London and the thrumming, traffic-clogged streets of Lagos. Again, Amoo is keen to stress that it is only partly autobiographical ('I felt close enough to get the realism and authenticity,' he says, 'but distant enough to know these were [fictional] characters'), but *The Last Tree* brought African private fostering out of the shadows with an acute specificity and skill.

The unexpected romance and freedom of the life that Femi (the film's protagonist and Amoo's on-screen stand-in) has with his doting English foster mother in predominantly White Lincolnshire; his struggle to adapt to the stricter, floor-sweeping household regime upheld by his birth mother; the conflicting currents of alienation and acceptance that visibly flow through him during a climactic first trip back to Nigeria: all of it has the feel of eloquent truth spoken by someone who lived through it. And though its release in the autumn of 2019 (opening in around 25 theatres nationwide in the UK) could be characterized as modest and outside the mainstream, it permeated the consciousness – earning lovestruck reviews from the *Observer* and the *New York Times*, plus Best Screenplay at the 2020 Writers' Guild Awards. It left a cultural mark, then – thus vindicating Amoo's circuitous career journey (via training as a journalist and time spent directing low-budget rap videos) and decision to take his time over how to tell his fostering story.

But perhaps more significant than this is that *The Last Tree* signalled a precise tipping point: the moment that African private fostering shifted from a muttered secret into something that was suddenly being thoughtfully excavated in films, books and an undulating wave of news articles. Whereas previously it had been a secret lurking at the fringes of Black British history – only mentioned, if at all, when related to the biographies of fostered Black celebrities like former sportsmen John Fashanu and Kriss Akabusi – during that autumn in particular, it was suddenly thrust into the spotlight. There was *The Last Tree* and *Farming*, a similarly themed, semi-autobiographical drama from the aforementioned actor-turned-director Akinnuoye-Agbaje, released in UK cinemas, in line with that maxim about long-awaited buses, just two weeks after Amoo's film. There was *That Reminds Me* by Derek Owusu, a slender, quietly devastating novel in verse, partly inspired by the Ghanaian-British author's formative experience with chain-smoking White foster parents in Sussex and the recipient of the prestigious Desmond Elliot Prize for debut fiction.

And then, in dialogue with these works of art, there were true-life accounts from adults who had been privately fostered as kids, unpacking their feelings of abandonment, cultural conflict and more on outlets like Buzzfeed, BBC News and ITV. Gina Knight, a woman fostered in the 1980s, left by her Nigerian birth mother and ultimately embroiled in a court battle that handed custody to her English foster parents, established an online network to connect others who had been farmed. A dam had clearly been burst. And each public account seemed to engender even more and shape what was being pushed out into the world, until all these stories morphed into a big, messy act of collaborative group therapy.

'What was amazing was the amount of people that I didn't know were fostered who would come up to me after the film came out,' says Amoo. 'I just had no idea. But that's the beautiful thing about sharing something like this. It just gives people that bit more space and comfort to be like, "OK, this is part of my story too."' I felt this personally. When I mentioned in passing that I was seeking out those who had been farmed, my mother breezily reeled off some family friends and at least one set of cousins that had done time with the people she pointedly referred to as 'English nannies'. It wasn't especially surprising. But it spoke to both the pervasiveness of farming as a practice and also, more broadly, the secrets that tend to lurk in the biographies of Black African immigrant families (and British Nigerian families especially).

At around eight years old, I remember being told by elder relatives that my cousin Tenne was going back to Nigeria on holiday when, in truth, he was moving back there permanently. The intention was that the falsehood would cushion the blow for me. In fact, it did the opposite – serving only to make his prolonged absence, and the slow, dawning realization that he wasn't coming back, more confusing and painful. I do not doubt that others in London's Black African diaspora have similar memories. Memories of atomized family units and well-intentioned parental decisions yielding unforeseen, occasionally traumatic repercussions. And this, I think, is what made the emergence of these farming stories so affecting for many like me. Private fostering may have only afflicted some, but the issues it brings into focus – of familial secrecy and dissonance between generations of immigrant settlers – are universal among many Black African Brits. To see all this thrust into the spotlight felt at once thrilling and transgressive.

Plus, that notion of dissonance is key. For the benign, decades-long conspiracy of silence around private fostering stories to be broken marked a fascinating cultural transition. Not just in the wider context of a media landscape where Black stories of all kinds had a new-found currency, but also in the sense that British-African identity was clearly undergoing a pivotal evolution. Or, in other words, there was a generational swing from the emotionally durable, necessary stoicism of those first West African settlers in the UK – with both the influence of colonialism and an omertà-like culture of respect and secrecy conspiring to produce the stiffest of upper lips – to a way of being that was more about openness, psychological curiosity and a desire to explore and, perhaps, heal past traumas.

Kemi Martins, when discussing the notion of witnessing any evidence of regret or remorse from her now elderly biological parents, puts it in simple terms. 'There's a different way of relating,' she says, describing that generational gulf. 'That idea of, "Oh we've reflected now so let's all have a group hug, cry and move forward" – that's not what it is. But I guess [my birth parents] are so used to battling through life and managing with what they've had that they're more on that survival level. Whereas we've had the luxury of being able to listen to emotions.'

There is an irony to this: to the idea that the gifts and advantages those African parents sought to bestow – through both farming specifically and, more generally, a life in Britain – have opened up a chasm of understanding and feeling between them and their children. Just as their parents' generation had found solace in stoicism and survival, this new wave of first-generation children, or at least some of them, found that they could not stay silent about what they had been through. Incidences of dislocation could not be brushed aside. Punishment beatings were not readily shrugged off as the gift of strict parenting. A settled, less itinerant life brought the space for introspection, growth and a yearning for answers. And in the case of farming specifically, in life as in art, the grief and trauma – for those who were not abused, of course – tended to attach itself to the moment when these children were brought 'home' by their birth parents.

In Kemi Martins' case, this unwanted return came when she was 11 years old, and took her from Canvey Island to the family home in South London. The relative ease of her life in Essex, where her younger sister and brother remained, was replaced by regular housework and learning to greet her elder family members with the deferential bow that's common in Nigerian culture. 'I don't know if this is me being bitter and twisted, but I always thought [they brought me back] because I was at an age where I was useful,' says Martins now, with a dark chuckle. 'At 11, you're fairly autonomous; you can get to school and start to do a bit of cooking and cleaning. And so it was probably seen as an age where I wasn't wayward and was still manipulable.' Elsewhere, in *Farming* – an unflinching and, truthfully, tonally patchy, primal yowl of a film – this enforced return to the biological family unit is depicted as even more extreme and traumatizing. In scenes inspired directly by Akinnuoye-Agbaje's tumultuous early life, Enitan (his on-screen avatar) is taken back to Nigeria by his parents at around eight, rendered mute by the change of environment, subjected to a tribal purging ceremony and swiftly deposited back in his old foster home mere months later, back in the violently racist wilds of 1980s Tilbury and even more maladjusted and troubled than he was when he left. Owusu's *That Reminds Me*, meanwhile, gives voice to the lingering feeling of cultural whiplash – and the sensory dislocation – that followed his sudden transition from White, rural Suffolk to Black, urban South London.

> This countryside melody played so loud it was years before the sound of boots on mud and friendly good mornings was taken over by sirens and the smell of booze and latex, a door buzzing instead of knocked, faces that were not hostile but indifferent.

But real life has the power to outdo art. And the story of Lola Jaye's post-farming reunion is a case in point. Jaye's family's life had always been, in her telling, somewhat fragmented and nomadic. While she lived in Blackfriars with her White 'Nan', two of her six siblings – ten and 15 years older than her – were living alone in Battersea, her oldest brother, 20 years her senior, was elsewhere in London, her father, 'who left when [she] was four and never came back', was in Nigeria, and her mother shuttled between Nigeria and the UK. 'I only briefly lived with [my siblings],' she explains. 'I mostly just visited and stayed the weekend sometimes. My brothers were men, my sister was a woman and my mum wasn't always there. So it wasn't really a "mum and dad" situation.'

This non-nuclear arrangement gave Jaye what she characterizes as the best of both worlds. But in the early 1980s, when she was nine years old, there would be a pivotal intervention. This was a period that saw a change in both the legislation and rhetoric around transracial fostering. On the one hand, the Children Act 1975 had made it easier for foster parents to be granted custody of children who had been in their care for more than three years (a move that led to a number of headline-grabbing 'tug-of-love' court cases pitting West African birth parents and English foster carers against each other). In addition to that, a more culturally sensitive approach to child welfare, shaped by influential figures like the late-1970s American sociologist and 'same-race' adoption advocate Joyce Ladner, began to take hold. In 1983, the Association of Black Social Workers and Allied Professionals was formed and mobilized to, wherever possible, place Black children with Black families.

For Jaye, this meant her situation with Nan and her husband Ted was scrutinized by social workers. And following a calculated charm offensive ('Those social workers, they were slick,' remembers Jaye with a laugh – 'they took me to McDonald's, which to a ten-year-old might as well have been the Ritz'), the authorities sought to place her with a Black family. Nan and Ted reacted with understandable anger and bewilderment. Then, once the case was brought to family court, Jaye's mother rushed back to London in order to take her back to Nigeria, lest she be taken into care while a foster family more palatable to the state was found.

It's fair to say that Jaye experienced this hurried, unplanned return as a violent shock. 'Mum came and she took me, and it was a horrible day because, obviously, it was under duress,' says Jaye. 'Nan was crying. I was crying. They took me to the airport and it felt like I'd been dragged from the only home I'd known and someone that was a mother to me. So it was like I was kicking and screaming, without being able to vocalize it.' The frantic nature of such a huge life change meant that things were all the more challenging in Nigeria. 'Mum wasn't set up because she wasn't expecting me, and so I was sleeping on the floor at one of her cousins' houses,' she adds. In the end, [my mum] got set up, got a business going and we got a place. But it was a culture shock. There were mosquitoes, I didn't have the mod cons I was used to, and I went to school there and got bullied for being the British kid.'

The history of private fostering is littered with tales like this – of children failing to acclimatize to West African surroundings, of social struggles and of those who, given the almost biblical choice of which parents they wanted to live with, chose their White foster families. And after a year of asking to be sent back to London ('Now I'm an adult, though I'm not yet a mother, I realize that it must have been so hard to hear your child say, "I want to go", she adds sombrely), Jaye's wish was finally granted. Her eldest brother became her legal guardian, sent money for a return flight, and she arrived – unbidden, and as if it were all a dream – back at Nan and Ted's red-brick council house in Blackfriars. 'Nan always reminds me that she almost fainted,' says Jaye with a laugh. 'I knocked on the door, standing there with my little wet look [hairstyle] and she said, "What the bloody hell are you doing here?" I was back. And it was just wonderful.'

If we push aside the issue of the social worker intervention that disrupted her life – a well-intentioned piece of welfare state heavy-handedness that actually created an inadvertent logjam of Black and mixed-race children in the care system right up until transracial fostering policy was softened again in 2014 – then the biggest question is this: what does an experience like that do to your relationship with your birth parents and wider biological family? And, perhaps, even more than that, what does it do to your own personal relationship to that side of yourself? To African culture and your associations with it?

In a 2012 conversation with the *Guardian*, at a time when *Farming* was still just the improbable life story he had already been trying to turn into a film for almost a decade, Akinnuoye-Agbaje touched on this phenomenon; on how his forced return to Nigeria as a nine-year-old, as well as temporarily robbing him of speech, hardened his attitude towards Africa and Blackness in general.

'Now I had a reference point, and that really heightened my cultural identity crisis,' he said, 'I wanted to assimilate and go back to the abnormal normality I knew. I wanted to wash off the experience of Africa, but obviously I couldn't, because that's who I was. As much as I wanted to deny it, it was plaguing me, and I was reminded by the images coming through the TV, people on the streets and in the end my [foster] family in the house.'

Obviously, Akinnuoye-Agbaje's response to this glitch of identity, which, in his case, was to become a self-hating skinhead, fighting shoulder to shoulder with the racists who once tormented him, was especially extreme. And it should be noted that plenty of kids, adrift in the choppy waters of private fostering, would have frequent contact with their biological family, and managed to find ways to have positive interactions with Blackness and African life ('My sister came over to plait my hair, I spent a lot of time with my brothers and they were all very instrumental in making sure I knew I was *Black* Black,' says Jaye, by way of explanation).

But this notion of the many lasting ways that a private fostering experience can leave its mark on an individual – and inculcate, at best, mixed feelings towards the people and the traditions that put them in that particular position – is one that sits at the heart of any conversation about farming. How do you square old traditions, values and personality traits with new ways of living and feeling? Who do you identify with, when you are too British to be accepted as African, and too African to be accepted as anything else? Is it possible, or even necessary, to seek answers from parents who gave you away to strangers? These are the issues that Owusu, Amoo, Akinnuouye-Agbaje and anyone else who has told their farming story is grappling with; the knot they have been vying to untangle.

And, again, it's notable that much of what relates specifically to private fostering also extends out, more generally, into what has come to define Black African life in the UK. Trying to establish yourself in a new country and culture; the difficulty of balancing the sleepless exertions of immigrant life with a settled family situation; Britishness as a covetable and socially beneficial commodity, but also something that can lead to the loss of connection with a part of your identity. All this is especially visible in the living histories of those who were farmed and have since been moved to share their experiences. In this, private fostering is like a cracked mirror held up to African London. And, long after it fell from favour as a practice, its shattered reflection would throw up just as many questions as answers.

Bim Babatunde doesn't quite buy it. The British-Nigerian PR executive and former actor is polite enough, listening intently as I chart the dramatic twists and turns of his life – being privately fostered as a baby in 1962, growing up as the only Black child in the White English, aristocratic Queensberry family, a brief, traumatic return to Nigeria with his birth parents – and wonder aloud at how they may have negatively impacted him.

Did he crave the sense of cultural belonging that may have come from growing up in a less homogeneously White environment? Does he feel any lack of affinity with his African side, having pleaded, throughout the four years he spent in Nigeria, to be sent 'home' to his foster mother? Is there any resentment aimed at his birth parents or regret that his childhood wasn't more settled and traditional? Babatunde laughs with recognition. But only in the abstract way of someone acknowledging a set of wholly logical emotions that they have never felt themselves. 'I feel that what happened to me was a divine thing,' he says. 'It was meant to happen, so I don't look at it negatively. I think it all boils down to a particular person's experience. And I don't think you hear about the positive stories that much. But, really, I had the best of both worlds. I had my birth parents that I loved, my adopted parents that I loved and I think, hopefully, I'm a bit more of a rounded, non-judgemental person because of it.'

Babatunde is a man of outward contradictions. Broadly built and with a prominent-browed, close-shaved head, he speaks in a rich, crisply enunciated baritone that betrays his aristocratic upbringing. There is, in his self-possessed energy and unhurried manner, the hint, perhaps, that he was a talented runner at school. That he is a Christian media entrepreneur who also had a teenage Teddy boy phase – complete with Dr Martens and earrings – tells you that he isn't hidebound by other people's expectations.

It's vital to make some distinctions with regards to Babatunde's upbringing. Though he initially came to his English family via an advert placed by his birth parents in *Nursery World*, he has always thought of himself as having been adopted in all but name rather than privately fostered; his White mother was his legal guardian and, to this day, people still mistakenly refer to him as 'Bim Queensberry'. However, Babatunde's story, and his particular take on it, is important in the broader context of farming narratives. Not every experience was negative. Not everyone feels that they missed out or struggled. Not all privately fostered African children think of themselves as particularly emotionally scarred. The grim tally of associated abuse cases cannot be ignored – a 2001 report by the British Agencies for Adoption and Fostering found that thousands of West African children were at risk of abuse or neglect through these kinds of unvetted arrangements. But the very fact that African private fostering stories are often flattened into tales of suffering is a point of contention for those who actually lived them. As Lola Jaye puts it: 'People assume, wrongly, "Oh, you poor thing, you must have been abused." And, it's like, "No. I'm so much more than that."' Multiple versions of a story – with their own texture, nuance and contradictions – can be true at once.

And yet, even in the accounts that describe a life mostly unaffected by being farmed (or even those that, like Babatunde's, weigh their experience in terms of what they gained, rather than anything lost), there is almost always a lasting impact; a legacy that can be measured in a person's sense of self or their understandable desire to reclaim power in stories that serve as the grimmest reminder of youthful powerlessness.

By 1964, organizations like the British Council were offering accommodation to West African students so they could keep their family units together; an example of the growing anxiety, in both the UK and Africa, about private fostering and what its social aftershocks meant for the supposed temporary status of Black Africans in Britain. Even at that relatively early juncture, societal forces understood that this seemingly straightforward childcare arrangement had unpredictable long-term consequences. And nowhere are those consequences more apparent than in the lives of those on either side of the farming equation.

Let us focus, for a moment, on the parents. Often absent in private fostering accounts that alight on the perspective of children, their apparent silence shouldn't be mistaken for getting out unscathed. Whether through feeling rejection from their own children, facing social stigma from all angles, or simply having to deal with widening familial rifts, it's hard to fully chart the impact on the parental side. And that applies to the White families as well, who found themselves inextricably linked to the Black experience (this is not the same as always understanding it or necessarily doing the work to educate yourself) and could feel the reverberations of their decisions in the most unexpected and unseen ways.

'One thing I noticed was that my nan had five or six siblings and I never met any of them while I was growing up,' says Lola Jaye. 'Maybe they didn't agree with what she did. It wouldn't be difficult to imagine a White working class family in the 1940s and 1950s as racist. And then when I got older I started to hear snippets and I put two and two together. The attitude to her taking all these Black kids in was, "What are you doing?" And, well, she was like, "Bugger 'em.'" She laughs fondly, remembering the spirit of her nan. 'That was her attitude.'

It's a memory that serves as a reminder of all the sacrifice – all the unwritten grief, acrimony and loss – that would have been part of the experience of many White parents who offered this care in an era of such flagrant intolerance. But it is the relationship between farmed children and their biological parents that has often proved the site of the most complexity and unresolved grievance. Put simply: neither party finds it easy to see it from the other's point of view, or understand the reason certain decisions were made. Or certain facts were withheld. In *The Last Tree*, Amoo worked to try to foster some of this missing empathy with his third-act depiction of Femi's mother in Nigeria. Ultimately, we see her as a diminished figure, no longer the strict firebrand of the London scenes, as she is embarrassed and ignored by a polygamist husband who long withdrew any form of support. As the director says: 'I wanted to pay tribute to that first-generation immigrant journey, particularly through a Nigerian lens, that you don't understand as a kid. The sacrifices and all of that. Because a lack of understanding is a firm foundation for a lot of that friction.'

And so, what about real-life West African parents who entered their children into private fostering arrangements? Have they been able to explain themselves and their actions, even as a finger of blame is raised in their direction? Do they even feel that they need to? The answer to that last question, anecdotally at least, would be a firm 'no'. While many farmed children called their foster mothers 'Mum' or 'Nan', African parents tended to prefer terms that conferred distance and status. If you continue to call a stand-in mother 'the nanny' then, in your mind, that is what she becomes.

Here, yet again, we find ourselves back at the disconnect between African-born parents and their British-born children; between a culture predicated on stoicism and respect and one that embraces introspection and emotional openness. One function of this disconnect is the way it has complicated some farmed children's relationship with not just their parents but their heritage. And for Kemi Martins, it's a feeling that goes right back to when she was first brought back into her biological family. 'For me, I never really learned Yoruba, and so when you don't understand the language of your parents there's a level of understanding that will never be there,' she says. 'And I feel it's the same from [my parents'] perspective, the way they look at us. They'll say, "You know you're not English? You're not White?" And I'll go, "Hold on, I've lived here for more than 50 years – how can you possibly think [I'd be any different]?"'

This inability – or perceived inability – to access African culture in the same way as the previous generation can yield multiple reactions. For Martins, it has led her to take what you could call an à la carte approach to her Nigerianness. 'I guess I feel more like a Black Briton than a Nigerian,' she admits. 'I have the curiosity about Nigerian culture of someone who has been raised in the UK and almost wants to cherry-pick the bits of it that will help me navigate my life.' But for Lola Jaye, acknowledgement and awareness of the unbridgeable gap between her experience and that of her biological parents has actually opened up a path to greater understanding and forgiveness.

'I have to accept [my parents] for who they are,' she says. 'If I have this image of it being this all-loving family like *The Waltons*, I need to get rid of that, grieve, and just love them for who they are. My mum has been gone for a while now, but I still speak to my dad. He's 90, has other wives and other children. So I need to take away my prejudices about that, forgive, and just deal with him as he is. He's a pensioner. An old man. So I'm going to do what I can for him, and I'm not going to have any malice about it, because that means I haven't truly let go.'

It is tempting to assume that it was this culture shift across the generations of West Africans – the handing of the baton from those first settlers to their children – that ultimately led private fostering to fall from favour in the 1980s, the 1990s and beyond. This, however, would be an oversimplification. Just as an unpredictable aligning of various post-war conditions led to farming's birth, a similar perfect storm signalled its downfall. First, there was, again, the Children Act 1975: new legislation that, among other things, brought standardization to an arrangement that previously only involved an advert in a newspaper and the transfer of a swaddled baby. This increased legislative scrutiny – paperwork, obligation to inform a local authority of a childcare arrangement, social worker visits – added a complexity to the process that, understandably, proved off-putting.

Then, of course, there was the shifting demography of the UK's Black African diaspora. Where once it was dominated by the West African student population who flourished in the immediate aftermath of empire – welcomed by bodies like the Colonial Office because they were thought to be politically useful, temporary guests in the metropole – after the 1960s especially, things had shifted. Soon, the emergence of universities in Africa and a Home Office-backed tightening up of overseas student policy meant that the students who would have required private fostering arrangements were quickly being replaced by a class of less prosperous African migrants, intent on improved economic prospects and a permanent stay. There was a transition, too, when it came to child psychology; a new-found appreciation of the potential lasting impact of a bad private fostering arrangement only stoked by chilling, news-making cases. In the year 2000, Victoria Climbié, an eight-year-old Ivorian girl, was tortured and killed by her great-aunt and de facto great-uncle.

'This was a time when the public discussion of [private fostering] got a lot more hostile,' says Jordanna Bailkin, author of *The Afterlife of Empire* and a historian with an expert grasp of this chapter of British African history. 'Because no one that I encountered earlier was really thinking this was a bad thing. It was more, "What are these parents supposed to do? They're here, they're learning." But I think those very prominent cases of tragic child abuse were a turning point.' In this context, farming's fall from favour is hardly surprising. With increased regulation, a vastly diminished population of West African students and the taint of criminal neglect, private fostering, by the turn of the millennium, did not hold the same appeal for Black African parents, the White caregivers, or the encouraging government powers that had initially thought it such a good idea. This is not to say it suddenly disappeared. The umbrella of private fostering, which could often involve children sent to study in the UK and entrusted to a Black African friend or family member who had settled in the country, has definitely persisted in different guises. But throw in the fact that a lot of those original White foster parents – the ones who were already pensioners when they were in their second decade of taking in West African children – will have passed away, and it is easy to see how something that was once so prevalent has been significantly transformed and, perhaps, pushed even further underground.

But, of course, farming's legacy is too huge and far-reaching for it to remain hidden. And it is, in many ways, reflective of the ways that the Black African experience has intertwined unexpectedly with the postcolonial British story. It is there in Bim Babatunde's memories of his first wedding, and both his mothers – the aristocratic White English one and the Nigerian Yoruba one – standing beside him. It is there in Shola Amoo's depiction of a small African boy, letting out a cathartic scream in the Lincolnshire countryside. And it is there in Lola Jaye's fond stories of her White nan, her Black siblings, and a childhood that had space for Judy Blume and Malcolm X, Public Enemy and Kylie Minogue. None of this is what anyone intended when all of this was first set in motion almost 70 years ago. But out of the chaos and hurt, remarkable, meaningful things still managed to bloom.

2

Market

London's markets can be a portal. I have slalomed past haggling Lewisham aunties on my way to the gym and, with a jolt, suddenly been a child again, traipsing after my mum on a Saturday morning, stepping over squelched tomatoes at Woolwich market and looking on at gnarled tubers of yam going into thin plastic bags. I have stumbled, a little tipsy, past Peckham salon windows where entire families loiter late into the night and a hair stylist sews in weave with a slumbering baby trussed to her back, and felt a tug of recognition, as oblivious White friends have wandered on. I have spied bundles of multicoloured scouring nets hung at the door of a Walworth Road Sierra Leonean supermarket and been reminded, with a shudder, of the adolescent bucket baths we endured when all we craved was the boundless luxury of a working shower. They are slippages really; moments when those of us who grew up immersed in Black African London, but now perhaps spend much less time in it, spot the seams between those worlds.

But if you have known these sites of Black African and Afro-Caribbean social interaction, commerce and cultural connection – if you have bought a phone card to make international calls, lingered by the tiny storefront that sells Ghanaian Kumawood DVDs or complained to a shopkeeper that the plantains are priced at more than the industry-standard three for £1 – then you will know that few places have the same transportive, polyphonic power of Dalston's Ridley Road. Officially ratified in 1926, but founded long before then in the late nineteenth century, this living, breathing strip of London history was not specifically established as a Black market. In fact, to the contrary, it has ebbed and flowed with the varying tides of British immigration, offering tailored goods, an entrepreneurial foothold and a meeting point to East End communities that have included White working class, Irish, Jewish, Turkish, East Asian, South Asian and more, as well as Black African and Afro-Caribbean.

Though, of course, if you have visited the market in the last 20 years or so, then you will know that there is a specifically West African tenor to much of its long, unruly stretch of stalls, shops and pitches. Because here, after the Kurdish butchers thudding their cleavers down, the tablefuls of bagged gold jewellery, and the stall that appears to sell nothing but net curtains, are the distinctive blue plastic drums of a cargo shipping company. Here are dried bales of Norwegian stockfish, spongey folds of honeycomb tripe, massed pyramids of hacked-off cow foot, and baskets of handle-less palm-frond brooms. Here, as any child who has ever been to Ridley Road will tell you, agog, are giant, live African land snails, writhing on top of each other in a cardboard box, and yours for £5 each amid an accompanying soundtrack of tinny Afrobeats, shouted Yoruba and stallholders crying out, 'Don't pass me by, my brother!' On more than one occasion, I have come to Ridley Road and felt, even if for a flickering moment, I could be back in Lagos's labyrinthine Alade market, walking its tight pathways and hearing the sing-song, hawker's refrain of 'Come-and-check, come-and-check'.

The temptation to exoticize should be resisted (land snails and goats' heads are, in their own way, just as ordinary and redolent of East London as jellied eels and salt beef). But that Black African-run businesses in places like Ridley Road can imprint a certain character on the London landscape, and serve, in some way, as conscious analogues of establishments in African cities, is significant. And you only need to spend some time in any of these places, among the jokes and arguments and constant phone calls, to know that they are about more than just purchases.

They, along with the neighbouring businesses of other immigrant diasporas, are spaces of political importance, as well as cultural and social significance. Or, rather, their presence often represents creativity and an indomitable, against-the-odds success. In 2013, the exploratory 'Ordinary Streets' project found that the practice of mutualism — namely subdividing commercial buildings on Rye Lane in Peckham into micro-premises able to house cupboard-sized phone shops, money transfer services and salons — meant that when it came to both number of businesses and people employed, Peckham town centre outstripped even the recently built Westfield Stratford shopping centre (2,100 and 13,400 respectively, compared with Westfield's 300 retail units and 8,500 jobs). Add the fact that many of these subdivided Rye Lane premises are rented on cheap, flexible, pop-up style leases, thereby circumventing the initial outlay that is another barrier to entry for immigrant heritage business owners, and they feel all the more nimble and ingenious.

However, to look at these African small businesses as merely representative of multicultural triumph would, again, be overly simplistic. True, the visibility of Black African and Afro-Caribbean-oriented shops and market stalls speaks to how well established London's Black community has become. What's more, the ready availability of ingredients and goods that previous generations of Black African settlers could only dream of accessing in the UK signals a hard-won collapsing of the distance between indigenous life and life in diaspora. And yet the complexities and challenges of this world can always be discerned.

High street remittance businesses – places, for the uninitiated, where you can send money back home – offer a daily reminder that a large portion of London's African immigrant population are constantly battling to send funds to those with even less. Subdivided businesses – hastily built structures where different entrepreneurs operate cheek-by-jowl – indicate the struggle to find space, in community markets that are increasingly under threat of effectively being gentrified out of existence. Black African entrepreneurialism, for all its supposed prominence in places like Brixton and Peckham and Dalston, is fraught with difficulty and impermanence; a harsh reality borne out by the fact that, as per figures released in 2021, just 11.2 per cent of Britain's Black worker population are self-employed, the lowest number by ethnicity, compared with 23.2 per cent of workers from the combined Pakistani and

Bangladeshi ethnic group. In these figures, we can glimpse something of the long-running, ongoing battle to assume ownership of the businesses that serve the Black community.

So, it is true. African and Afro-Caribbean traders lining streets like Ridley Road are a vivid, evocative sign of Black fortitude, adaptability and connection to home. But they are also symbols of continued struggle; sacred, emotionally resonant and fundamentally egalitarian spaces mortally threatened by the ravages of urban regeneration and a social landscape redrawn by the pandemic. Yes, Black African presence in London's markets can be a portal to many things. And you only need to look back to see why these are portals worth preserving.

I am pretty sure that the first time I ever tried genuine West African suya, the thin-cut, fearsomely spiced Northern Nigerian barbecued beef sold all across the world, it had been smuggled into the country by a relative. Bought on a Lagos roadside, frozen pre-flight and stashed in an odour-blocking tin within their hand luggage, it had nonetheless lost nothing in transit; brown, peppery strips of meat, almost transformed into a bovine crumb, and crash-landing on the palate as an intoxicating rush of salt, Cameroonian pepper heat and groundnut sweetness. It was the catalyst for a long-standing addiction that has involved eating it at Peckham hole-in-the-walls, on Nigerian beaches and at more than one funeral. But what I didn't realize at the time of that first, contraband delivery was that I was actually playing my part in a long-standing tradition of indigenous foodstuffs being muled from Africa to the

UK. Because the available historic record is pretty clear on this: before there were African restaurants, specialist African supermarkets or even Afro-Caribbean fruits and vegetables readily available on London's streets, there were ingredients either posted or surreptitiously stashed in suitcases.

'I write my mother that I was in White country, and I miss ... our African food,' that was how Opeolu Solanke-Ogunbiyi, matron of the pioneering West African Students' Union (WASU) hostel and author of a 2009 memoir, described the yearning she felt while in London during 1933. She and her husband, WASU founder and barrister Ladipo Solanke, were there establishing their headquarters and a vibrant social hub for the interwar period's growing community of Black African overseas students. Later in her memoir, Solanke-Ogunbiyi goes on to describe the consignments of specific ingredients her mother dries and ships to Tilbury ('Dried fish, dried ewedu, dried okra, dried bitterleaf [spinach-like greens used in West African soups] ...') not just to sate her own cravings but also to help fuel the small restaurant within WASU. The sense is that these deliveries were legal. But, food writer Yemisi Aribisala, in her book *Longthroat Memoirs*, encapsulates the situation that those in the nascent Nigerian diaspora would have experienced during much of the early to mid-twentieth century and beyond. 'If Nigerian restaurants were so easily replaced by others,' she writes, 'we would not need entire Nigerian food sections in London's Brixton Market, or customs officers at the airport collecting bribes to turn a blind eye to dried afang wrapped in old newspapers and hidden in underwear bags.' It's a vivid description of the lengths Africans in London would, anecdotally, routinely go to (and, as evidenced by that smuggled suya, will still go to) in order to scratch a particular culinary itch. But, more than that, it tells you something of the importance that specific ingredients and tastes held for Black African and Afro-Caribbean communities in London, particularly during the interwar and post-war periods; how they tried to combat the unfamiliarity of life in the cold, perplexing and demanding metropole with some form of familiarity on their plates.

And in this, the fake-it-until-you-can-make-it era, Africans and Caribbeans would have to get especially creative to make versions of their food with what was available in Britain. Solanke-Ogunbiyi describes using ground rice instead of gari – the fermented cassava flour whipped into a smooth accompaniment for stews – in dishes during the 1930s. Bernice Green, a participant in the British Library's oral history project examining Caribbean foodways in Britain, explains how in 1960s London her family grated carrot into a dish to impart the orange tinge of pumpkin stew in lieu of any actual pumpkins.

In the end, though pioneering food stalls in places like Brixton and Shepherd's Bush began stocking products to appeal to an increasingly West Indian clientele, salvation came in the form of other immigrant communities. Specifically, it was butchers and grocers serving London's Jewish diaspora who recognized shared tastes – for oxtails, old layer chickens, tongues and trotters – among their traditional customer base and both Afro-Caribbean and Black African locals. Green, again, talks about Ridley Road being one of the first places where predominantly Jewish traders began, in the late 1950s and early 1960s, to source produce specifically geared towards the Black diaspora. 'There was a Jewish man on the corner, Regent Groceries,' she says. 'And when I explained to him the rice I wanted, he used to get things to suit me . . . It was lots of stalls with Jewish people. There was not a Caribbean person selling in the market there. All Jewish. And they would ask you what you want, what you're missing, and they would make enquiries about getting them for you. And that is how Ridley Road spread to being such a market for Black people.'

This status that Ridley Road, and other markets like it, held as a rare place where an atomized and often harassed Black population could freely congregate is key. Procuring non-native ingredients became something of a sacred weekly act; particularly vital because of the possibility it afforded to connect to both your roots and other Black Africans and Afro-Caribbeans making their bewildered way through the capital. As the African American writer Henry Louis Gates Jr put it in *Black London*, his 1976 dispatch from the capital's unlicensed 'blues parties', African churches and 'the ritual of the gut' that occurred in places like Ridley Road and Brixton: 'Market Day means keeping one's stomach in tune with the Islands, at the expense of salted fish and chips or steak and kidney pie.'

There was a power in the availability of Black produce, then. But the hands that this power was concentrated in came to be an issue. 'We used to go to a shop called Charlie's in Kilburn,' explains Nky Iweka, a British-Nigerian chef, cookbook author and restaurateur who grew up in 1980s London. 'Charlie was a White, Irish guy, and I remember that he'd have the red onions and would be like, "Oh, they're from Nigeria." And they would be so expensive. God, he made a fortune, that man.' This point about the inflated sums African Londoners would willingly pay for specialist imported goods is delivered with a smile. But it conceals an important truth. The sense of gratitude and migrant fellowship that shoppers like Bernice Green felt in the post-*Windrush* era began to dwindle; White traders profiting off London's Black community became a point of contention and, you imagine, the subject of much disgruntled teeth-kissing in the queue. And by the time the 1980s and 1990s rolled around, when shops predominantly run by the South Asian community had effectively cornered the market on cassava, plantain, palm oil and any number of other Black household essentials, it had become a widely acknowledged sticking point. Why, came the repeated question, were Black Africans and Afro-Caribbeans lining the pockets of shop owners and stall holders with no connection to the community or affinity with the products they were selling their Black customers?

In the field of Black hair and beauty products – a billion-pound industry in the UK alone – this frustration has, at times, felt especially pronounced. With Black women spending six times as much as their White counterparts on hair products, the historic lack of genuinely Black-owned cosmetics businesses on London high streets has come to carry a deeper significance within the community. You could say that this issue is about purchasing power, ownership, cultural pride and an intangible sense that, beyond the cold, hard transactional process of money changing hands for goods, you should only offer your eager patronage to someone who understands and appreciates your need.

As the writer Yomi Adegoke noted, in a 2016 story on the issue, 'Many of the existing male vendors [in South Asian-owned hair shops] simply don't know enough about Black female hair because, well, they don't have it. And unlike e-cigs and electronics, there's no shorthand guide on how it all works.'

It is worth treading carefully here, with full awareness that tensions between London's Black and South Asian diasporas have traditionally been rooted in misplaced intra-ethnic bigotry and suspicion. But the idea that the Black community could move to the other side of the counter, and seize control of the businesses that were increasingly central to their lives in London, was clearly a hugely meaningful one. That was the broader context, anyway. For Eugene Takwa, a Cameroon-born shopkeeper who opened Woolwich's African Cash and Carry, initially alongside his brother, in 1987, establishing a Black-owned retail business was a simple matter of recognizing what was missing from the landscape.

'At that time, you had to go to Dalston, Brixton or Lewisham, and most of them were Asian shops,' says Takwa, from behind his counter, lean and stern in jeans and woollen black hat, in an accent that still carries more than a hint of his homeland. 'Very few Africans had shops. And it was more that there were certain things that Asian [shopkeepers] wouldn't know to import. Things like African vegetables. Yam and cassava was already coming from South America. But certain things like African spices, and ewedu and bitterleaf. Those were really out of the question, and you couldn't get them unless you travelled.'

Over in West London, a few years later, Nigerian-born Monsurat 'Iyabo' Obisesan was having a similar epiphany about another relatively untapped part of town. 'My aunt used to live in Chiswick, and she told me there were no African shops in Shepherd's Bush,' she explains. 'Just an Asian one. But because they don't eat our food, they wouldn't have all those fresh vegetables. That was what pushed me and encouraged me.'

Obisesan is small and bustling, with a strikingly beautiful face beneath her tight-wrapped headscarf and the fast, easy intimacy of someone who runs a public-facing business. By 1996, she had opened her first stall in Shepherd's Bush market. And this era of the late 1980s and early-to-mid 1990s can be viewed as a specific boom time for African-owned and specifically African-oriented businesses, encompassing Takwa's and Obisesan's, plus John & Biola's Foods in Camberwell, and Bims African Food Store, a neighbourhood institution on Peckham's Rye Lane, run by the politician and community fixture, the late Bola Amole.

You could say that this surge of business ownership was merely a reflection of the stage Black African settlers – and, primarily, West African settlers – had reached; an inevitable marker of the social progression of the generation that arrived here in the 1980s. Yet the speed at which many of these ventures were established – the ambition and desire that is embodied in each bakery, remittance desk or burgeoning import/export empire – speaks, to me, of an acute, deeper yearning among Black Africans to be their own bosses. Nigerians especially are, in my experience, entrepreneurial to an almost pathological degree. In addition to their day jobs, my older relatives have, at various points, run franchised pick-and-mix kiosks, hired out crockery for events and offered computer training classes on the side.

After receiving a voluntary redundancy payout from her administrative job at the Commonwealth, my mother opened an internet café that, though it ultimately became a costly and burdensome enterprise, still ranks to her as the realization of a lifelong dream. I cannot picture myself at a family party without also hearing a bellowing chorus of uncles, talking all at once about their hypothetical business ideas.

Obviously, this kind of industriousness is a universal hallmark of the immigrant experience; a means to combat the foreign newcomer's unfavourable odds. But active side hustles – driving taxis, catering parties, working evening cleaning jobs – have long cut across class borders and been part of the accepted reality of what it is to be Black African in diaspora. It is a proactiveness shaped by both natural, burning ambition and the understanding that, within the disorienting machine of traditional Western employment, opportunities will not necessarily be meted out fairly. 'I used to work in a bank in Nigeria,' says Obisesan, who also spent some time selling jewellery in Italy and Switzerland. 'And I was thinking that I wanted to do that in this country. But, you know, at that time it wasn't easy for a Black person to get work in a bank.' She laughs. 'And most of the time that I tried to work for other people, I would just get fed up with it and something would make me leave the job.' In this light, London's African-owned businesses are really just the most obvious, visible expressions of a deeper, intangible longing. Namely, a desire for agency, for autonomy, and for the kind of cash-in-hand, person-to-person businesses that could prosper away from the restraints of White society.

Interviewed for Gates Jr's *Black London,* the Jamaican-born photographer Armet Francis lands on the idea that, for the older generation of *Windrush*-era migrants, the Caribbean way of life was something to be actively sustained and sought out in specific Black spaces; that it was 'an alive thing . . . in the form of a memory they nurture through dances and through the marketplace, and especially through the church'. The same, you'd venture, can be said of the more Afrocentric Black businesses that have proliferated in the last 30 years.

Yes, they are significant in terms of the customer and the relative ease with which Africans can now access ingredients and products that would once have had to be smuggled into suitcases, privately shipped here in dried form, or inventively synthesized from what could be found in a British post-war larder. But London's Black African shops were and are just as significant for the person on the other side of the counter. Not just because there was a good deal of collective self-esteem bound up in seizing control of the businesses that most actively served the community, but also because they offered an alternative route to employment, social advancement and the promised land of self-sufficiency in the metropole; a space and localized, diaspora-specific economy where the Africanness that made the world of mainstream work harder to access could be repurposed as a huge financial and professional benefit.

It is notable that, in contrast to the South Asian and East Asian communities that gained a generational foothold in the UK through establishing mass-appeal businesses in the fields of retail, restaurants and takeaway food, African British entrepreneurialism has historically been centred on specifically African (and, by extension, Black) need.

Or, as a woman called Maria, the squat, beanie-hatted proprietor of Victory Convenience Store, a crammed cornucopia of African goods on Ridley Road, put it to me on a blustery winter morning: 'It's not so easy to get a job out there these days.' She gestured with her head beyond the open doors of her shop; out towards the frustrating, unfair Western world that lay beyond the dented tins of Milo instant chocolate drink, the bags of dried crayfish and the Sellotape-wrapped bales of stockfish that marked this little, raggedly cultivated patch of African familiarity. Ultimately, Black African-owned high street businesses offer a chance for customer and trader alike to do things as they would in their respective mother countries. To find, as Gates Jr had it, 'a city block full of Black folk who speak the same tongues'. What the shops in African London's market spaces offer, really, is the chance to conduct yourself as you would back home. But that, as these traders would learn the hard way, is a proposition racked with its own unique difficulties and complications.

Even on a quiet weekday morning, TM African Foods is a scene; a whirl of colour and dazzling brightness and the kind of brusque, warm interaction that feels definably African. In this space, set hard against Goldhawk Road in West London and beyond an unremarkable blue-on-yellow sign, are bottles of luridly orange African Fanta, heaped sacks of Tilda rice, display baskets of smoked mackerel and gilded packets of dried spices all flashing beneath the clinically white strip-lighting. Here, despite the teetering roll call of familiar labels on the shelves – Ovaltine malted chocolate, Exeter corned beef, Robb muscular ointment – is atypical order and cleanliness; a scent that holds freshness and a back note of ginger, rather than the mothballed dankness that generally accompanies imported African goods and leaps unbidden from the suitcases of just-arrived relatives from the motherland. And here, conducting it all as customers file in and out seeking pale garden eggs and okra and squishy loaves of sweetened bread, is Obisesan, a fixture of this neighbourhood for more than 25 years and the diminutive force who maintains some sort of order.

'Mr Chas,' she calls out to the tall, only sporadically seen man who appears to be her sole employee. He skulks into view near the back of the shop, beside the clear bags of raw shea butter. 'Please. Bring two boxes of chicken Indomie up from downstairs,' she says, referring to the Indonesian instant noodle brand that is wildly popular among Nigerians. Then she is pricing up a sheaf of foil takeaway containers for a woman making moin-moin (the pale orange Nigerian bean curd cake) for an event, confirming to a passing man that, yes, the plantain is still three for £1 and beckoning in a pensionable shopper in a drooping face mask. 'Your chair is there, sister,' she says gently, as the older woman takes a seat at the back, amid some boxes. Later on, Obisesan will talk about the unusually close, reciprocal and almost familial relationship she has with her customers 'They were the ones that really encouraged and supported me to start,' she says. On the rare occasions she has returned to Nigeria on holiday, she has received multiple panicked messages from regulars who fear she has closed down forever.

The same is true south of the river, in Takwa's shop, where the bundles of potato leaf often come with a side order of philosophy, a revealing nugget of information about the local community's buying habits (West African palm-frond brooms are, apparently, increasingly popular among South-East London's Chinese population) and some jockeying over price. And so, to stand among the happily chaotic thrum of these places is to seal it: Black African and Afro-Caribbean shops are about much, much more than the act of merely buying goods or services. They are that rare place where the impersonal, clenched world of London recedes and is replaced with something warmer, louder and more familiar. To put it simply, you cannot sit down and hang out for a while in the middle of Tesco; you cannot, as Obisesan's customers do, call ahead on the phone to ask for some jollof rice seasoning or premium Ghana gari to be put aside for you.

'Sometimes when you're in these places and observing what's going on, there's not even a money exchange,' says the Jamaican-born historian Aleema Gray. 'People just go in there for a chat. Or because they're building a house back home and want advice. These places are central to how people in a community thrive and survive.' Gray would know this more than most. Quite some distance from the stereotypical idea of a museum worker – the island lilt of her voice and her thickly bundled dreadlocks act as clues that she was raised as a practising Rastafarian by her Jamaican parents – she was nonetheless the driving force and curator behind Feeding Black, an exhibition that ran at the Museum of London Docklands between 2021 and 2022, and sought to explore the significance and impact of four Black-owned, South-London-based food businesses. Through recorded oral histories, photography, and artefacts plucked from the shelves of the businesses, Feeding Black underlined the acute closeness of the customer–shopkeeper relationship within London's Black African and Afro-Caribbean communities. 'Brother Junior [the Jamaican-born owner of long-standing Woolwich-based greengrocers Junior's Caribbean Stall] described his job as being like a social worker,' says Gray with a smile.

But even that might be selling it short. Black shopkeepers, and by extension their shops, act as a mirror for the ebb and flow of their communities as they evolve over the years. Obisesan, who has had to keep pace with demand shaped by a growing Congolese and Sierra Leonean clientele, notes that most of her products are 'things people have asked for'. In the 1990s, Takwa's product knowledge had to adapt to a sudden influx of Ugandans displaced by Idi Amin's regime. And, as Gray explains with a laugh, even Brother Junior affects a fake West African accent when he is serving Nigerian customers. These businesses, as borne out by their money transfer capabilities and the often bewildering array of items crammed into a small space, are crucial points of crossover and interchange for linked but distinct Black cultures. It is not especially surprising, for instance, to learn that the Ordinary Streets project discovered that 61 per cent of Peckham Rye's largely foreign-born business owners speak two to three different languages.

Takwa is in no doubt about the importance of his role in the community as sage, interpreter and human hard drive for a quarter of a century of mostly ignored Black British history. In fact, he sees his intimate, hyper-specific knowledge of the largely Black African clientele that he serves as the most valuable remaining weapon in his arsenal, amid rising competition and brutal pricing wars. 'In the last ten years, there have been more than twenty other Asian-owned shops that have opened in the area,' he says. 'I can't compete with them when it comes to price. But [I'm] still hanging on because of the product knowledge. Because I know what different countries go for, and if someone picks the wrong thing, I will tell them. One of the things that most customers know is that I won't lie to them. You can go to some African shops and they'll tell you anything in order to make a sale. But I won't. My goal in life has never been to be rich.'

However, one of the more crucial functions of these businesses brings us back to the lady taking a load off in TM African Foods. Simply put, Black African small businesses in particular, and local Black businesses in general, are spaces that are consciously set apart from the strictures of the White Western world. The behaviours that are implicitly permissible within a Black-owned shop – unhurried lingering, haggling on price, speaking at volume in thick-accented patois or pidgin or, perhaps, not even in English at all – signal a rare and treasured atmosphere of Black freedom, forged in these ostensible sites of commerce. Gray describes Brother Junior's stall as a place that, in contrast to her working life as a historian, 'makes me feel real'. Set against a historic backdrop of a Black London subject to colour bars, prejudice and overzealous policing, they are points of unobserved congregation; urban oases where you can unclench, exhale and be the unmodified version of yourself that wider British society implicitly asks you to muffle. I have felt it myself, pushing through the door at my barbers and entering an exclusively Black, male world of cranked dance-hall music, arguments, free-flowing Wray & Nephew rum, and, on some days, very, very few people actually getting their hair cut.

But what of the traders and business owners who find themselves conscripted into maintaining these precious (but, at times, quite challenging) spaces? The ones tasked with balancing the needs of their livelihood and a disinhibited clientele that, occasionally, expect bent rules, credit and abundant discounts? Well, for some, it is a tacit social contract that they understand and are (just about) happy to honour. 'Some people will come in, skip the queue, put any coin down and just say, "Take," before they walk out,' explains Obisesan, with a shake of her head. 'I don't take that from them any more. But sometimes, I will take some money off [the price of an item], just to keep the customer and make them happy.'

Takwa, who first came to London in 1986 to study marketing, takes a more hardline approach. And it is one that I see first-hand, when a bustling young Nigerian woman attempts – after much grousing about the unfairness of Takwa's prices – to pay one pound less for the three drooping bundles of potato leaf she has put on the counter. 'That's not my price,' says Takwa, calmly but firmly. 'That's your price.' After much clucking and complaint ('Don't be letting our things be too expensive, *oga*') she grudgingly pays, gathers her plastic bag and hustles out into the roar of Woolwich. To Takwa, stand-offs like this indicate both the tricky balance he has to strike as a Black shopkeeper and, in his view, the changing demographic make-up of his particular patch of African London.

'There has been an influx of people from African countries since the year 2000, and a lot of them behave like they are back home,' he says, citing 'aggressiveness' and customers that have attempted to get a refund on previously bought, perfectly fine vegetables he has sold. 'It's not even a question of class,' he adds. 'You see people who are hustlers; people who have crossed the Mediterranean or come through the desert and have that animal, survival instinct. [It's] something that you didn't have in the 1970s, 1980s or 1990s. But they have brought it here.' Though Takwa has a better vantage point on the community than most, it seems an extreme stance on what is, at its mildest, the theatre of haggling and a friction between buyers and sellers that has probably existed as long as markets have. But, for him, it isn't just about this perceived sensibility change among Britain's Black African diaspora. No, for Takwa it is also that the behaviour of some of his customers – the feeling, in his words, that 'they are doing me a favour by shopping here' – points to a deeper tension between Africa and Britain; between the old ways and the new.

'The thing with some Africans is that they want to be African when it suits them and European or English when *that* suits them,' he says, with a mischievous chuckle. 'Some people will come here and say, "The customer is always right." And then, these same people will say, "This is an African shop, you shouldn't do this. Your prices don't change. You're too stiff." To which I say, "Well, we either do it the European way, where the customer is always right and you don't argue about the price. Or you don't ask for a discount. Because you don't ask for a discount when you go into an English shop. You take the price and you pay it."'

Again, it is worth acknowledging that Takwa's stance on this is probably heavily flavoured by his 25 years of service behind the counter. For all the shared history and friendship he clearly has within the neighbourhood – for all the Woolwich locals who, like Gray, have known him since they were children – his is a world of shoplifters and counterfeit notes and customers seemingly always looking for confrontation with him. However, his portrait of the demands of his clientele helps to illustrate just how freighted with emotion and cultural importance Black African businesses can be. They are places where people go to be themselves. Places where they expect an unwritten, amorphous set of traditional expectations and needs to be met. They are, really, a locus for both the longing for home and the tussling contradictions of what it is to be simultaneously of both Africa and Britain. 'For some people', as Takwa observes, 'the body is here, but the mind is back home.'

By this logic, Black African-run shops and market stalls are environments where both body and mind can briefly be in concert. But serving this function for the community is clearly difficult to begin with: a study by the British Business Bank found that, in 2019, the average annual revenue for Black business owners was £10,000 less than that for White entrepreneurs – and especially draining to sustain. 'It's very stressful,' admits Obisesan, as she buzzes around her shop, calling out occasionally for the elusive Mr Chas. 'The customers, the deliveries, getting staff – those things are very challenging.' She pauses. 'But I have a passion for it. A lot of people open shops without that passion, and in the next six months it will close.'

Here we see the fragility of the ecosystem of Black shops and businesses in places like Shepherd's Bush, Woolwich, Dalston, Peckham and beyond; that, for all their cultural significance, they are really just one overworked person, trying to appease a community while swinging from one bill to the next. So what happens to these businesses when you throw in the transformative force of gentrification? Or a post-war Black African diaspora that is ageing, evolving and, in some cases, moving away from cities like London? How about if you add a generation-shifting pandemic, and all its unanticipated difficulties, consequences and social reconfigurations, into the mix? These businesses may embody bedraggled, purposefully laid-back sanctuaries of tradition to many, but – as evidenced by the complex, contradictory demands of the British Africans in Takwa's cash and carry – at some point the realities of the world outside tend to encroach. The march of time, especially in a city like London, cannot be outrun. And if the market is the beating heart of African London, then, in recent years, its fading pulse has been a little concerning.

Ridley Road Market's history has always been as much about conflict and politics as produce and community. In the early 1900s, when it was a ragged collection of traders controlled by the police force rather than the council, morning disputes over who got the best pitch would be settled with fist fights. In 1962, the British aristocrat and former MP Sir Oswald Mosley's British Union of Fascists, who had taken to staging neo-Nazi rallies on the street, were forcibly beaten back by a local consortium of Jews, anti-fascists and stallholders in an incident that made national news.

And so it holds that, on a bright, blue-skied late summer day in the second year of the coronavirus pandemic, the first thing I see at Ridley Road is a protestor, standing on a bench opposite Dalston Kingsland Station and addressing an ambivalent lunchtime crowd from his improvised pulpit. 'Leave our children alone,' he says into a raised megaphone, as other protestors circulate with pamphlets. 'No vaccine for our children!' Covid vaccine hesitancy in multicultural communities like this one is not exactly what has brought me here today; that, specifically, is a meeting with a local activist called Kieran Kirkwood. Yet this scene feels like a fitting metaphor for both the unpredictable crackle and energy of the market and what has been an especially fractious, challenging and emotional last few years for spaces like this. Not to mention the people who cherish them.

'When I think of the London that I love and that I'm a bit nostalgic for, it is the market that I think of,' says Kirkwood, once we have made contact, laughed a little at the scene around the protestors, and then made our way to a nearby café. 'Now I'm seeing it change every day and watching people getting displaced from these areas. And places where they can gather socially or get affordable food and drink slowly ebbing away.' Kirkwood, who prefers gender-neutral pronouns, is young and compact, of both Black Jamaican and White English heritage, and with hair combed into a striking blowout Afro. They grew up nearby in Stoke Newington and had history working with the (ultimately successful) campaign to save Tottenham's Latin Village from redevelopment. But, by their own admission, it was an incident in 2018 that finally prompted action closer to home and gave other members of the local community

– which had been gentrifying at a frightening rate for at least the past 20 years – 'a catalyst and a clear point of resistance'. Specifically, the spark came in October of that year, when all the businesses within Ridley Shopping Village (a market-adjacent, indoor space made up of lots of Black African and Afro-Caribbean small businesses, plus affordable local artists' studios) were informed they would need to vacate the premises in two weeks as it was being turned into a mixed-use office, retail and housing block.

'We thought it must be illegal,' says Kirkwood of the eviction order. 'But it turned out their contracts did say [they were subject to only] 14 working days' notice. Which is fucked up, considering these are people's livelihoods we're talking about.' At that time, by Kirkwood's admission, the Shopping Village needed 'paint, new toilets, proper investment'. But this, in their view, is an example of 'managed decline'. The proposed new development would have featured five luxury flats and just 10 per cent of its workspaces designated as affordable.

It would not stand. And so, organizing under the umbrella of a newly formed group called Save Ridley Road, Kirkwood and other local activists protested against the move, organized a rally for the following week on 27 October 2018 (attended by more than 200 people) and, alongside the London Renters Union, marched on the West Hampstead offices of Rainbow Properties, the managing company representing the landlord of the building. This resulted in Rainbow withdrawing its eviction notice, a symbolic retreat that Kirkwood theorizes has had huge ramifications for all of Ridley Road Market, beyond the specific short-term future of the Shopping Village. 'If people from the community hadn't stepped in, the Shopping Village wouldn't be there, it would have been turned into some bullshit, and that would have been a big nail in the coffin for Ridley Road Market because it would have meant loads of disruption.'

When we meet, edging into late 2021, Save Ridley Road are celebrating another victory of sorts. Rainbow Properties has agreed to enter into a period of consultation with the campaign and Hackney Council, to discuss the future of redevelopment plans it had updated. Kirkwood, though wary of the ensuing consultation becoming 'a one-way thing from them', points to this recent success – the fruit of almost three years of campaigning – as an example of what it takes to prosper against those riding roughshod over a city's history. 'It feels like the fight to save Black London, basically,' says Kirkwood. 'Because where our communities live is in those social spaces, in markets, and in affordable housing and retail. The story of Ridley Road recently, and of this campaign, is something I use to talk to people who feel they haven't got much to believe in. The traders are still there. The market is still alive and kicking. If it wasn't for the campaign, I don't know what this place would look like, to be honest.'

That the complicated issue of urban regeneration affects all manner of communities, not just Black ones, is worth stressing. What's also notable, amid all this, is that it has taken activists like Kirkwood to fight on behalf of the traders and artists in Ridley Road Shopping Village. For the traders, the people these changes would most directly affect, the threat seemed intractable and hard to fully comprehend. And, again, this brings us into contact with the way Black businesses – and especially those adjacent to markets – often exist at a conscious remove from mainstream society. 'There was a lot of defeatism from the [Black] traders I spoke to,' adds Kirkwood. 'Some wanted to fight, but lots of them were talking about feeling this pressure of, not even the developer, but just society in general. When they say, "This is too big for us," they're talking about the whole system. There was a lot of mistrust as well. And mistrust of "activists" even coming and talking to people.'

This feeling of scepticism and wariness towards any form of authority – no doubt heightened by the legal grey area that trade around markets has traditionally occupied – is important. It is something I definitely felt as I roamed the market in the months after meeting Kirkwood, asking traders about the redevelopment plans, only to be met with either stony silence or the sort of noncommittal, one-word answers you'd imagine are reserved for particularly blatant undercover policemen. Maria, at Victory Convenience Store, when she wasn't ducking basic questions about how long she'd lived in London ('That's my privacy. You're going too far into my privacy'), only seemed dimly aware of the battle over Ridley Shopping Village in the sense it was something that might affect local parking. And this wariness towards, or lack of engagement with, the forces shaping their livelihoods, was a stance that Gray also discovered, throughout the interview process of Feeding Black.

'There's definitely an ambivalent relationship that Black-owned businesses have with the state,' she says. 'And there's an ambivalence within the community. It's like people saying, "You know, we're not sure about this vaccine thing. We're going to just be using our ointments and drinking our herbs."' With that, we are back to the anti-vaccine protestor with the megaphone standing at the mouth of Ridley Road, and the relevant issue of what effect Covid had on the Black African and Afro-Caribbean entrepreneurs in this already threatened ecosystem. The truth, as is often the case, is more complex than it first appears.

Naturally, months of lockdown, government-mandated closure, tricky-to-access financial support and staff and proprietors either falling ill or being forced to isolate represented an extinction-level event for plenty of Black high street businesses. A British Business Bank survey in 2020 found that 61 per cent of Asian and other minority-owned business enterprises had either paused or stopped permanently because of Covid. I saw my own universe of regular Black stop-offs shrink a little (either through a barber who never returned to his shop post-lockdown or Nigerian bakery Angel's keeping the shutters down on its Peckham branch for an indefinite period). And it seemed, thanks to both the crowded public spaces that are especially important to those of African and Caribbean heritage and the fact that those communities were in the high-risk category for the virus, that Covid carried an acutely high toll for the Black marketplace. 'People were already being isolated because of social cleansing,' suggests Kirkwood, 'and so the pandemic meant they were even more isolated because of social distancing.'

However, the contrasting view to all of this is that markets and shops became all the more crucial in this period. Especially during those fearful, early months of the pandemic. At a time when Britain's large supermarkets were characterized by long queues, jittery, ill-tempered shoppers, and shelves ransacked by people panic-buying flour, yeast and toilet roll, London's local cash and carries became comparative nirvanas: dizzyingly well-stocked lands of plenty that were cheap and quick and offered a lifeline in terms of both specialized produce and human interaction. When I think of late spring in 2020, I think of myself roaming the aisles of a Turkish-run African supermarket in Catford, heaping a basket with the yams, Scotch bonnet peppers and bottles of palm oil I would regularly deliver to my mother as she spent the first throes of lockdown alone in her house.

What's more, money transfer businesses became even more of a lifeline throughout this period of global difficulty. Particularly for those Black African diasporas for whom remittance is especially crucial. 'Sending money home, whether you're Ghanaian or Somali, is a huge aspect of the economies of diaspora,' says Ismail Einashe, a British-Somali writer who wrote a 2020 article for the BBC about the strain felt in the money transfer pipeline during Covid. 'But Somalis transfer more than a billion pounds every year to Somalia – which is more than the country receives in aid. They are really important payments.' This was doubly true at a time when people on both continents were falling ill, losing work or, in many cases, having to find ways to help fund the family funerals that they would only be able to attend via Zoom. It's a reminder of just how vital the connection offered through businesses like Obisesan and Takwa's is. Not just to African London's well-being but also to its sense of self.

And what is striking is that the personal difficulties felt by London-based Somalis (and others in the community) during the pandemic – loss of work, the need to isolate or shield – did not impact the flow of money as drastically as many expected. 'At the beginning, in spring 2020, the World Bank and the IMF were thinking a lot of these crucial payments were going to end,' explains Einashe. 'But actually it didn't happen. The drop in the amount of money sent wasn't as bad as had been predicted. [The payments] didn't stop, because people in the diaspora made huge sacrifices.'

Of course, one of the other ways the pandemic affected business at African shops in particular was through the embrace of the herbal and natural remedies Gray references. Obisesan did a brisk trade in oruwo, the dried-bark anti-malarial that she keeps in plastic bottles behind her counter (next to the Agbo jedi root that's supposedly a remedy for piles). And Takwa lights up when I ask if he saw an uptick in demand for goods linked to health. 'Oh, the things we were selling,' he says with a gleeful whistle, before detailing the immunity-boosting kola nuts and tubs of the anti-inflammatory muscle rub Aboniki balm that were flying off his shelves. In the months before there was a readily available vaccine against Covid, these purported herbal solutions – covering everything from turmeric and ginger to plants with proven, if mild, anti-malarial properties – were heartily embraced by the Black community around the world. And then, in the months that followed November 2020, after the Oxford/AstraZeneca vaccine had been approved, fondness for these non-pharmaceutical protections – and misinformation about Covid disseminated on WhatsApp – was blamed by official bodies for the high rate of vaccine hesitancy among Britain's Black population. (By April 2021, 64 per cent of Black over-50s had been vaccinated, compared with 93 per cent of White people in the same age category). If you spent any time with Black Africans or Afro-Caribbeans throughout that first phase of the pandemic, you will know the pronounced, unwavering scepticism the emergence of the vaccine seemed to rouse in many of them. At this time, Black businesses offered a solution and a balm (often literal) to those worries.

If you are, as I am, a British-Nigerian with faith in both science and the vaccine – and you have been socialized and educated to implicitly trust institutions – it is tricky terrain to navigate. There is, of course, historic justification for Black communities displaying healthy suspicion when faced with medical remedies pushed by governments and big business. In 1994, for instance, a Pfizer anti-meningitis drug was responsible for 11 deaths in the Nigerian state of Kano. Further afield in the US, the notorious Tuskegee trials – which, starting in 1932, misled Black men in order to observe the effects of untreated syphilis – led to a 40-year scandal and dozens of preventable deaths. It is no surprise that these stories had particular weight in the midst of a global health crisis. But it is hard to shake the sense that, alongside the social disadvantages and employment patterns that made Britain's Black population especially susceptible to the virus, unfounded rumours about a perfectly safe vaccine were just another way for disadvantaged communities to bear the brunt of Covid's ravages.

Specifically, this applied to transmission-prone, multi-generational households that were the long-term consequence of prejudice within post-war housing.

Elsewhere, it was unconscious ethnic bias within the NHS (in 2021, a Race and Health Observatory report found that 'ethnic inequalities in health outcomes are evident at every stage throughout the life course, from birth to death') fostering ill health and a justified sense of apprehension. As the historian David Olusoga noted in a 2021 *Guardian* column on the issue: 'The pandemic has acted like a vast searchlight, sweeping across society, illuminating unpleasant truths that were lurking in the darkness.' Decades of building inequality within society, so entrenched that successive British governments had struggled to identify it let alone meaningfully address it, were clarified by Covid. It was a tragic perfect storm, with Black life at its centre.

The altered landscape of lockdown and the drift towards those natural Covid remedies (however contentious they were) gave small, market-adjacent Black businesses an undoubted boost. But if we are to take anything from London's shifting landscape – and, specifically, the succession of campaigns launched to try to preserve these markets and cherished immigrant-run businesses – then it can look as though these spaces are fighting a losing battle. The tide of history might be against them. Partly this is generational. As is often the case with immigrants who establish small retail businesses so their children may have better opportunities, there is a question of succession. 'My children are not interested in taking over,' says Obisesan, with a tinge of regret. 'Before they went to uni they used to really help me, but now they are really not interested. This is the problem. Sometimes I sit down and think, "Let's say tomorrow I retire. Is there a young person to take over the shop?

Or even anybody my age?" It's a lot of challenges and it's hard. My brother, it is not easy.'

Gray, for her part, tends to agree that the people currently running these businesses in the Black community – and those frequenting them – may represent the last of a dying breed. 'I'm quite pessimistic because, really, these places are only appealing to the older generation,' she says. 'I don't want to generalize. I'm young. But we care more about pictures, what we can put on the 'Gram and that whole performance. I think we're making a move towards things that have that online appeal.' This is a theory borne out by the emergence, in recent years, of Black African and Afro-Caribbean services like the app Oja and the online grocery delivery operation Trap Fruits: slick, digitally savvy companies that carry some of the spirit of the Black businesses that are their forbears without replicating their dusty, defiantly analogue personal touch.

And then, of course, there is the unstoppable, oat milk tsunami of gentrification. Early 2022 brought the welcome news that, thanks to the Save Ridley Road campaign, Hackney Council agreed to take over management of the Shopping Village, listed it as an Asset of Community Value and vowed to sensitively update facilities, offer stability to current tenants and preserve it as an indoor market for the next generation. But, just to further highlight the game of redevelopment Whac-A-Mole that tends to dog immigrant-run businesses in London, Takwa has learned that the days of his cash and carry are numbered. In late 2021, long-brewing plans to transform the area around Woolwich Arsenal Station, a vital connecting point for the delayed, £18.7 billion Crossrail project, were approved by the council.

Subject to the signing of a compulsory purchase order (as detailed on a crumpled letter that is pushed my way over the counter), Takwa's place, and many of the other phone shops, butcher's and takeaway businesses that have stood near it for years, will in the coming months be moved on, replaced by a £400 million development comprising accommodation, a restaurant and a cinema. More than 25 years of local immigrant history is about to be razed or relocated. But Takwa is typically sanguine and unemotional about his disappearing business and legacy – and whether there would be any value in mounting a Ridley Road-style objection.

'Whether you fight it or not, it's not going to change anything,' he says. 'The council has approved the plan, and it will be a maximum of two more years. I still want to retire. I'm sixty-five and I'll be sixty-six this year.' Add in the fact that the pandemic has led to Black Africans and Afro-Caribbeans of all generations leaving the country ('I really think the pandemic has made people question this idea of home,' says Gray. 'Lots of people [my age] are going to Nigeria, they're going to Jamaica') and it makes the Black marketplace that has grown so impressively in recent years look all the more endangered.

However, I am not so sure. Yes, in contrast to the boom years of the 1980s and 1990s, it seems to be getting increasingly difficult to sustain these businesses. The odds remain firmly stacked against Black entrepreneurs trying to build an empire from nothing more than a market stall and a bulk order of imported goods. And, true enough, there is clearly a generational drift from the tradition of aunties proudly wheeling a granny bag to places like Peckham or Brixton or Ridley Road.

But the embrace of herbal Covid remedies during the pandemic, for all its attendant issues, showed the enduring power and importance of these spaces, and that, amid the grief, chaos and restrictive isolation of the pandemic, Black Africans and Afro-Caribbeans clung to the traditional and the familiar – found solace in solutions steeped in a precolonial past and ancestral knowledge. If something is already old, and proven, then it never goes out of fashion. It's relevant that, more often than not, African supermarkets are places to get traditional brooms, the chewing sticks, or *pako Ijebu*, that West Africans use as an oral hygiene aid, and calabash bowls made from hollowed-out gourds. And so as long as there are Black African Brits craving connection, a portal, and that intangible sense of home, there will be these businesses and people running them.

Because, really, if these places are anything, then they are purveyors of cultural continuity; spaces that uphold the important idea that, even in a world of Dyson vacuum cleaners, electric toothbrushes and expensive ceramics, there is a value, grace and power in the old and supposedly outmoded way of doing things.

3

Boat

There is something transgressive about being in an open nightclub in the daytime. Beneath the grey skies of a Sunday afternoon, I arrive at South London's Studio 338: a vast, squat dance paradise, daubed in peeling black paint, set beside the A2 and its tide of vehicles surging towards the Blackwall Tunnel. All around is an industrial, slate-grey jumble of retail parks, pedestrian walkways and a North Greenwich car park temporarily converted into a drive-through Covid testing centre. Noses wrinkle at an unwelcome, stray plume of sewage on the autumn air. And though there were no official signposts, the boxy frames of idling security guards, and a steady flow of smartly dressed women walking at a purposeful clip, were the first clue I was on the right track.

The sensory hit beyond the metal detector arches at the door confirmed it. Here was music at sternum-juddering volume, fake palm trees swaying in a bedraggled roadside terrace and, back inside, a sunken seating area holding a gathered, almost uniformly Black crowd of early arrivals, availing themselves of bottomless mimosas in white plastic flutes. This, in all its wonky, unexpected majesty, was DLT (or Days Like This) Brunch: a wildly successful event series that is at the vanguard of a 'day party' scene that has experienced a particular boom among young Black Brits in recent years.

This moment could easily have been expressly designed to highlight multiple facets of London nightlife in the early 2020s (the drift towards clubbing venues that are less susceptible to neighbourhood noise complaints, the topsy-turvy embrace of 'day partying', the all-conquering nature of brunch as both between-meals portmanteau and way of life). But if there is one social phenomenon that it highlights more than any other then it is this: the dominance of African culture within the UK's Black spaces and beyond. Because everywhere you look, Africa is visible. It is there in the steaming mounds of jollof rice that people are shovelling in from brown paper cartons; it is there in the Africa-shaped jewellery glinting around necks and dangling from earlobes; and, most of all, it is there in the Afrobeats music that dominates the sound system, whumping out of speakers and setting girls off dancing in a low crouch as their braids swing behind them. 'Give it up to all of those celebrating Nigeria's 61st anniversary,' says the DJ into the microphone at one point, acknowledging this particular event's theme to loud approving whoops from the crowd.

It's easy to imagine that, in another era, a party like this would have been more obviously in thrall to identifiably Caribbean or African-American references. But here and now, as British-Nigerians fill out the crowd and a Wizkid song sparks fevered singalongs, this is Black Britishness with a distinct African accent; the manifestation of a prolonged pop cultural rehabilitation that nobody really saw coming and reflective of a broader power shift within the UK's wider Black community.

'For a long time, Black Britishness was defined by the *Windrush* generation,' explains Akemnji 'AK' Ndifornyen, Cameroonian-British actor and co-creator of the BAFTA-winning sketch show *Famalam*. Blessed with leading-man looks, expressive features and eyebrows that seem perpetually arched in anticipation of a droll aside, Ndifornyen has a clown's spirit and a restless, academic mind. To speak to him is to head off on meandering comic digressions that give equal weight to Langston Hughes quotes and East London grime crews. It is not always clear where you are going. But it is always fun getting there. 'Now, the common thread', he continues, '– and this is not a shot at my West Indian brothers and sisters – is that Nigeria, Ghana, the Ivory Coast, Congo and Gambia rule the roost in terms of successful Black representation. In terms of music, it's Dizzee Rascal, Tinie Tempah, Skepta, Little Simz, Dave and Stormzy. And then from a film and TV perspective, it's Daniel Kaluuya, Michaela Coel, Idris Elba, Chiwetel Ejiofor. I could go on.'

He could. Just as many of us who have noticed the rise of this visible new breed of Black African heritage stars could reel off our own roll call of high achievers, with Ugandan, Zimbabwean, Somali or Sierra Leonean heritage making their mark in a variety of fields. But what is striking about the wave of the last decade or so – especially in relation to West African visibility – is that it does not seem to be slowing down or levelling off. It has come to resemble a series of infinite tipping points; a cresting wave that refuses to break.

And so, what do we second-generation British Africans think, as we survey this fresh landscape of African ubiquitousness and supremacy? This representational land of plenty, where detailed explorations of Black African diaspora life are so commonplace and prominent and prized as to barely warrant a mention? Well, honestly, we feel immense pride. But, also, perhaps, a sense of core-shaking bafflement. Because the truth of it is this: if you have Black African ancestry and you grew up in the UK during the past half-century then you will know that African identity has not always been regarded this highly. You will know, in fact, that not only was it decidedly uncool to be from Africa, but it also carried all manner of negative associations and stigmas, ranging from famine-ridden destitution to backwardness. And you will know, ultimately, that in the hierarchy of Black British communities dominated by those originally from the Caribbean islands, Africans of every stripe had come to be viewed, through the prism of mainstream culture at least, as the whipping boys of the diaspora.

This transition, and its deeper significance, is what makes the historic interaction between London's Black African and Afro-Caribbean communities matter. To put it simply: it is an issue that strikes to the heart of shifting notions of Black Britishness and what its future may hold. To truly understand the situation now, I and others like me have to look back to the difficulties of the past. No matter how personally painful that may be.

It was a Jamaican girl in my Year 7 class who first told me I was an African. Don't get me wrong. I had, of course, for a long time before that known that my family – as evidenced by each of the exuberant weekend functions that were the drumbeat of our lives – was an extremely Nigerian one. But it was this girl, let us call her Sabrina, who first let me know that I was an African in a conspicuous, detectable way. And it was she who informed me that this was not something I should be remotely happy about or proud of.

'You've got a proper big African nose, yuknow.' Those are words that I dimly remember her saying, with a squint and a menacing smile, early on in Year 7 when I'm pretty sure we had barely been introduced. Big, quick and motormouthed in a draining, utterly devastating way, Sabrina was the undoubted alpha of the class; the verbal sniper we all prayed wouldn't aim a laser-sighted hollow-point in our direction. And so, when she commenced abusing my African nose, I think I probably dismissed it as a random non-sequitur designed to unsettle and disorient me.

But then it happened again. And again. And the jibes about the massiveness of my African nose, the size of my lips or the heft of my African '*bubu*' head kept coming, until one day, as we were waiting to go into some lesson, she cornered me with a gathering crowd around us and a glint in her eye. 'Is it true,' she said, cracking a smile, 'that Africans eat *bright* orange rice?' The smirk switched to a repulsed, pantomime grimace. Now, from the vantage point of the present, the notion that jollof rice – a pretty much universally beloved dish that is practically a byword for mainstream West African deliciousness – would be viewed as some comically disgusting piece of culinary exotica is, of course, patently ridiculous. However, in the less enlightened surrounds of majority-White, majority-English, suburban South-East London in the mid-1990s, things were different. I recall some revulsed, quizzical noises from people within earshot. And I think my immediate impulse, like a cornered politician caught in a lie, was denial and deflection.

'W-what?' I said, flustered. 'No, we don't. Well, it's not ...What?' I have an image of myself, practically pressed back against the door jamb of an open classroom as we waited to file in, stammering until Sabrina lost interest and went to find some other target. In truth, set against my various other school run-ins with her (which came to include a pattern of her professing her love for me one day before swinging back to vicious bullying and threats of physical violence the next), it was reasonably mild. However, it is an incident I have repeatedly scoured for meaning. One somewhat fixed in my mind. And the reason, I think, is that it was one of the first times that the compartmentalized African and British sides of me were brought into sudden, glitching conflict.

I had, like a lot of second-generation immigrant teenagers, sought to keep the Nigerian version of myself (the one at home, who went by 'Folajimi' and jostled for space in a noisy house where English was often the second language) somewhat concealed. But now, here was Sabrina and her (I imagine, deliberately) shaky grasp of West African gastronomy. Ready to whip off the veil, put me in my place in Britain's Black hierarchy, and introduce me to the fact that it wasn't just White people who could be xenophobic. The 'orange rice' moment had such an impact because it viscerally confirmed something that I had perhaps always slightly suspected would be a governing force in my life.

However, the key thing to note here is that, though this moment left a lasting mark on me, it was far from unique. Because, unbeknown to me, all across London and the UK, other kids of Black African heritage were fighting similar daily battles in playgrounds, classrooms and buses. Our big, supposedly undesirable African features. Our strange, unpronounceable names. Our coarse, just-arrived freshness. Some of the Caribbeans in our orbit were introducing us to a whole new lexicon of ridicule. And the effect, for many of us, was more than a little confusing.

Take Nels Abbey, for example: an author and former banker who, after a period living with White English foster parents in Oxfordshire, moved to West London with his Nigerian family in the late 1980s, started at a new school, and experienced a flurry of different culture shocks all at once. 'The first thing I remember when we came to London was that I was relieved I wasn't going to be the odd child out,' he says. 'I was no longer the only Black child, and so that was a big burden off my shoulders. But I didn't know anything about Africans being one thing, and Caribbean people being another.' He laughs knowingly. Abbey has small, rimless glasses, a bearish stature and an infectious knack of gleefully barrelling towards taboo topics others would actively avoid. 'I remember getting in class and for the first couple of days it was going well,' he goes on. 'But then it just became apparent to me that to be African was frowned upon. The Jamaicans were the thing to be. And if you were not Jamaican then you at least had to be from one of the other islands like Barbados.'

And so what did he do, having recognized that his heritage was a kind of social poison? Well, he effectively went into the closet. 'My name is Nels Abbey, right?' he says, with a grin. 'So when I first saw that it was the Jamaicans who were winning, it dawned on me that my name would make it pretty damn easy for me to blend in. And so I just blended in and became a Jamaican. No, in fact, I didn't pick Jamaica, because I didn't feel that was my position.' He laughs again, at the ridiculousness of it all. 'I started to claim Barbados. Even though my mum had this flawless Nigerian accent back at home.'

What may sound a preposterous act of social contortion was actually a common survival method for lots of African kids growing up in London schools. 'There were so many Kwames, Kwekus and Femis at my school who hid their names and tried to Anglicize them,' adds Akemnji Ndifornyen, who grew up in Dalston in a similar era to Abbey. 'My name is this unpronounceable thing and my mum didn't allow me to Anglicize it,' he continues. 'She was doggedly resilient about it – and that prevented me from being able to blend in to a degree.' Anecdotally, some young African kids adopted some of the protective stance and swagger of Black American culture. Others veiled themselves in the Caribbean cool that was dominant at the time. Ultimately, it didn't matter, as long as nothing gave you away as identifiably Black African. Although, naturally, hand in hand with this closeting came the daily threat of exposure.

'If ever my mum wanted to punish me for misbehaving, she would have my Nigerian clothes ironed out and ready for school the next morning,' says Abbey, chuckling at the memory with a kind of delighted horror. 'And I would just beg and beg. "I won't do it again. *Please*." She would ultimately let me wear my normal stuff. But she always knew that she could out me.' It sounds extreme; like the darkly absurd pinnacle of what it was to hide your heritage during this period. Yet you only need to look around at the depiction of Black Africans during this time – and, to be specific, the entire, oversimplified concept of 'Africa' as one indistinct entity – to see why the fear was so real. Because the Afrophobia of Sabrina, and all those like her, did not just come from the ether. It derived from a society that was shockingly lacking when it came to positive, mainstream depictions of life and culture on the mother continent.

'Look, the portrayal of Africa has always been vicious,' notes Abbey. 'Just dark, backwards people, flies on faces, poverty, war and famine – you name it. And then came the [email] fraud wave. There was nothing good in terms of how we were portrayed.' None of this was especially new. As far back as the 1920s, Western fascination with Africa had been bound up with its reputation as the largely uncharted Dark Continent – an alien zone that sparked conflicting notions of disease, savagery, hardship and a kind of exotic, mysterious nobility. But it's notable that the 1980s and 1990s (ironically enough, a period that saw a marked increase in immigration from African countries to the UK) represented a curious nadir for African representation in the mainstream. To put it bluntly: Black Africans were generally there to be either rescued or ridiculed.

And through the precise prism of Caribbean-dominated Black British pop culture, the bias could be especially stark. This is, after all, the era that gave us Lenny Henry shrieking '*Katanga!*' in tribal paint and a grass skirt as his trademark 'African' character (a lamentable, extremely of-its-time decision he has since expressed regret for). Elsewhere, in 1991, the landmark Black-oriented sketch show *The Real McCoy* gave us the other end of the caricatured African spectrum with Felix Dexter's popular creation, Nathaniel: a thick-accented, self-important

African 'h'accountant', fond of scolding gathered members of the live audience for their crude manner or improper grasp of the Queen's English. To the Black British community of that time, depictions like this acted as both transmitter and megaphone. They broadcast and amplified stereotypical views about Africans (namely, that they were either screeching savages or comically haughty, over-educated nerds) that were already widely held and discussed within the Black community's barbershops, churches and trinket-stuffed living rooms. But, in an era when any Black representation on television was strictly rationed, these views invariably felt deeply embedded and much harder to challenge.

Which is not to say that there were not dissenting voices within the mainstream. For instance, Channel 4's *Desmond's* – the pioneering, Peckham-set sitcom about a Black barbershop and its dysfunctional family of employees, customers and hangers-on – gave us Matthew: the Gambian-born mature student who had an old African proverb for every occasion. Though he was a fundamentally broad character, Matthew was also afforded a degree of nuance atypical for screen representation of a Black African at that time. And this was very much by design, according to Trix Worrell, the show's St Lucian-heritage creator. 'I found it so difficult that, at that time, West Indian Blacks weren't honouring Black Africans,' explains Worrell, an engaging ball of profanity and anecdotes who has since swapped the South-East London neighbourhood he made famous for Hastings. 'That they were so dismissive of them used to vex me. I just felt that [African heritage] was a strong heritage. It was our heritage. And I wanted people to know that.'

In collaboration with cast member Gyearbuor Asante, the late Ghanaian actor who brought the character to life, Worrell set about imbuing Matthew with both recognizable traits and humanizing contradictions, and, in doing so, hopefully portraying some of the multiplicity of a Black, largely working-class South London neighbourhood. 'For me, there was a dignity in the African student,' he adds. 'In the way that they held themselves and in the fact that they weren't economic migrants.'

This point brings us to an important aspect of this debate. Because, in many ways, it is the story that each of these founding Black communities in the UK has told about itself – broadly speaking, that Caribbeans are children of *Windrush* who arrived to rebuild post-war Britain, and that Black Africans are primarily foreign students who came for better education – that has occasionally set them in opposition. It's a perceived ideological stand-off that takes in other related issues (class, displacement, the trauma of slavery), and lies at the heart of so much of this conflict. And what's more, crucially, it nudges us towards the fact that this intra-ethnic discrimination didn't just flow in one direction.

'It was very much a two-way street,' says Abbey. 'African parents took pride in the fact that they came here for education whereas Caribbeans generally came here to work. So there were two different routes. And so, of course, the more learned a person is, and the more Western education they have, well, with that comes arrogance.' If this African sense of superiority can be called arrogance then I definitely experienced it when I was growing up. Whatever Afro-Caribbean kids like Sabrina had been told about us – that we were strange, that we were ugly, that we were uppity – it met its match in what many Black African parents had to say about our counterparts within the West Indian community. We were told that 'Jamos' (a contraction of Jamaican that added insult to injury by not delineating between different islands) were shiftless, coarse-mannered future criminals that we were not to mix with. To even write it feels painful and absurd. But there is no denying that there was an entire generation of Black Brits who were pretty much kept apart because of the seductiveness of these damaging stereotypes. As Jeffrey Boakye writes in *Black, Listed*, to be segregated from one faction of Blackness, while living in such close proximity, could be more than a little confusing: 'Growing up on an estate in Brixton, my senses were overwhelmed with a combination of African and Caribbean cultures; the smells, the signposts and signifiers, but they were seldom reconciled. We simply didn't spend time in each other's homes.'

A vignette like this highlights the ridiculousness of two groups that were so inextricably linked – two groups that were and are, in essence, one group – working to maintain some distance. But if there is a seriousness underpinning it all then it comes from what these anxieties say about Black Caribbeans and Africans alike. On the subject of education, for example, Worrell surmises that some of the stigma and teasing that Afro-Caribbeans aimed at those studious Black Africans, in thrall to academia long past adolescence with their many, many useless degrees, could almost be attributed to a sense of rueful recognition. 'For my generation of West Indians, education was key,' he says. 'But that was beginning to be knocked down, because the feeling was that no matter how many A-levels you got, you still weren't getting a job.' The 1970s and 1980s brought prejudiced banding of Caribbean heritage students and the scandal around the educationally subnormal (ESN) pupil category that was disproportionately applied to Black kids. Simply put, West Indian settlers bore the brunt of structural disadvantage that their Black African counterparts hadn't yet experienced. They were the lifers on the wing, trying to educate greener new arrivals about the oppressiveness of the system they were entering.

For the Black Africans, meanwhile, the notion that those of Caribbean origin signified trouble or criminality is also worth some scrutiny. First, it should be pointed out that this view is probably, again, as much about class as it is about culture (thanks to the landscape of decolonization, many of that first post-war wave of West African students would have been drawn from privileged or aspirant upper-middle-class families who brought with them all manner of notions about status). Yet it is striking that, in attaching some of the most damaging stereotypes to Afro-Caribbean men in particular, Black Africans were simply parroting the suspicions and assumptions of a racist, White society. Some Afro-Caribbeans, in their own way, were enacting a different version of the same thing; making fun of our collective African foreignness and inability to integrate. In this sense, both sides were punching and jibing at something that didn't exist, thanks to their own anxieties about prospering in an inhospitable country. These confected, limiting ideas of Blackness on both sides of the divide were so accepted – and, in some cases, so alluring – that they could be uniquely damaging.

'What was actually funny,' begins Abbey, 'was that it was only in later life that I realized some of the more vehement "I am Jamaican, shut the fuck up" kids at my school were actually Nigerian.' He laughs again. 'So we had actually just wound ourselves up. I even got sent to Nigeria because of the amount of trouble I was getting into, and it was just from trying to live out a vicious stereotype of a Jamaican person based on what I'd been shown on TV.' It's a revelation that, as well as forcing Black Africans who attended London schools in the 1980s and 1990s to wonder how many of their playground tormenters were actually Caribbean, cements the harmful absurdity of this feud. It shows that bitterness between West Indians and Africans was, ultimately, a triumph for those who sought to keep the Black community in limiting boxes.

And it also makes me think of Sabrina, who, in her own way, was a prisoner of these constrictive societal prejudices. I'm pretty sure she really was actually Jamaican. But, despite her cruelty during school (not just to me but to anyone who managed to be within the radius of her sprinkler system of fury), I can now see that she must have been fighting her own battles as a young Black woman, perennially bracketed as loud and disruptive by classmates and teachers alike. Ultimately, the Black community in this era was kept apart by wider societal forces and a narrow perception of the ways in which one could be Black. It was pride in cultural difference and fond, interfamilial teasing allowed to curdle into something far more volatile. And, as one millennium tipped into the next, it was going to get a whole lot worse before it got better.

Tragic, untimely deaths always leave questions, but Damilola Taylor's seemed to leave more than most.

Injured on his way home from school on 27 November 2000, the Nigerian-born ten-year-old slumped in a stairwell near his Peckham estate, bled profusely from a severed artery in his leg, and was near death by the time he was found. Initially at least, the details that led to his killing were murky. Who inflicted the fatal wound? Was the weapon a knife or a broken bottle? And, most pressingly, why was he killed? Some answers would come, of course, with the delayed trial of Richard and Daniel Preddie, the sibling perpetrators found guilty of manslaughter in 2006.

But the cloud of doubt lingered around Taylor's death, as if mirroring the intractable, bottomless nature of a nation, a community and a family's grief. There would be no satisfying answer to why he lost his life. Even so, there was no alternative but to keep looking. And so it tells you something about the rifts within parts of London's Black diaspora at the time that one of the motives to gain the most traction in the months after Damilola Taylor's death was this: that he had been wounded by children of Afro-Caribbean heritage because he was Black African. This was the persistent word on the street, as winter crept on, what would have been Damilola's 11th birthday passed, and Christmas came and went. In a lengthy *London Review of Books* story, published in January 2001, the journalist and legal expert John Upton reported from Peckham and alighted on this mood during conversation with the owner of a local chip shop.

He says he'd like to put his point of view. Several newsmen have wanted him to say that what is needed is more police on the streets, but he doesn't think this will stop bullying; and when I ask him about that, he says it's the Jamaican boys wanting to copy the New York gangs. They pick on the Africans – and the Africans, well they're not violent but they're all benefit fraudsters.

Though presented with a sceptical, comic glint, these reported quotes hint at what Upton later acknowledges as 'anecdotal evidence of tensions between the Afro-Caribbean and African communities on the estate'. Yet it wasn't only opinionated local observers who appeared to believe that the bullying and teasing Taylor faced at school, and the violent encounter that led to his death, had their roots in wider discord within Peckham's Black population. 'Nigerian people are not popular in this area because they try to fit in and do well,' said the British–Nigerian politician Lola Ayorinde to the *Sunday Telegraph* in an article that appeared a few days after Taylor's death. 'The West Indian community likes to pretend there is racism everywhere and Black people are being held back. Anyone who doesn't subscribe to that point of view suddenly becomes a target.'

Even now, these quotes – the equivalent of hurling a bucket of petrol on dangerously flickering flames – are shocking to read. But, putting aside the deeply unhelpful nature of Ayorinde's views (and there will be more from her in a moment), it is not hard to see why the tragedy of Taylor's death had many in the West African community walking this particular path of blame, prejudice and suspicion. Something about the sad, random injustice of Taylor's killing punctured and disturbed the national consciousness. Yet, for the Black Africans who were part of the great migratory wave of the 1980s and 1990s, you can imagine that the front-page images of his smiling face were all the more acute; that the lack of any intervention as he was attacked in broad daylight spoke to London's lack of community. Looking at the details of his short life that were being repeatedly combed over – his studiousness, his Yoruba mother anxiously awaiting his return as he perished, the fact that his family had only arrived in London three months earlier so they could access better healthcare for his sister's epilepsy – would have only cemented the feeling that it could just have easily happened to any one of their families. My middle name is Damilola. For my mum I imagine it felt especially close to home.

Coupled with the earlier 1993 killing of Stephen Lawrence, Taylor's tragic demise seemed to confirm the worst suspicions about the haphazard cruelties of Black life in London and the ills of inner-city living in general. This confirmation bred understandable fear and a grief-stricken search for a viable culprit or societal boogeyman. And so it holds that West Africans like Ayorinde would look at Damilola Taylor's violent death on one side, look at the undoubtedly very real tension between Black African and Afro-Caribbean settlers in some London neighbourhoods at that time on the other side, and make the assumption that one must be related to the other. Because who is to say that what starts as teasing and bullying could not spill over into fatal violence?

Well, the truth is that this theory can quickly be dismissed as bogus. The testimony and investigation that followed Taylor's death found no evidence to prove that any of the occasional taunts he experienced on the estate were about his heritage. Damilola's late mother, Gloria, released a statement saying that she did not think racism (of any sort) was a factor in her son's death. The Black newspaper *New Nation* conducted a survey on the streets near Damilola Taylor's estate and couldn't find one respondent who thought the Africans vs West Indians theory had any credence. As Mike Eboda, *New Nation*'s British-Nigerian editor, put it in a *Guardian* column published six days after Taylor's death:

> All of a sudden we are left talking about whether there is a rift between Britain's West Indian and African communities. And more importantly whether this was to blame for the killing of the little boy. Next thing you know, activists on either 'side' receive phone calls from journalists. Leading questions are put to them. 'All West Indians are troublemakers,' says the Nigerian one. 'Nigerians are just arrogant,' retorts the Jamaican. Divide and rule was always the colonial way.

'Divide and rule' is a phrase often deployed when discussing this issue. And the image it conjures – of the mainstream press, standing in the middle and stirring things up, like the kid in the playground gleefully screaming 'Fight!' – is a convincing one. However, it's significant that it is a term that has its roots, as a saying and an idea, in the transatlantic slave trade. It comes, specifically, from the way plantation holders in the Caribbean used a suite of sophisticated, psychological methods – including pairing workers from different African nations together and instituting rivalries by offering preferential treatment to some but not to others – to maintain control and minimize rebellions among a slave population that often vastly outnumbered its White overseers.

And so, if we shift beyond Damilola Taylor, and zoom out to the defining tragedy of Black enslavement, then we also find the root of much of this conflict and rumour. Slavery is, in effect, the inciting incident in this long-running saga. And it starts with the belief, surely held in certain quarters, that some Africans were complicit in the enslavement of those who would become West Indians.

'The whole idea that Africans sold Caribbean people into slavery was the most seductive and successful piece of Western propaganda I've ever seen in my life,' says Abbey, explaining the crux of so much of this tension. 'It really forced a wedge between us for so long.' This falsehood about Africans effectively selling out their own people – which is tied, historically, to an oversimplification of kinship-based enslavement and the use of war prisoner labour in precolonial West Africa – has somehow long been passed across the generations, becoming more sacrosanct and widely accepted as fact the further it gets from the truth. This sense of a misdirect is key. Because it is often the case that, just as those plantation owners intended, a point of tension between different contingents of Black people maintains the status quo and obscures a legitimate grievance. Confusingly, beneath the ping-ponging accusations, there is often a kernel of truth.

And nowhere is that truer than in the case of Lola Ayorinde (yes, her again) and Labour MP Diane Abbott engaging in a war of words in 2006. It began with a column written by Abbott entitled 'Think Jamaica is bad? Try being a Nigerian' and published in a Jamaican newspaper, which took aim at corruption, oil industry pollution, intra-religious turmoil and other societal ills in Nigeria. Needless to say, Nigerians did not take kindly to this. Yet while the more reasonable among them mostly took issue with the impolitic tone of the piece (not to mention that Abbott had chosen to air these legitimate grievances with Nigerian governance in a Jamaican publication rather than in the House of Commons), Ayorinde went for the jugular, accusing Caribbeans of – among other things – effectively monopolizing access to resources in the UK. 'Anything that's supposed to go to us goes to the Caribbeans,' she said during a debate on the BBC's *Politics Show*.

Again, it is hard to imagine a less edifying way for representatives from the same marginalized group to interact with one another (a point deftly made by Abbott in a second column that requested unity and decried the 'silly myths and antagonism' resurfacing within the Afro-Caribbean and Black African diasporas). But Ayorinde's position highlights a relevant issue, even if it isn't the one she thinks she's highlighting. Ultimately, it is revealing that she gives voice to anxieties over the scarcity of resources like jobs, housing and social support. Some of the perceived differences between Black Africans and Afro-Caribbeans in the UK speak to the divergent circumstances of their initial arrival and are actually borne out by the numbers (for one thing, a 2016 article in the *Economist* notes that less than one-quarter of Black Africans are the owner-occupiers of their homes, compared with nearly one-half of Afro-Caribbeans; an oddly fitting manifestation of the supposed transience of one group versus the permanence of another).

However, the key mistake is to assume that scarcity of adequate resources for the Black community is a sign of one group hogging more than they deserve; that a limited share should lead to a fight over the crumbs rather than unified action to bring about more for everyone. In this sense, in turning one longer established group against newer settlers, the feuding feels like a way for prejudice to keep being rolled down the hill; for the cycle of blame and suspicion to never be broken. And nowhere is this more evident than in the other Black groups that arrived in considerable numbers after both Caribbeans and West Africans – those from Francophone nations, East African countries like Uganda and, perhaps most prominently, the Somali population that arrived after fleeing civil war in the 1990s – and struggled, in some instances, to integrate in the face of discrimination from both sides.

In 2004, the late Darcus Howe created a documentary on racist infighting among British minority communities (provocatively titled *Who You Callin' a Nigger?*). And in a preview column in the *Guardian* he recalled a real-life encounter that truly solidifies the surreal nature of Black immigrant groups punching down in this way.

I journeyed through Woolwich and Plumstead, where thousands of Somali refugees are settling. The Caribbean community is mostly unwelcoming. Some visit on Somalis the same kind of racial abuse we suffered in the period of early migration. Dissenters to this reactionary view are few and far between. 'They are taking our houses. They are getting social benefits which are denied to us. Their children are overcrowding our schools.' And more . . . One middle-aged West Indian woman capped her experiences at the hand of a group of young Somalis with [an] uninhibited outburst: 'I hate Somalis. They should go back to where they came from.' She did not bat an eyelid . . .

Having grown up around this particular part of South-East London, I remember both the influx of Somali refugees and the prevalence of these sorts of attitudes well. Aware of my slight punchbag status as a West African, I met the arrival of this new group – so culturally and physically distinct that they were even easier to spot than those of us with supposedly conspicuous Nigerian features – with something like shameful relief. Shameful, because I had the sense that I was slightly off the hook. But the struggles faced by groups like those Somalis, and the echo of post-war xenophobia they prompted in some Afro-Caribbeans and other Black Africans, effectively clarify this issue. Because the first great lie of this period was that all the various designations of Blackness in London at that time needed to remain in conflict and competition with each other to get on in life; that we needed to jockey for power and control. And the second was that all of this was fixed. That tension between communities could not be eased, that the way a culture was perceived was set in stone, and that there wasn't a way we could all assert our individuality while also being part of a bigger, more meaningful whole. As Abbott noted in that 2006 rebuttal column, by that midpoint of the 2000s this pushback was already manifesting in a new generation that 'share a common Black youth culture, wherever their parents come from'.

A time had come when the seeds of deception that were first sown on sugar cane plantations, and bloomed amid the challenging atmosphere of the postcolonial metropole, were beginning to be questioned. Though, of course, to overcome these tensions, we would first need to actually discuss them. Something that, on occasion, has been easier said than done.

Even further back than the 1990s, the tension between Black African and Afro-Caribbean cultures was set to a low, steady simmer. In his posthumously published 1964 book, *Toward the African Revolution*, the pioneering, Martinique-born Black psychiatrist and Marxist thinker Frantz Fanon suggests that these attitudes took particular root in the era that preceded the Second World War, arguing that 'In Every West Indian, before the war of 1939, there was not only the certainty of a superiority over the African, but the certainty of a fundamental difference. The African was a Negro and the West Indian was a European.'

Fanon, it should be said, was an anti-colonial revolutionary with a knack for provocation; a man who rarely saw a hornets' nest he didn't want to kick. It is also worth noting that, in this particular essay, the issue of discord and suspicion among the global Black diaspora is employed to, among other things, present what is ultimately a compelling, hopeful case for Black pride and unity. But, even so, it is striking to see these views expressed in this way, even at this point in history. That the same attitudes and taunts about Africans that flourished in the British school playgrounds of the 1990s – the implicit and explicit reminders of your place in the immigrant pecking order – have such deep roots is not especially surprising. But the shock is there all the same.

As we can see, the tension between Britain's Black African and Afro-Caribbean immigrant communities has, at times, spilled over into matters of life and death, with the jokes and jibes and whispers tending to be the manifestation of far more serious anxieties about assimilation, class, loss of culture and the fight for access to the insufficient social resources doled out by a discriminatory government.

These are the painful realities of life in diaspora; things we do not necessarily want to sit with. And so I have found that few outside the Black community would even be aware of this tension between Black Africans and Afro-Caribbeans, which tells you something interesting too. Historic infighting and bad-mouthing among the Black British diaspora is that rare issue that is both commonly discussed in private spaces and recognized as extremely taboo. I lost count, for instance, of the number of times a broad conversation for this book inevitably wound its way back to a whispered, off-record account of what some in the Black African community would once say about Afro-Caribbeans, and vice versa. It is a topic, I soon learned, with its own irresistible pull. Everyone wants to talk about it. Nobody wants to talk about it.

And, truthfully, there is a temptation to maintain this air of public silence. What good can come from reopening old wounds or bearing any grudges? Isn't a degree of tribalism, infighting and jockeying for superiority within immigrant communities (or all communities, for that matter) simply a fact of life? And shouldn't the surging African renaissance of the last decade or so – the events like DLT Brunch, the Afrocentric TV shows, films and songs and the prolonged, brightly garbed jamboree of *Black Panther*'s

2018 release – be interpreted as an unambiguous happy ending? A reflection of a hard-won unity that could only be weakened by the dredging up of old feuds?

Honestly, solidarity within the Black British community has never been a more vital resource. Recent public outcries concerning racial justice in the UK – encompassing both the Black Lives Matter marches of 2020 and the 2019 *Windrush* immigration scandal that preceded it – have been characterized by a cross-diaspora unity of feeling and purpose; shoulder-to-shoulder protests against government indifference from both Afro-Caribbeans and Black Africans (not to mention White Brits, South Asians, Poles, East Asians and others freshly acquainted with the concept of allyship and the role we all play in maintaining a racist status quo) reaffirmed the idea that infighting is a misdirect – and any anger and frustration should be aimed, not at other cultures caught in the societal machine, but at the powers that be pushing the buttons. This is the crux of it. And the reasonable concern of those who would prefer Afrophobia and intra-Black hostility in the UK was left in the past, lest it cause more division.

So, yes, there are many valid reasons to cautiously back away from this centuries-old unexploded bomb; to uphold the long-standing taboo status that tends to shroud it as an issue. But I think to do that would be to ignore what can be learned. Because, as we have seen, what may appear to be solely about Black British culture's conflicting relationship with Africanness is actually about so much more. It deals with internalized prejudice and the long-term ripple effects of the transatlantic slave trade. It touches on colonialism, the 'We were here first' hierarchy that tends to exist within all immigrant communities, and the ways both Black Africans and Afro-Caribbeans have come to be defined by the initial circumstances of their settlement. It tells us a little about conflicting notions of assimilation, what constitutes 'Blackness', and the ways in which perceived proximity to Whiteness has traditionally tended to confer superiority. And it even, perhaps, teaches us a little about class, education and the members of other Black diasporas still fighting to make it to these shores in boats far less accommodating than the *Windrush*. As Darcus Howe put it, after first exploring these issues in that 2004 documentary: 'Dirty linen needs airing.'

The journey that Black Africans and Afro-Caribbeans have been on – from the internal prejudice and hostility touched on by Fanon to the joyful release and exuberant pride on display at DLT Brunch – is a long and winding one. It is, in truth, a road that can look a little like a gauntlet: fraught with tensions, bad feeling, accusations, self-hate and lasting incidents of childhood bullying and trauma. But, treacherous as it is, it is a path that ultimately leads us towards a reconciliation that deserves to be explored and exalted.

Back at DLT Brunch, as the relatively sedate, sit-down event slides into a more raucous early-evening party, the afternoon's bottomless carafes of Prosecco elicit predictable results. Chair-dancing in that sunken pit of a dining area evolves into giggling, full-scale two-step. The DJ takes to the mic for a third time, pleading with the dawdling crowd to vacate the brunch area so the tables can be cleared and removed. And outside, in Studio 338's strange, Astroturfed paradise, girls guffaw and stumble from the pedestal of a specially installed

360-degree photo booth, while a nearby catering truck offers barbecued suya beef, meat pies, fried plantain skewered with chicken gizzards, and little doughnut-like balls of puff-puff, heralded by a sweet, fatty scent drifting through the air.

'This is cute,' says another girl, leading her friends out past me and towards a standing table, shivering a little, as the sound of South African *amapiano* music drifts from the indoor area. 'Cold, but cute.' It would be hard to imagine a scene that, after the difficulties of past decades, more forcefully expressed how far Black African culture has come. Or, for that matter, the joyful, multifaceted inclusivity that has come to be synonymous with what it means to be Black British at this particular moment in time. Celebration, individuality and an unashamed pride are everywhere you look. As Anthony Iban, one of the group of British–Nigerian friends who founded DLT in 2016, puts it to me later: 'I think that now, African culture just *is* popular culture.'

It's a contention hard to argue with. Not just in light of, say, grime and British rap's distinct links to the Black African experience in the UK (as evidenced by Afroswing, Afrobashment and any number of Afrobeats' subsidiary genres that may have been minted in the time it's taken me to write this sentence), but also in the context of more global examples of Africa's shift to the forefront of the collective consciousness; whether that means the rumbling juggernaut of *Black Panther*, John Boyega wearing a traditional Yoruba outfit to the premiere of 2019's saga-capping *Star Wars* film (and inspiring countless other actors from other diasporas to follow suit), Beyoncé using a role in a remake of Disney's *The Lion King* as an excuse to create a sonic tribute to the multiplicity of the continent's music, and even Donald Glover, co-opting the shirtless, revolutionary stance of Fela Kuti for his internet-breaking video for 'This Is America'. From the dark days of African representation in the 1980s and 1990s, a corner has been turned. No one can deny that. However, identifying precisely when it was turned is a trickier proposition.

'The rise of broadband internet, localized documentary makers, better writing and better researched history has definitely made it better,' says Nels Abbey, noting that this moment for Africans has coincided with a tandem boom in mainstream media reappraisals of Black British history at large. 'And also, if I think of a cultural turning point, Afrobeats clearly played a role. The sound being a fusion between traditional African music, hip hop and Caribbean music brought African culture more into the mainstream.' Akemnji Ndifornyen, who has mercilessly ribbed much of this Black British culture through *Famalam*, agrees that visible, mainstream expressions of a proud, cool, aspirational African Blackness have helped to embolden a generation and smooth that long-standing rift.

And, in fact, he goes further, pointing out that the confidence we are seeing now is a result of a deeper, more varied breadth of Black British representation making its way on to both mainstream TV channels and online platforms. 'We were governed by the bandwidth of media where there were only four channels before 1997,' says Ndifornyen. 'And of those four channels, you'd get maybe two hours of programming a week that might be relevant to you as a Black person. Now, if you're 20 years old, then you've grown up without ever knowing a world where you can't see as many

Black people [on screen] as you want. And Black British people in particular.'

Naturally, we shouldn't present mainstream representation of the Black experience as being in some utopian state of perfection; there is still work to be done, and greater opportunities also place greater emphasis on the need to resist tokenism and fight for continued, more nuanced portrayals of Black British Africans on screen. Much more needs to be done, for instance, to reflect the experience of East Africans, Central Africans and those from the south of the continent.

However, Ndifornyen's point about a generational shift is key. Because the positive strides of the last few years have been as much about the determination and unwavering pride of a new, younger breed of Black Africans – and the readiness of their Afro-Caribbean counterparts to unite with them in that cultural celebration and, in the process, perhaps, create something new. Yes, the sight of proud Afrobeats stars on awards show stages and acclaimed Black African actors in native wear will have helped spur people on. But the positive movement of the last decade or so has been instigated by a younger generation with no sense that there were any old battles to be fought or scores to be settled between different factions of the Black community. 'There was a point at which young African kids weren't having it any more,' says Ndifornyen. 'And by not having it, I mean that they were no longer going to be bringing up the caboose of Blackness. They were going to be at the forefront.'

Moreover, this power shift – no doubt helped by the fact that, of course, by 2011, Black Africans were the dominant Black group in the UK – helped take the sting out of any intra-ethnic rivalry. 'By the time I got to university, the talk of "Oh, you're African and you're Caribbean" just didn't exist,' says Abbey. 'We were fairly well-educated people and we would joke about each other; Nigerians and Ghanaians joking about each other was the source of belly laughs for days. But the key thing here was that things were just moving away from that primary school, secondary school-type rift to where we're at now: just pretty much becoming one community.'

And that sense of convergence is often literal, with this new generation engaging in the intermarriage that finger-wagging elders once tried to protect a generation from. 'With me, I'm engaged and my fiancée is Jamaican,' says DLT's Iban. 'My parents are the most Yoruba people you could meet, and yet there's an understanding and they don't mind.' Abbey too, reports of family functions during which he keeps having the same misunderstanding with men that he presumes to be Nigerian. 'My younger aunties bring their Jamaican husbands along and they're wearing the coral beads [jewellery worn by Nigerians at celebrations as a sign of prosperity] and everything else,' he says with a laugh. 'They've just embraced it, and that's the beauty of intermarriage.'

It is quite a journey. To have gone from a place where young African men were hiding their identity from their Caribbean classmates to one where those whose heritage links to Africa were broken by slavery are donning the African garb (both literally and figuratively) to participate in something that many in the community once kicked against. In this reading, the tensions and sniping of previous decades can be attributed to the growing pains of a reunited diaspora sorting through how they might coexist in the UK. And the current moment of African celebration and reclamation can be viewed as a family reunion of sorts; the forging of a blended identity with which to join together and heal the wounds of the past. And if other African cultures, with their own stories to tell and gifts to contribute, can be added to the mix, then all the better.

Abbey perhaps encapsulates it best. 'Let me put it this way,' he begins, with another grin. 'The biggest Black population in the Caribbean is, I believe, Jamaican. And the biggest Black African population in Africa is Nigerian. Do you know when the first direct flight between Jamaica and Nigeria took place? December 2020. Now, Blackness in Britain is synonymous with West Africanness, and by that I mean West Africa and the diaspora. Because even when you're looking at the enslaved Africans in the Caribbean, they're pretty much coming from the West African coast. So what we actually have now in Britain is these two massive diasporas that are realizing that not only do we look the same but we are the same. We were just separated by White supremacists. And now we have to find a way to make it work for ourselves collectively as a group of people. Maintaining what we all bring to the table but making something beautiful in the overlap.'

It has been a long and at times painful road, riven by fear, tension and suspicion. But Black Africans and Afro-Caribbeans in Britain have, for the most part, found peace and created something that is greater than the sum of its parts. And the specific things each culture seems to have learned from the other feel, to me, especially significant. Central to some of the difficulties that emerged between post-war West Indians and modern West African settlers was a difference of approach to the challenges of British life: the contrast between Caribbean realists who had experienced a structurally unjust system and African strivers with more faith in the innate fairness of institutions and a tunnel vision approach in the face of prejudice. This current moment of Black British cultural plurality seems to rest on each diaspora drawing important lessons and taking influence from another. African culture really has become popular culture. But what's key about this era is that Black Britishness is imposing itself on its surroundings and exerting its influence, rather than the other way around.

Success is now measured not in terms of integration, edges sanded off or which immigrant population has the deepest roots in the host country. It is rather an exchange between different influences, underpinned by the faith that core identity doesn't need to be diminished. And in fact, outside influence from another Black community – the thing that parents of a different generation fretfully warned their children about – is something to be encouraged rather than feared. That, ultimately, there is an opportunity to jointly create something new. And that at parties, and in life, those of us of African heritage are, at long last, dancing to the same beat.

4

Cell

If you are young and Black, then the moment that you realize how the police see you can feel like an inevitable rite of passage. It could be a stop-and-search in the street; feet kicked apart from behind and the brisk accompanying explanation that you match a witness description. It could be barely concealed disinterest when reporting a crime. Or the wail of an approaching siren and the needless car inspection that makes you late for your Saturday job.

But, for me, the realization came in the late 1990s, at the precise moment that mugging started to sweep the pocket of suburban South-East London where I grew up. If that phrasing makes it sound like a teenage fad then that is absolutely how it felt at the time. One moment the practice of relieving another young person of money or belongings didn't seem to really exist. And then, all at once, like trading stickers, digital pets or dance routines linked to novelty pop songs, it was everywhere, and the only thing that people in the playground or out in the wilds of Bexley borough's shopping precincts could talk about; a constant lurking threat that simultaneously felt not that big a deal and also a dark new escalation in the context of the simmering beefs, school rivalries and occasional running battles that were an accepted part of teenage life.

I do not remember exactly when this particular incident occurred, and the precise location is hazy. But I know it wasn't the first time a stranger had used the veiled threat of violence to try to get money out of me. A handful of friends and I were sitting on the top deck of a bus at the weekend (it is significant that I was the only Black kid in the group that day). Suddenly, as the bus idled at a stop just outside Bexleyheath, a crew of twice as many, slightly older boys got on and thundered upstairs with purpose. One of them, a mixed-race boy with pale eyes, sharply drawn feline features and a slight lisp, slid in next to me, pushed up uncomfortably close and told me at a whisper to hand over all my money. I told him I didn't have any, which may or may not have been a lie. And at this, he pulled at a thin, silver T-bar chain I was wearing and ripped it off my neck. My response, as I looked around desperately at my friends coming in for the same treatment and bystanders on the bus nervously averting their eyes, was to scream. In fact, no. Shriek is probably a more fitting term. 'What are you doing? What are you doing?' I asked, over and over, my voice emerging as an unnaturally high, panicked and screechy wail.

'Shut up, man,' he said, again trying to whisper, but sensing that more people on the bus were taking notice of the commotion. He nudged the front of his head towards my temple with a painful little jutting motion. 'He's just headbutted me!' I screamed, voice somehow even higher. 'Why have you just headbutted me?' I think I was aware, even in the moment, that it was an especially uncool way to react to a mugging; the kind of thing that would prompt ridicule at school unless I took ownership of it and got out in front of the joke. But I couldn't help it. The incredulousness, the sense that a stranger couldn't just do this, was pure and involuntary. And, perhaps strangest of all, it worked.

The bus had travelled to the next stop, but now the engine had cut out and it wasn't moving. Then came the muffled voice of the driver or one of the other passengers, invoking the police and claiming that they had been called. And from there, in a flurry, my chain was dropped, I was loudly cursed by my attacker, and the crew of muggers went sprinting down the steps and out of the door. After that a decent stretch of time must have elapsed. However, from there, the next thing I remember as the adrenaline left me was standing on the pavement with my friends, nursing a sore head where I had been butted, and clutching my broken chain while sharing details and descriptions with a pair of police officers. That is when it happened.

'So,' said one of the policemen, taking me to one side, a little bit away from my friends. In my recollection he was young, slim and fair, with what I took to be the slightly over-eager air of a recently qualified recruit. 'Can I just ask whether you've always been with this group?' He looked over at my White friends and then back at me, eyes narrowing. It took me a while to fully understand what he meant. To register that, in the midst of reporting a traumatizing attempted robbery and assault, I was being accused — merely because I was Black — of being the perpetrator rather than the victim. That his assumption was that I could have been a criminal mastermind, cunningly embedding myself among the nice White boys I had just tried to mug, in order to evade capture. Because, of course, the alternative – that I was a scared teenager, who happened to be Black, looking for reassurance and protection from an authority figure after a traumatic ordeal – was too implausible to be taken at face value. I sensed, vaguely, that I had reasonable grounds to be outraged. But the shock of it all had a numbing quality. And so I nodded and trudged back to my friends, too sad, exhausted and hurt to tell them the truth of what had just happened.

It is strange, with an adult's eye and sensibility, to look back at a formative experience from childhood. That I remember so much about the emotional experience of that day tells its own story about the impact of that attempted mugging, the sense of isolation and the grim plot twist of that policeman's racist suspicion. However, as is often the case with the stories of prejudice that Black Britons will share with each other like grisly scars, what seems personal and distinct is actually grimly commonplace. Because what I felt during that exchange with that Bexleyheath policeman, but couldn't possibly have articulated at the time, was the many, many years of blame and suspicion and structural Black oppression at the hands of law enforcement.

Look back to 1919 and the case of Charles Wootton, a Bermuda-born sailor killed by a racist mob in Liverpool, overlooked by police officers who failed to make a single arrest. Or turn to targeted campaigns of anti-Black police aggression in Brixton in the 1960s (referred to by the officers involved as 'nigger-hunting'). Direct your gaze to the 1970s and 1980s abuse of sus (suspected person) laws that effectively legalized police harassment of minorities, to the New Cross fire, and to the Stephen Lawrence investigation. Or, for that matter, to more than a century of 'race riots' that have often been collective community responses to sustained periods of violent persecution. The African and Afro-Caribbean settler story is rich with cultural triumph, successful organizing and an ingenuity that has led subsequent generations to thrive in all manner of unexpected ways. But it is hard to look at the modern history of Black presence in Britain and not see it undergirded, and somewhat defined, by the mechanisms of a policing and criminal justice system mobilized to maintain the socioeconomic status quo.

That Bexleyheath policeman's racist assumption, alongside all those other incidents of state-backed prejudice, is not a stray coincidence scattered through the decades. Rather, they are linked examples of a system that has long seen Black presence in cities like London as a problem to be solved. In that moment, I saw, for the first but not the last time, one of the most sophisticated and enduring machines of control and division ever created. Or, as it was presented to the Royal Commission on Criminal Procedure in the opening line of a 1979 report on the Black and Asian experience of British policing: 'If, as our researches show, Britain is moving towards "two societies, one Black, one White – separate and unequal" – the police will have had no small part in that polarization.'

And what's perhaps most notable, more than 40 years after those words were first published, is that the issue of overzealously policed Black communities is getting worse. Or, at least, it is not improving in the way you might expect, as the arc of history supposedly bends toward multiculturalism, equality and racial justice. If we start running through the damning statistics we could be here all day. But suffice to say: Black people in England and Wales are nine times as likely to be stopped and searched by the police (particularly for drug offences, though statistically they are less likely to use drugs than their White counterparts). In London, they are five times as likely to have tasers used against them during arrest. They are consistently over-represented in prison inmate numbers (in 2015/16, Black, Asian and minority ethnic men and women accounted for 14 per cent of the general population but 24 per cent of its prison population) and, at the overlap between criminality and ill mental health, Black people in the UK are four times more likely to be sectioned.

They are depressing figures that, though they fluctuate from year to year, reveal a fixed societal truth that may as well be carved in stone. This is who we are. This is how we are seen and what is meant for us. There is no way to change it, so we must learn to survive, even while we are grimly aware that we are only ever a moment from experiencing the sharp end of an institution that consistently shows itself as equating Blackness with criminality. When the case of Child Q – the unnamed Black 15-year-old schoolgirl who, while on her period, was degradingly strip-searched by Hackney police officers who wrongly suspected her of cannabis possession – shocked a Covid-weary Black British public in early 2022, it was no accident that her reported response became a rallying cry. 'I can't go a single day without wanting to scream, shout, cry or just give up.' Here, she spoke for all of us. From the docks of Liverpool and the Mangrove restaurant to the streets of 1980s Brixton and the flame-lit skies of 2011 Tottenham, we were and are, perhaps more than anything, just exhausted. To live your life under such sustained suspicion, and to have to fight the same continued battles for basic shreds of respect and humanity from police, is draining; to be exposed to the same repeated lie about your nature is to feel yourself giving in to the apparent truth of it.

And it is here that we alight on another interesting legacy of Britain's dark history of racial disproportionality within policing. Because one of the most insidious victories of historic police and government profiling of certain Black groups is this: it has presented such a deviously convincing stereotype that even Black people themselves have unwittingly accepted it. This, I think, brings us to one of the ways that British policing and the judicial system has come to specifically affect the Black African diaspora. And it is also part of why the realization I had in the aftermath of that late-90s mugging carried such sting and forcefulness. It was almost certainly my first meaningful interaction with a police officer. If my mother had engaged me in any sort of discussion about what to expect from dealings with the Met – if she had given me her own version of 'the talk' that is now a mainstay of African American parenthood in particular – then it wasn't comprehensive enough to plant a lasting memory. In fact, contrary to that, my mother and the other senior members of the freshly settled middle-class Nigerian community I grew up in defined ourselves as set apart from the sort of people who would necessarily need to worry about victimization at the hands of the police. Criminality, in the cheerfully bigoted telling of my elders, was the principal concern of our Caribbean counterparts in London. And as long as we made sure we stayed away from them (at the same time, ironically enough, that their parents were saying a version of the same thing about us) then we would be fine.

In *The Black Cop*, director Cherish Oteka's BAFTA-winning short film about the life of British-Nigerian former Metropolitan police officer Gamal 'G' Turawa, there is an early moment devoted to Turawa's childhood awakening to the depths of racism within the force he would one day join. In the clip, Turawa's White Irish friend had just bounded up to a passing bobby to say hello and been rewarded with a ruffle of the hair and some money. Impressed, Turawa skipped up and tried the same playful greeting to the officer. 'And then he just looked at me and said, "Fuck off, you little Black bastard."' The face-slap of shock hits him all over again as he recounts it. 'That was the first moment that I realized I was Black.'

It is a chilling insight into the petty cruelty that existed and flourished both in British society and within the police at that time. And while I can't claim my own encounter as having the same seismic impact on my sense of self (it is also relevant that Turawa had been farmed to White private foster parents as a child), I feel some recognition in the sense of a certain, definably Black African innocence being shattered. Bundled up with the implicit understanding that race wasn't an excuse to underperform or underachieve, the lack of warning or fear of the police among that cohort of West African immigrants conferred a kind of bulletproof obliviousness on second-generation kids like me.

This could be a useful tool as we made our way through the world. But it also, I think, made us completely unprepared for the lacerating dose of truth served by authority figures that could only see us through a lens of suspicion. And that is the issue that has faced London's Black communities – and, especially, its Black African communities – as they have come into increased contact with the vicissitudes of policing and the criminal justice system. If your self-image is contingent on faith, respectful industriousness and a life set up in opposition to the postcolonial stereotype of the invading Black criminal, what do you do when arrest or even incarceration upends that? What do you do when the stresses of diaspora – whether through socioeconomic circumstances, school exclusion rates or ethnic disparities sewn into the very fabric of policing – seem to be drawing more and more Black Africans into one system or another? How do you deal with a sectioned child when your culture has no readily available language to discuss it? These are the added stresses that come into play for many Black African Londoners who find themselves becoming one of the men or women behind those dismaying annual statistics. Throw in the fact of the attached social stigma and shame that is especially pronounced within some recently settled Black African communities and you have the situation as it is now: a huge social problem and cycle of deprivation that no one wants to necessarily talk about or address.

Because, ultimately, the forces of control do not care about your particular cultural needs, your designation of Blackness or, in many cases, your obvious innocence. There is no level of well-spoken respectability, studiousness, or non-threatening presentation that will prevent you from coming up against a policing machine where your presumed guilt has been engineered by centuries of history. That was the lesson delivered to me on that Bexleyheath pavement all those years ago. And it is a lesson that Black Africans and Afro-Caribbeans, whichever side of the law they are on, have had to learn again and again.

In some ways, Victor Olisa owes his 35-year career with the police to the comparative boredom of professional biochemistry. True, the Nigeria-born former borough commander with the Met had a grandfather who was in the force back home. But it was only after a six-week work placement midway through his course of study for a biochemistry degree at Royal Holloway University of London in the early 1980s that Olisa realized his calling might lie elsewhere. 'Studying biochemistry was really exciting,' he says now. 'But the reality of it was that I was going to be stuck inside for the rest of my working life. And that just did not appeal to me at all.'

In the end, it was a friend from the university football team – who happened to be fresh from his own three-day taster session with the police – who decisively nudged Olisa towards a future in uniform. 'He came back talking about how wonderful it was; serious investigations, getting taken to crime scenes,' says Olisa. 'I thought it sounded really exciting, and so I made some enquiries.' Historical context (specifically the landscape of British race relations amid the wreckage of 1981's Brixton uprising) ensured his enquiries found a receptive audience. 'The police were doing then what they are doing now, 40 years on,' he notes. 'They were looking to change their reputation, culture and everything else. And one way of doing that was to get graduates that were, back then, predominantly Black people.' Within weeks, Olisa had heard back from

Surrey Constabulary; within a month, after training at the Surrey Police's Mount Browne headquarters, he had been accepted. And if Olisa's family were concerned about what he'd face as Surrey's first Black police officer ('They were worried about the racism and the danger – that I'd stick out like a sore thumb and become an easier target'), then their apprehensions were justified pretty swiftly.

Olisa would have to look on in the briefing room as colleagues freely used the n-word in reference to suspects; he would sit in patrol cars and watch as members of the public completely ignored him, preferring to address whichever White officer he was with; and during a defining moment, Olisa arrested two drunken men who had been racially abusing him ('You niggers are a disgrace. You shouldn't be wearing the uniform'), only for one of his colleagues to suggest that he 'should be able to take that sort of language'. This was the lot of the Black policeman in the 1980s: a wearying world of tension and ostracism where aggressions, both micro and macro, lurked at every turn. Olisa, who has neat salt-and-pepper hair, chiselled features and a low, throaty baritone, generally has the measured, articulate comportment of someone used to public speaking. Yet there is a rawness to his voice as he reflects on those early years. 'There wasn't a day,' he says regretfully, 'when I went out on patrol that I didn't have butterflies in my stomach thinking, "What am I going to face today? What kind of language am I going to need to deal with?"'

Still, he persisted. Olisa would rise through the ranks in the following decades – though not nearly as quickly as his White colleagues. He moved from Surrey as a sergeant and on to the City of London (where his applications for senior posts were bounced for 14 long, dispiriting years) before, via a period at the Home Office and a posting in Bexley, he was named as borough commander for Haringey in 2012. Figures like Olisa, Turawa and Leroy Logan (the Caribbean-heritage former Metropolitan police officer immortalized by John Boyega in Steve McQueen's justly lauded 2020 anthology *Small Axe*) hold a unique significance in any discussions about Black Britain's historic interaction with police. They are human lightning rods whose struggle seems to reveal something about the depth of prejudice within a British police force that is stubbornly unrepresentative of the public it serves – in 2020 a mere 3.5 per cent of Metropolitan Police officers were Black, despite the fact Black individuals made up 13.5 per cent of London's population. Their stories, of unbowed determination in the face of extreme hostility – from both White colleagues and large sections of an understandably mistrustful Black community – shock even as they inspire. However, you only need to look back at the entwined histories of modern inner-city policing and Black settlement to know why life proved so difficult – and any attempts to shift the culture of law and order in the UK proved to be such a Sisyphean task.

Put simply: for as long as there has been a meaningful modern population of Black people in the UK, policing has existed as a means to manage, control and contain them. This goes all the way back to the end of the First World War, when the population of long-settled Black seamen and naval veterans that had proliferated in British port areas like Liverpool, Cardiff and Canning Town found, suddenly, that peacetime had turned their presence into a problem.

Accustomed to plentiful employment during the war years, Black dock workers were quickly displaced by demobilized White servicemen who saw themselves as having been usurped by racially inferior foreigners. Those Africans and West Indians who wanted to stay – and many did, having long established themselves in Britain and also, in many cases, having somewhat contentiously started families with White women – could find no work, while those who wanted to return to their countries of birth struggled to find White crewed ships that would accept them. Requests for government intervention, like the Liverpool Ethiopian Association's suggestion that these 'practically starving' men should be given a £5 repatriation fee by the Colonial Office, went unanswered. Throw in the presence of similarly displaced (and often intolerant) White foreigner seamen and persistent local tensions over interracial relationships and you get a sense of the societal powder keg that preceded the violent unrest of the summer of 1919: shocking escalations in South Shields, Wales, Liverpool, Limehouse and beyond that followed a familiar pattern of White mob aggression, Black reprisal and disproportionately weighted blame from the police, government and press.

It is instructive to learn that the death of Charles Wootton, the Bermudan ship worker chased along the docks of Liverpool and victim of a lynching if ever there was one, was sparked by a chain of events. Specifically, this involved the stabbing of a Black man who had apparently refused to give some Scandinavians a cigarette, a brutal retaliatory strike enacted by others in the West Indian community, and police raids of Black boarding houses that resulted in injuries on both sides. If the Black experience at the turn of the century sounds like one of displacement, violent lawlessness and deprivation, then it was only that way because state negligence and public racism allowed it to be. Britain's nascent Black population (which had swelled to 20,000 by the end of the war) had effectively been abandoned by the state and then blamed for the inevitable social consequences of that abandonment.

Throughout the other flashpoints of the twentieth century – 1948 disturbances in Liverpool mere months after the *Windrush* had arrived; 'riots' that spilled over in Nottingham and Notting Hill thanks to Teddy-boy-led violent attacks in 1958; the uprisings of Brixton in 1981 and Tottenham in 2011 prompted, in each instance, by accusations of Black mistreatment at the hands of police – the pattern of 1919 would repeat itself. But the discord amid the rubble of the war effort is key. It is the moment at which a number of powerful, enduring ideas about Black interaction with the police, and Black settlement in the UK in general, really took hold. The first of these is the notion that Black people were somehow responsible for their persecution; that the blame for the bloodlust they roused in White aggressors lay in the jobs they were taking, the racial intermingling they were indulging in, and the mere fact of their presence.

Given that much police work during the disturbances of 1919 was reportedly centred on protection of buildings (a *Western Mail* story on the sustained anti-Black attacks in Wales noted that 'the efforts of police were confined to keeping the White men from damaging property'), the prevailing logic, even in supposedly liberal circles, was that the quickest way to stop the unrest was to remove Black settlers from the equation.

This thinking manifested most troublingly in proposed plans – spearheaded by the Lord Mayor of Liverpool and the Chief Constable – to evacuate the city's entire Black population (many of them subjects of the British Empire) to unused army bases for internment ahead of repatriation. Thankfully, this idea, highlighted by David Olusoga in *Black and British*, was abandoned. But the thinking took root in the wider consciousness. Black seamen were held up as incompatible with British life; a transfusion rejected by the host. Their settlement, rather than White prejudice, was the issue to be resolved.

Another long-standing contention that flowered at this time, within the police and White society at large, was Black proximity to crime, violence and undesirable, ghettoized parts of cities. Incidents where Black African or Afro-Caribbean men injured or even killed White aggressors (often in self-defence) fed the colonial idea that members of the Black population were dangerous, backward savages; that they were often forced by employment colour bars to earn money through less than legitimate means underwrote the sense that immorality and licentiousness seemingly came naturally. The Black British settlers of this era were not perfect or morally unimpeachable; to expect them to be would be to rob them of the human right to be a fallible individual rather than a representative of an entire race. But if the culture of presumed guilt and limited life opportunities for Black settlers takes root anywhere in British history, then it is here, in the first years of the interwar period.

However, if there is one aspect of the 1919 riots that proved especially prophetic in the field of the policing of the Black population, it is the language of war and the lingering shadow of wartime thinking. It isn't just that the presence of discharged Black and White servicemen shaped both the motivation and texture of the street battles raging in British cities (it is hard, for instance, to read reports of uniformed ex-soldiers leading attacks on Cardiff's Black neighbourhoods and not feel that many in the White community were not quite ready to leave active service behind). It is also that the urban battlefields of this era yielded decades of 'conflict zone'-style policing in domestic spaces. The 1948 disturbances played out to an atmosphere of battering-ram raids, planted evidence and forced confessions from the police; in 1977, riot shields were introduced to mainland Britain for the first time and used at both Notting Hill Carnival and a Lewisham anti-fascist protest; and by the early 1980s, as recession deepened and tensions rose, paramilitary police Special Patrol Groups adopted crowd-dispersal, ringleader kidnap and stop-and-search techniques perfected during the Troubles in Ireland.

We tend to think of militarization of the police as a modern phenomenon tied to tactics first deployed in faraway theatres of conflict like Afghanistan and Iraq. But Black Britons have long felt the reality of this invading, baton-wielding heavy-handedness. As Peter Fryer notes in *Staying Power*: 'To the Black communities the police had become, in effect, an army of occupation charged with the task of keeping Black people in their place.'

Naturally, to behave like an occupying force you need to continually convince yourself of the dangerous volatility of those you are seeking to bring to heel. And if you can find no evidence of the necessary danger, the machine of history gives you the tools you need to concoct it, create it or see it where it doesn't exist. There are examples, throughout modern Black British history, of this method of self-justification happening at both a large, policymaking level and in those street-level interactions like the one I had as a teenager. But few feel quite as revealing as the lamentable tragedy of David Oluwale.

Having arrived from Nigeria to Hull in 1949 as a sharply dressed aspiring engineering student, Oluwale fell into the justice system, first as a prisoner repeatedly charged with disorderly conduct and then, for a two-year spell, as a detainee at a mental hospital, and emerged 20 years later as a vagrant who slept in Leeds shop doorways and was routinely tormented by police officers Geoffrey Ellerker and Kenneth Kitching, as well as other members of the local force. For many years they harassed him, tortured him, beat him up and even, in Kitching's case, urinated on him as he lay on the floor. In 1969, Oluwale was found drowned in the River Aire. A resulting 1971 court case ended with Ellerker and Kitching sentenced to time in prison (despite the fact initial charges of manslaughter and perjury against the officers were softened to charges of assault) and drew headlines, outrage and a broader inquiry into the conduct of the Leeds police force.

As the campaigner Ron Phillips noted in a lengthy, incendiary 1972 article published in *Race Today*, for all the horror embedded in the details of Oluwale's fate, it only served to confirm what the Black community had long known about what the police and British society thought of them.

David was dying of racism anyway. The fact a number of policemen who had been given the power to do so chose to hasten his death says something about the way police see their role in society. If the entire society defines a group as a threat, then the police forces have a vested interest in reducing that threat by a positive policy of attack.

While Oluwale's fate revealed an extreme depravity and racism among British police, there were persistent signs that the problem was structural, rather than merely to do with the behaviour of individual officers. Anti-Black mobs in the 1950s and 1960s were, as Fryer has it, 'the racist tail [that wagged] the parliamentary dog'. Yet the dissemination of these bigoted ideas and attitudes – the calls for immigration controls and the feeling that Britain was under siege, despite the fact that the Black population of the 1960s was about 190,000 among more than 50 million – flowed both ways. When, in a 1978 appearance, the then future prime minister Margaret Thatcher fretted about the country being 'swamped by people with a different culture', it was wholly consistent that, in 1981, a Brixton police force blitzkrieg of stop-and-searches was known as 'Swamp 81'. Here, the 'swamping' was probably twofold: police invading and flooding an area synonymous with Black sanctuary as well as fighting a more general sense of being overrun in 'their' country. These ideas and associations, forged across the reign of three separate monarchs, would prove stubbornly hard to shake no matter how many inquests and scandals there were. And it was something that Victor Olisa discovered first-hand, again and again, throughout his time in Haringey.

'There was mistrust both ways,' he says. Mistrust on the side of the community and mistrust from the officers who, although they worked in Haringey, had minimal contact with Black people and so had formed this stereotype that they were against them. One of my most difficult tasks was getting officers to actually behave professionally. Some of them would say to me, "I've been here many years, I know what the community is like, they're likely to assault us."' Olisa shakes his head, still incredulous a decade or so after these conversations. 'And I would say, "Borough commander, tell me the last time you were assaulted by a Black person?" And they wouldn't have an answer.'

This is how it goes. Years and years of mutual tension between Black settlers and White police have elicited what can feel like a fixed atmosphere of animosity. From early twentieth-century Liverpool to modern-day London, the criminal Black boogeyman of the collective imagination has been hard to shake. And so, as a new generation of young Black men and women came of age in this landscape, more and more of them understandably wondered if, rather than trying in vain to change the minds of the police, maybe they would be better served making the system work for them. Maybe, if society insisted that you were a criminal, the best course of action was to be a successful one?

Hassan Ali had seen all the same hard-hitting TV dramas and films as the rest of us. Before he actually went to prison, the Somali-born West Londoner had a vision of it as a starkly lit, cramped world of stifling misery, sadistic prison guards and toothbrush shanks; he imagined it would be survival of the fittest and that he would be lucky to escape without a slashed face or worse. And then Ali actually went in to serve a four-and-a-half-year sentence related to drug offences, which meant that he could discover that the reality was, if not exactly stranger than fiction, then at least a lot more comprehensible and not quite as irredeemably hellish.

'I thought it would be like *Gladiator* or something,' he says now, flashing a smile. 'Don't get me wrong. Prison is tough. But then when I went [in], I was so surprised because, actually, it's a simple place.' He leans forward to lay it all out for me. '30 per cent of the people are crack addicts who are recovering and are shells of human beings. Another 30 per cent are middle-aged guys who got caught for corporate crime, and they just want to get home to their kids. 20 per cent are gang members. And then the other 20 per cent are people like me who are like, "Yeah, I used to sell drugs, but if you don't bother me, I won't bother you."'

Just as prison's hierarchies held some surprise, you could probably also say that the circumstances leading up to Ali's eventual arrest also buck many of the usual clichés.

For one thing, his was a mostly very contented childhood. Dressed almost solely in black, with a carefully cropped beard at his chin and a ready, toothy smile, Ali cuts a friendly but occasionally edgy presence in the busy Paddington branch of Starbucks where we've chosen to meet. Born in Somalia but brought to the UK at the age of five, he remembers growing up in a Hayes house where, despite the fact his late father had seven other children split across three marriages, he never wanted for anything growing up. 'My mum was on benefits,' he says, 'but she was one of those people who was good at saving, and she'd have little hustles; she'd be sewing on the side for people.' Hayes was a comforting, majority-Somali bubble of family gatherings and weekends of Quran lessons, while his actual school was 40 minutes and a world away in leafy Uxbridge. Though he was aware of a local gang, who would skulk in the park when his mum took them there to play football, criminality didn't hold any real appeal for him as a younger kid.

At least not until, at the age of around 16 and not long back from a brief period living back in Somalia, Ali realized many of his friends were making money from either selling drugs or other less than legal means. He had shown an aptitude for both maths and science at school. And so the realization that peers, who 'were not as smart as I was', were making enormous sums awoke his competitive side. 'I just used to look at them and think, "OK, you're making £500 a day, fam? I can make a grand. Guaranteed." And I really was.' Money, he says, was always the primary motivation from day one. ('It's not about power,' he notes. 'For Somalis it's always about money.')

This attitude perhaps makes Ali's chosen path, and its inevitable outcome, seem less about police prejudice than his mindset. But then you hear about the schoolfriend who was so terrified of Hayes that he spurned an invite to come and play basketball with Ali ('That made me realize people were scared of where I lived'). Or the fact that, by his mid-teens, he was accustomed to being routinely stopped by police because 'somebody got mugged and I matched the description'. And you realize that environment, state hostility and historic expectation played their part in making him feel crime was a viable, or even inevitable, outcome. However you look at it, the money he was suddenly earning illegitimately – not to mention the fact he was no longer having to cadge fivers and tenners from his mum for train fare – was what ended up bringing the contrasting worlds he was inhabiting into contact with each other.

While sorting through the house one day when he was around 18, Ali's mother found £2,000 in cash in his bedroom. 'I think we might have robbed someone and I ended up taking the lion's share,' he says, at a low whisper. 'And she was like, well, this is obviously not halal money.' This added cultural and religious component feels, to me, like a particularly intriguing additional wrinkle when it comes to Black African Londoners and criminality. Lots of children of immigrants live double lives of one sort or another. We are accustomed to oscillating deftly between the very different person we are with our parents and the one that we are out in the world. But these lurching shifts of personality are especially acute, I'd say, for the post-1980s wave of Black Africans whose lower position in the settler hierarchy necessitated chaotic working rhythms and fragmented family units. As Peter (not his real name), a Zimbabwean-heritage young man from East London who served two years of a seven-year sentence on drug-related charges puts it: 'My parents would work from morning to night, I'd be getting in at about three in the morning, and so we could go the whole week without seeing each other. [That's why] we didn't get along. 'Cause in their eyes I'm not really doing anything.'

Similarly, with my own mum, there was a period when she was working an evening cleaning job in addition to her main job at the Commonwealth. As children we were given a long leash because there was no real alternative. The onus to behave and not abuse that trust was on us (and, speaking personally, it was mostly heeded, bar the odd falsehood about a friend's sleepover that was actually a value-cider-fuelled party at the house of some girl whose parents were away). Though, of course, this level of obliviousness in relation to your children's lives can make the moment of discovery feel all the more shocking.

In *This Is London*, Ben Judah's hard-boiled exploration of the capital's hidden immigrant underbelly, a Nigerian policeman in Peckham details how he has seen African mothers at the station 'shouting, screaming and slapping' their sons when they come to collect them from custody, because they 'have brought shame on the whole community'. Peter's mother only found out that he knew how to drive when the police raided the family home and used a warrant to search the motorbike and two cars that were in his name. While he was on bail, following other arrests, he was thrown out of the house; left to sleep in his car, in hotels and at friends' houses. During his time in prison he had no contact with his parents and only one conversation with his sister. He had been somewhat cast out. But he understood and didn't bear a grudge. 'I just thought, I put myself in this situation, so I just need to get through it.'

Things were a little different for Ali. Though, of course, incarceration would ultimately be his fate as well. Not long after his mother found the £2,000 he was sent back to Somalia ('The family didn't know what to do with me,' he says), but soon returned to London and fell back into the rhythms of selling drugs: the graveyard shifts working out of a car, the out-of-town excursions, the close-call police operations that saw lots of friends caught by undercover officers wearing hidden cameras. 'There were so many times when I should have got arrested,' he admits. 'So I just felt like I was lucky. Like, God's got me and prison's not meant for me.' Until, that is, his luck ran out. He had temporarily relocated to Brighton for the mythical last big score ('I thought, "Let me just go hard, see if I can make a million and then just stop"') when he was stopped on the beach by police and subsequently had premises that he was selling out of raided. It was a wake-up call. But not one that immediately prompted him to be honest with his family.

'I'm quite a good liar, so even when I was selling drugs I'd always tell my mum I had a job and was doing night shifts,' he says. 'But with the Brighton thing, I was on bail for two years and I didn't even tell them. I was properly stressed out, getting letters from the CPS [Crown Prosecution Service] and snatching them up before anyone could see.' Ali hoped that he would get a not-guilty verdict and, as he says, 'no one would have to know'. Clearly, it didn't go that way. However, gratifyingly, when he did finally tell his family what had happened they continued to support him, albeit in a way that was kept very much under wraps. 'Part of Islamic faith is that you don't cut the ties of kinship,' he says. 'So my family would never do that. But what they do more is that they don't talk about it.' He laughs darkly. 'I've got a friend I grew up with who, as far as other people in the family know, has been on "holiday" for eight years.'

Ali credits his relatively positive prison experience to a number of factors: his agreeable cellmates, his focused, head-down approach to serving time, and the fact he was shipped out to HMP Littlehey in Cambridgeshire, out in the countryside and far away from the territorial beefs and smuggled contraband drops that tend to be especially prevalent in London prisons. But it seems obvious that the emotional ballast he received from his family helped a great deal too. There were regular visits and, just before he went in and was very fearful about what he was going to face, an aunt said something that proved pivotal. 'She said to me, "Prison was made for men – and you're a man, aren't you?" And that just stayed with me. I thought, if I'm going to prison then I must be the sort of person that can handle it.'

Moreover, in contrast to Peter's experience, Ali knew that this access point to his culture, support network and sense of self would be waiting for him when he left. It is not especially surprising to learn that close family links have long been identified as a key contributing factor in lower reoffending rates among British prisoners. In fact, a 2017 study found that offenders who maintained ties were 40 per cent less likely to reoffend. Here we see one way in which those established, traditionally African methods of dealing with a family member in the justice system – namely, ostracism, intensified prayer and the proverbial clump around the ear in the custody room – come up short. Few parents will want to shout the news about an incarcerated child from the rooftops. But I can't help but feel that, as Britain's prison population – in line with its broader Black population – comes to include more Black Africans, increased honesty and forgiveness between parents and children can only be a good thing.

For young Black African and Afro-Caribbean men especially, a degree of police control really can feel like an inevitability. That was the reality I was roughly acquainted with in Bexleyheath all those years ago. It is also a lesson that Ali remembers learning as a teenager, out on the road. 'After a while, we realized that police would just stop us, push it, and try to get a reaction so they could arrest us,' he says. 'It got to the point where I'd seen friends getting bent up and handcuffed so many times that I just realized, there's no point in arguing with them. It's either you get one over on them and you get away, or if they get you, they get you. There's no point fighting. If you overpower one, another will come. If you overpower two, five will come.'

This sense of powerlessness in the face of police aggression felt, all at once, both wholly understandable and personally alien. I cannot say that, insulated by the respectability and discipline of my middle-class Nigerian upbringing, I ever felt the police force were out to get me or there to be outwitted; beyond that incident after the teenage mugging, encounters with racial profiling and police mistreatment in my life have been blessedly rare. But it's hard to deny that this illusion, of being out of the grasp of the police, is one I have probably absorbed from those around me and cultivated through my life choices.

I still remember, during a summer holiday in America, an uncle chiding me for wearing my jeans sagging halfway down my backside. Did I know, he wondered, that this style came from male prisoners who had been relieved of their belts? Those lessons tend to stick. Criminality and its associations were something to be avoided at all costs. In this sense, my approach was the flip side of Ali's attitude, though it was still shaped by the same racist stigmas. Whether you are aiming to subvert an ethnic stereotype or wearily conforming to it, it is still governing the way you move through the world. Through this lens, all Black Brits are imprisoned by the expectations attached to their race by police.

This feels like an issue specifically related to diaspora. And, in fact, the more you look at it, the more it can seem that the stresses of a modern immigrant existence are uniquely calibrated to draw the Black community into systems they are ill-equipped to fight. Or, truthfully, that if we are looking for the defining factor that led both Hassan Ali and Peter down their chosen life paths, we might justifiably point to the harsh socioeconomic realities of London as a whole.

The chief White anxiety underpinning all the unrest of 1919 was that Black settlement might be, in some intangible way, bad for the well-being of Britain. But what if the opposite were true? What if the status quo of British life was bad for the soul and psyche of the Black community? What if it was diaspora itself that was turning criminality into such an issue? What if, ultimately, the only way to be truly free was to take those that were at risk as far away from the system as possible?

When we think of Black Brits coming into contact with the law, our minds tend to drift towards the most dramatic examples. It is county lines drug operations and political activists facing down riot shields; it is Doreen Lawrence, Darcus Howe and Mark Duggan. But for Black African Londoners especially, some of the most seismic encounters with policing and detainment can also feel like the quietest. Namely, the immigration status letter from the Home Office landing on the doormat; the phone call from the child services worker using concerning words that you do not fully understand. Or, if you are Sylla, a Guinea-born charity organizer and FGM campaigner, it can come during a routine antenatal appointment that, out of nowhere, pivotally reorients your life and work.

It was 2015 and, pregnant with her first child, Sylla — affectionately known as Mama Sylla to those who work with her — had gone to see the midwife. Unexpectedly, a woman called Joy Clarke, at that point the leading specialist midwife for female genital mutilation in the country, appeared and Sylla was asked if she was from West Africa and if she had been 'cut'. She replied yes, allowed herself to be examined to identify the type of cut she had (it was type one, the least severe), and then watched on as Clarke turned to her with a serious expression. 'She said that the reason they had called me in was that in the UK they don't cut girls,' says Sylla, picking up the tale. 'Everybody is cut in Guinea, and I grew up thinking it was normal. But she said to me: "We're not sure yet whether you're having a boy or a girl, but just to let you know, if the baby happens to be a girl and you go to Guinea to have her cut — even if your mum or one of your relatives does it without you knowing — when you come back you'll be sent to prison for 14 years."'

To say that it was a surprise would be to understate it. But, having already established the Francophone African support charity Fraternité, Sylla sensed that, within that shock, there was the opportunity to act. 'I was just like, "Wow",' she says. 'So when I came out, I did a kind of survey and asked women I knew from Guinea what type of cut they had. Nine out of ten of them didn't know the types, let alone the punishment. And so we started doing this campaign in our community in 2016.' In the intervening years, Sylla's remit with Fraternité has continued to grow. Now, as well as educating French-speaking, predominantly Muslim West Africans on the illegality of FGM, her organization offers advice that encompasses immigration rights, housing, accessing benefits, interacting with police and safeguarding children. Really, Sylla and her colleagues are giving Black African women (and it is mostly women) the tools to survive and thrive in London.

'We just realized that these women didn't know,' she says. 'And coming from Africa, people hear social services, they think it's people coming to take their kids and they just run away. They don't know that those people are here to protect them and put the child's safety first. Or it could be housing, wanting to change the doctor you see, the system itself. It's basic stuff. But they are scared and so we help them.'

In the sense that it empowers people to make the system work for them, rather than living in fear of it, Sylla's work with Fraternité links directly to the broader idea of Black interaction with the police. The history of the Black community not receiving the same treatment as their White counterparts within British institutions is long and lamentable. It manifests not just in things like stop-and-search statistics but also in, for example, the fact that Black women in Britain are four times more likely to die in pregnancy or childbirth than White women (social disadvantage and unconscious bias within healthcare have been put forward as likely contributing factors). This reality breeds understandable but, ultimately, damaging wariness. And so organizations like Fraternité are a means of breaking the harmful cycle; an important bulwark against the idea that the Black community should just accept these disproportionately negative outcomes as a fact of life in diaspora.

On top of that, the need for a conduit between forms of behaviour that are acceptable in one culture but unacceptable, and perhaps even criminal, in another is hugely relevant. Here we strike at an issue that goes to the very heart of the ways in which immigrant communities have been policed (and occasionally struggled with that policing) in the UK. Because long before FGM policy had been written into law, much of the anxiety around Black immigration rested on the idea that inevitable lawlessness would spring from a failure to adjust culturally. Never mind that the bulk of Black African and West Indian newcomers were arriving from outposts of Empire where White people lived and the Union flag flew.

In the 1950s, amid rising cases of African students having to be repatriated following psychotic episodes, plans were put forward to deport those who had been in the country for less than five years and were convicted of a crime. Later, in 1962, plans to expel Carmen Bryan, a 22-year-old Jamaican woman imprisoned after she had been caught shoplifting items having been sacked from her job, were abandoned after public outcry. This attempt to effectively revoke citizenship from British subjects who had got into trouble with the law was simultaneously a back-door means of introducing entry controls, an attempt to selectively thin the herd of Black settlers, and a way to remind the UK's Black community of something they had always sensed: that their stay in the country was very much probational and subject to the whims of a government ready to bow to racist invective. Deportation linked to criminal convictions was, as Jordanna Bailkin notes in *Afterlife of Empire*, viewed as 'a palliative for the highly vocal anti-immigration lobby, and as a filter to improve the quality of the migrant population'.

Reverberations of this tactic could be seen years later in right-wing Brexit campaigns that blew a dog whistle at the supposed coming swarm of unvetted criminals from EU countries. Or, more recently, in the Home Office deportation flights – often scantly filled with offenders being returned to countries they had no material relationship with – that caused uproar in 2021. And by the time of the 1962 Commonwealth Immigrants Act (which restricted entry to those who had been issued with employment vouchers), police and immigration officers' powers had been significantly increased. The Black population's second-class citizenship had effectively been written into law. Removal from the country was presented as the best solution for Black men and women under attack from both the police and racist factions of wider society.

However, what's fascinating about this thinking is that it isn't just limited to government policymakers. In the modern era there are widespread instances of Black African parents taking the decision, as Hassan Ali's did, to send children who were getting into trouble with the law back to their ancestral homeland. In fact, amid London's East African community especially, it has been a long-established last resort to save Black kids from drugs, imprisonment and violence. Interviewed in a 2019 exploration of the issue for the BBC, Rakhia Ismail, the Somali-heritage mayor of Islington, addressed what was prompting families to take such drastic action. 'Does the parent wait for her child to be killed?' she asked. 'Or does the parent take a decision – quite a drastic decision – to take him all the way back to wherever that child is from originally?'

As a trend, it highlights the desperateness of the situation and the ways in which Black families are trying to evade the gravitational pull of the system. But on top of that, it feels like Black African Londoners retreating from the contaminations of a world they don't understand into one that, whatever its hardships, at least makes sense. Dr Fatumo Abdi, a Somali mother quoted in the same BBC piece, puts it in even starker terms: '[Youth violence] is a British problem, and it's a problem that we've fallen into.' It is an interesting argument. And one that highlights the way that some of the difficulties that characterize much of African London life – the long hours in menial jobs, the inadequate housing, the overzealous policing of Black communities – seem to be actively engendering the issues with violence and imprisonment among young Black men especially. What's more, although these returns are especially prevalent among the Somali diaspora, they seem to me to speak to a broader yearning among Black African parents to recreate the social circumstances they themselves grew up in.

'When I look back to my childhood in Nigeria, I spent the majority of it living with my grandma in a compound,' says Victor Olisa. 'And if she was travelling for work, though the other family didn't look after me, they kept an eye out. They made sure [I was] safe. We don't have something comparable here. And now, with families working so hard, kids come back, there isn't that close family unit, and so they want to spend time with their friends. They want to stay an extra hour in between finishing school and getting back because they want to walk around with them. That just leaves them exposed to things that would happen that probably wouldn't happen if they were coming straight back home.'

Naturally, being sent back to Africa isn't a magical cure-all (as Ali notes, remembering his return to Somalia as a 19-year-old, 'they sent me back to punish me, but you can end up getting into trouble anywhere'). But another benefit it has is that it can foster a deep connection with a culture and life beyond Black settlers' comparatively brief story in diaspora. It can remind you how lucky you are but, also, that you are not defined by the circumstances and stresses of the city. During his time in Somalia, Ali visited relatives who still live as nomads in the village his family hails from. He rode through rural areas precariously balanced on the outside of a truck with seven other men. His government worker uncle speeded their path through police checkpoints with nothing more than a wave. 'I realized that, being here, part of it is being on the bottom rung of society,' he says. 'And so going back to Somalia changed me, because I realized, like, I have value. But also that, even compared to how tough we think it is in London, some people really don't have anything.'

This sense of appreciating the plentiful opportunities in a city like London – not to mention the sacrifices older generations made to enable their offspring to benefit from them – is key. Though it can cut more than one way. Appreciation of past settler hardships can help to keep you on a righteous path. Yet, equally, the feeling that the younger Black generation have nothing much to complain about – particularly when related to mental health – can be the kind of unhelpful taboo that ultimately fuels all those concerning statistics on detainment by mental health services. In her essay in *The Colour of Madness*, an anthology of essays and poetry themed around race and mental health, the writer Ololade A. gets to the nub of this issue.

> Our collective strength can also be a thorn in our side. A tough-love attitude manifests through the brushing off of complaints. We just get on with it like we always have, whatever 'it' is. A mindset persists that your Goliath isn't as bad as you're making it out to be. We shall overcome, right? Fears and anxieties threatening to swallow you whole get dismissed by elders who barely bat an eyelid. Cue ever-so-subtle victim-blaming. They tell us our worries are unfounded, that our generation's lives are easy, that we should be happy and grateful.

It's a reminder of the additional stigmas Black Africans, and recently arrived settlers in particular, have to contend with on top of other societal disadvantages. But also, it is proof that a new generation is challenging the old restrictive ideas. Because maybe certain forms of Black British struggle are not predestined. Maybe, rather than shipping children back to Africa, the response to dwindling community support networks is to forge new ones. And maybe, the centuries-old battle for more humanity from those who are supposedly tasked with protecting us is a fight we can still win.

If there is something keeping Hassan Ali on a law-abiding path – if there is a single factor that has helped to keep him from reoffending this past two years – then it is the memory of the middle-aged inmates he met when he was inside. Yes, his experience of incarceration wasn't anywhere near as bad as he thought it would be. True enough, he and his cellmate had access to a contraband phone, a TV loaded up with thousands of films and a rice cooker they once used to make pancakes. But if there is one thing stopping Ali from going back (beyond, it should be said, the support of Key4Life, the young offenders training and employment charity he's part of) then it is the vision of those older men who would end up back inside every few years.

'I just thought to myself, do I want to be 40 and coming back in here with people saying, "Wa' gwan, you're back again?"' he says. 'I didn't want to be that guy. And, secondly, I just thought that, yeah, I could sell drugs, but what would that say about me? That's why I'm moving differently.' The same is true of Peter who, since leaving prison and signing up with a different prisoner leaver mentorship initiative called Switchback, has trained as a plumber, found a place of his own and even begun to build bridges with his family. 'I walked to my mum's house one day, she was happy to see me, and so we just went from there,' he says. 'With her, she just wants to see me on a straight path. That's all it is. Nobody in my family even smokes – so the lifestyle I was living before is not one she grew up with or knows.'

Both Ali and Peter's willingness to walk their respective paths is admirable. Still, to talk to them is to get an understanding of just how easy it would be to stray. Frustrations and indignities lurk at every turn.

Peter was homeless for a week after he came out of prison, and had trouble opening a bank account. Ali has gone from the heights of earning as much as £1,000 a day as a drug dealer to working in security for an investment bank in the City, feeling the perplexed stares of fellow commuters in the morning as he heads to his workplace in a suit.

There is, of course, justification for them to lose some life privileges as a punishment for having engaged in illegal activity. Even so, it is an indictment of the state that it takes charities like Key4Life and Switchback to support them. And it is hard to shake the feeling that administrative challenges for prison leavers are part of a reconviction mechanism designed to keep certain demographics in the system; that the difficulty of life on the outside as an ex-offender is a feature, not a bug. 'I have good days and bad days,' admits Ali. 'Some days I just can't believe I'm starting from the bottom. And I just think that if I'd started a legit hustle from way back when, then I'd be doing better now.'

Still, while there is positivity to be drawn from individual cases like this, the bigger picture of policing and Black people in the UK looks more than a little bleak. George Floyd's killing may have sparked a global conversation, but meaningful change has been harder to come by. Incidences of intolerance are rising. Cases of shocking police mistreatment of Black people – like that of Child Q or Bianca Williams and Ricardo dos Santos, the athletes handcuffed while simply driving home with their three-month-old son in summer 2020 – still arrive with the regularity of buses. And, as Victor Olisa points out, even as Black Lives Matter protests were sweeping Britain's cities, the fact that Black people were disproportionately being issued with fixed penalty notices for apparently breaking lockdown rules only highlighted just how ingrained police biases still are. 'The Commissioner [Metropolitan Police Commissioner Cressida Dick] was asked, why is there this disproportionality?' he says. 'And her response was, "My officers are policing high-crime areas." So what she was saying was that high-crime areas equals more Black people, and they're being dysfunctional.' He shakes his head. 'And what really hurt me about it was that it went beyond the bounds of criminality. Subconsciously she was saying that, not only are Black people more likely to commit crimes, but they're not looking after their health by breaching regulations brought in to protect them.'

Even new legislation, it seems, can be bent to the will of a structural prejudice many senior figures in the police are still reluctant to publicly acknowledge. And it is this that also concerns Olisa, who retired from the Met in 2017, about any hopes we may have of improved relations in the future. 'I hope the culture [of policing] will change, but I don't have faith that the change will endure,' he says. 'We've seen all this stuff now, over the years. In the 1990s it was Macpherson [the 1999 police inquiry that followed the investigation into Stephen Lawrence's death]. A real focus on removing discrimination and disproportionately unfair behaviour and treatment, and the government probably were really focused on trying to remove the imbalance. But you look at what's happening now and it seems to be increasing again with impunity.'

Having said all that, Olisa does add that, in his view, the disciplined nature of the police means that behaviour could shift. 'If the police as an institution said they will not tolerate racist behaviour, and that officers would be sanctioned and punished for it, it would change,' he says. 'We could eradicate it if we really wanted to. But the will is not there to do it consistently.'

I choose to be cautiously optimistic about the situation. Not just because you have to be, but also because persistent, voluble uproar and anger about racist treatment at the hands of the police – while not a solution to the problem – at least shows we are collectively on the right path. One of the sadder facets of that formative moment with the policeman in Bexleyheath was that, for years and years after, I never told anyone about it. Maybe I didn't want to cause trouble. Maybe I didn't think I would be believed. Maybe I just wanted to pretend it hadn't actually happened, and that the ugly truth it revealed was something that could be locked away in a box.

Whatever it was, I think that impulse of stunned acceptance or denial doesn't really exist any more. With social media as a loudhailer and organizing tool, a new generation is taking up the mantle of Black British militancy established in the post-war era and fighting to initiate real, lasting change. In real time, the bad-faith boos that were aimed at British footballers taking the knee before matches were turned, by and large, into supportive cheers. On the advice of an independent inquiry, the UK's most senior police leaders are considering a public admission of institutional racism. And in early 2022 Cressida Dick – who, as well as her comments around discriminatory issuing of Covid fines, also claimed racism wasn't 'a massive systemic problem' – stepped down from her post, in part thanks to her failure to seriously deal with issues of ethnic disproportionality within the Met.

Change is coming. Even if, more than a century after Charles Wootton was chased to his death by an angry White mob, it isn't coming quite as quickly as many of us would like it to. The challenge now is to continue to exert pressure, to put one foot in front of the other and to keep trying to shake the narrative that has long been shackled to us. 'Sometimes I'm like, fuck this nine to five. Why am I living this life?' said Hassan Ali, right at the end of our long conversation. 'But then I've come to realize, yeah, it may be shit, but look at this lady working here.' He pointed to a barista behind the hissing coffee machine. 'Look at this guy out here.' Now he nodded to a rapid grocery delivery rider in bright purple uniform. He smiled mischievously, hinting, perhaps, at the fact there would be no neat, Hallmark closing line delivered for my benefit. 'Life is hard. So you might as well do something where you can put money in the bank, have fun, and not worry about who is coming for you.'

5

Worship House

More than anything else, it is the collective murmuring
that stays with me. In the faded interior of a premises
on Hoe Street in Walthamstow, beyond grimy white
stonework and a sign missing a decent proportion of
its letters, the Sunday morning service at Kingsway
International Christian Centre's London outpost has
been underway for close to an hour. It has, at times,
felt more like the finale of a gospel concert than the
prelude to worship. My mother and I have strapped on
our face masks and joined the socially distanced crowd
of congregants in the stalls of the two-level auditorium;
we have stood and watched the master of ceremonies,
pristine in auburn corduroy blazer, crooning along to
soulful hymns booming forth from the speakers; we
have sat and looked on as the church news bulletin
– something traditionally delivered at a tremulous
whisper by a parish administrator reading from a piece
of paper – is broadcast on one of multiple TV screens,
pulsing and strobing with high-level visual effects. The
mood here is slickness, professionalism and bombast. It
may not surprise you to learn that the official name of
this building, a derelict cinema until 1963 and a bingo
hall after that, is the Land of Wonders.

But, yes, the murmuring. After the master of ceremonies and his backing singers have left the stage – and it slowly becomes apparent that, rather than an in-person pastor, we will be watching a live broadcast of the service at KICC's larger church, 36 miles away in Kent – the screens suddenly fill with a denim-clad woman, pastor Yemisi Ashimolowo, approaching the end of a sermon themed on the fledgling year's coming financial and spiritual blessings. And then it begins: a building swell of muttering that I initially take for people in the crowd having whispered conversations. Then I look around, at scattered congregants with their eyes closed and palms upturned, shuffling from foot to foot, incanting repeated phrases, and I realize. It is the hypnotic, collective sound of individual prayers repeated aloud; 200 people lost in their own individual reveries, speaking desire into being. Later, the murmur will begin all over again, when founding pastor, and Yemisi's husband, Matthew Ashimolowo takes the stage for a long sermon and invites us to pray, with notable specificity, for a member of the flock suffering with a hernia and another with an eye complaint.

Worship is worship, at the end of the day. And given that a lifetime of grudging church attendance has taken me to both marathon funeral services in the sweltering Lagos heat and Pentecostal shacks on the outskirts of Detroit, KICC's earthbound Land of Wonders doesn't even rank as the strangest congregation I've experienced. But there is something about its cumulative impact that feels distinct; something about the desperate murmuring and the corporatized sheen and the scale implied by a room of people gathered to essentially watch a sermon on YouTube that, taken all together, underscores the enduring influence and importance of faith in Black

African London. Because here, if you choose to see it, is the extraordinary story of one of the more visible, powerful and contentious examples of Black settlement and success in the UK in the past century. To put it simply, in the past 30 years especially, London's Black African churches have boomed in a way that no one seems to have quite been prepared for.

The numbers bear it out. In the London borough of Southwark alone, it's estimated that there are more than 250 Black majority churches; a figure that means this corner of South London represents the highest concentration of African Christianity outside of the actual continent of Africa. At its height in the late 2000s, KICC drew a weekly congregation of 8,000 that made it the biggest church in Western Europe. What's more, as evinced by KICC, in their capture of disused cinemas, bingo halls, banks and community centres, these groups are effectively remaking the capital's landscape in their own image. Yes, in terms of financial clout and dizzying success within London's African diaspora, faith has long been the only game in town.

'There's a powerful mission idea behind them, but a strong sense of entrepreneurship as well,' says William Ackah, a British-Ghanaian senior geography lecturer and Black majority church expert at Roehampton University. '[These people have been] shut out of certain areas, whether that's mainstream business or mainstream work. But then they've transferred that talent into religion by then forming churches that perform a social function and also an economic function.' This wild success – both in a business sense and in theological terms – has not been without its detractors. With evangelical religion and megachurches growing in influence whether back home, in African nations or in the secular atmosphere of Britain (in the 2011 UK census, the number of Black African Christians rose by more than 100 per cent while, in the same period, the number of White British Christians fell by 6.2 per cent or 5.8 million), prominent figures have expressed a degree of disquiet. Especially in situations where faith has started to seep into politics and other areas of life.

'Religion has become the number-one problem for Nigerians,' said the Nobel prize-winning Nigerian author Wole Soyinka in 2021, in comments that caused inevitable consternation within African media. 'Hope is all very well; but hope itself can become putrid. Especially if it is hope for unearned advantages in society. If religion becomes an excuse for flouting the law, then that religion has got to be tackled head-on.' There is some ethical tension, then. And much of it stems from how these churches make their money, the ensuing scandals they have been engulfed by, and the supposed crookedness of a school of wealth-focused Black Christianity that has come to be known as the prosperity gospel.

It was hard to avoid the spectre of money and the weekly 'tithing' donations (normally, by spurious biblical decree, 10 per cent of a congregant's wages paid to the church) that are the funding mechanism for these establishments, during that service at KICC. The traditional collection pouches were accompanied by a screen flashing KICC's bank details and a special text-to-pay number; there were repeated requests for any new members of the congregation to make themselves known and provide their contact details (at my mum's urging, I was told to keep quiet lest I wanted to be bombarded with donation emails); and though

Matthew Ashimolowo cannily pointed out the elephant in the room at times ('I know what people say:"Pastors are hypocrites, churches are liars, they just want my money"'), the financial offering was unquestionably the crescendo and focus of his sermon.

We will come to the specific difficulties that KICC has encountered when it comes to its use of donated funds. And we will also come to the wealth it has amassed since Ashimolowo first founded the church in 1992. But it tells you something of the hold that faith has over many in London's Black African diaspora that, even in areas where the population is generally deprived, congregants are willingly giving up a healthy chunk of their salaries. That many of these lavishly remunerated West African pastors wear their wealth somewhat ostentatiously – driving expensive cars, flying in private jets and, in Ashimolowo's case, sporting sharp, double-breasted suits – can feel especially shameless.

However, as Daniel Jordan Smith, a Nigeria-based professor of anthropology at Brown University, points out in a 2021 examination of prosperity gospel's emergence and rise, the success of this school of worship actually rests on this supposed brazenness. In Smith's view, those Nigerians who are not cynical about prosperity churches (and, it should be noted, there are many, many of them who are) 'interpret the riches that accrue to church founders, pastors and successful fellow congregants as evidence of God's blessing'. That they are not yet obviously wealthy, despite all the tithing and the prayer, does not stop them from seeing 'their own faith as yielding many benefits'.

It is an important reminder. Not just of the fact that faith and logic often run contrary to one another, but also that, beyond the emotional ballast of belief, Black majority churches offer immigrants access to a powerful social network and readily available advancement narratives that aren't present elsewhere in society. Ackah, solidly built with small, rimless glasses, a neat goatee and a gift for wry observations trailed by a husky chuckle, sees this as key. 'Black churches, particularly in their early formation, are one of the few places where the cleaner sits next to the doctor, who sits next to the bus driver,' he says. 'So you see that aspiration in front of you. And when you hear someone's testimony about, I don't know, how they were sweeping the streets, prayed to God, and now they're an accountant, well, it's going to give you that momentum. It's like the Nigerian dream.'

In this, we get a sense of what churches like KICC offer. We understand, perhaps, why they had to form in the first place, and why the roots of Black majority churches in London actually stretch back longer than a century. But what were the societal forces that ultimately shaped the explosion in Black African faith in the UK? How do we square the good that many of them do, the literal devotion they engender, with the justified criticisms about how some of them have been run? And how do Black majority churches move into the future, faced with an increasingly secular British society and a city in which they are, all of a sudden, being squeezed out?

Truthfully, that was the other thing that was evident on that Sunday morning, standing amid a ragged crowd in Walthamstow's crumpled Land of Wonders. After unbelievable growth and expansion, London's Black African faith groups find themselves at something of a crossroads; hobbled by the increased scrutiny of wider society, recovering from a pandemic that forced them to close their doors, and beset by questions of how best to modernize, adapt and wield their considerable influence. It will not be straightforward. Or particularly easy to rationalize. But, as you soon learn when it comes to Africans and religion, very little is.

The godfather of Black British Pentecostalism was not a man untroubled by personal demons. Born to a wealthy Ghanaian family in 1865, Thomas Brem Wilson lived out much of his life in early-twentieth-century London as an itinerant entrepreneur and habitual philanderer, locked, for much of his later years, in an especially tempestuous marriage with a Jewish stage performer called Ettie Cantor. In his youth, he drank alcohol and engaged in indigenous religious rituals. He was once, as the historian David Killingray notes in a 2019 essay accompanying Brem Wilson's diaries, so short of money that he pawned his own overcoat in winter.

Not, on the face of it, an especially pious figure. And yet it was Brem Wilson who, in 1906, gathered individuals to found Bethel Chapel (occasionally known as Sumner Road Chapel): an institution widely regarded as London's first ever Black majority church. As recorded in a history of the church's beginnings (thought to have been written in the 1940s and, again, highlighted by Killingray): 'In 1906 Brother Wilson . . . gathered together with a few devout men and women and formed the first Pentecostal Church in London; meeting in Peckham Road [Bethel/Sumner Road Chapel] . . . the Lord blessed them, the Fire of the Lord fell, and strange things began to happen, people began speaking in tongues.' This entry – striking in the sense that it shows Peckham has been a cradle of Black African settlement and faith for well over a century – gives an idea of how unusual the exuberant style of Pentecostal worship was at that point in history.

Brem Wilson, who had international links to pioneering Pentecostal figures like the Sunderland-based minister Alexander Boddy and the firebrand Scottish-Australian faith healer John Dowie, rode this wave of notoriety and novelty. By the 1920s, as well as his work at Bethel Chapel, he earned fame (and Cantor's disapproval) as a kind of fervent guerrilla preacher; a loud, fiercely devout curiosity who toured the country and was arrested and imprisoned in 1922 for preaching outside the Royal Exchange.

Thanks to Britain's relatively small Black population in this era (thought to have been around 5,000 people), Brem Wilson and the Bethel – which was locally known, somewhat pejoratively, as 'the Black man's church' – were seen as rare oddities. It would take another couple of decades, and a Black community swelled by the concurrent waves of post-*Windrush* migration and freshly arrived African overseas students, for the next big boom in Black majority churches. And that boom would be one forged in the fires of rejection. Because of all the shocks that Black Africans and Afro-Caribbeans in post-war London faced, few were as pronounced and visceral as the ostracism they encountered in majority White Anglican churches. There was precedent for this jolting racism in supposedly holy spaces (the Jamaican poet Una Marson's provocative 1933 work 'Nigger' ends with the image of a church congregation filled with: 'Those who preach Christ/ And say with churlish smile/ "This place is not for 'Niggers."') But even so, it brought home the fact that even these houses of love and Christian fellowship offered no protection from London's daily smog of hostility.

If London's Black Africans and Afro-Caribbeans wanted sanctuaries – and places to practise the religion that, ironically enough, had been brought to them by English missionaries – then they would need to build their own spaces. As Ron Ramdin puts it, in *The Making of the Black Working Class in Britain*, 'At once, it was clear that the White Christians were not practising what they had been for centuries preaching.'

As with most Black socializing at this time, things shifted to the home. By the 1950s (alongside outliers like Bethel Chapel, by that time settled at the Sumner Road site in Peckham), a scattered constellation of 'house-meetings' in living rooms had sprung up to serve these diffuse, majority Black congregations. As the Black population continued to grow, these worshippers migrated from front rooms to disused White churches and other buildings, formalizing and growing their congregations as they went. The expansion of these Black church sects was rapid: between 1962 and 1966, the estimated number of West Indian churches in Britain surged from 77 to 390. In 1970, the American-affiliated West Indian mega-sect the New Testament Church of God had an active following and membership that, in the intervening decade, had swelled more than tenfold to nearly 25,000. This extraordinary growth can be attributed to several different factors.

On the one hand, strong diaspora links to international Black church denominations, like the Church of God in Cleveland, and the Redeemed Christian Church of God and the Yoruba Cherubim and Seraphim church, both in Nigeria, led to the founding of affiliates and satellite branches in London that were supported and sometimes funded by a global network of pastors and missionaries. What's more, the ecstatic, clamorous and fulsome form of worship generally favoured by Black Africans and Afro-Caribbeans – the same style that had caused the Bethel Chapel to draw complaints from neighbours and, on at least one recorded occasion, a brick through the window – was specialist enough to be a particularly prized commodity amid a growing Black populace. The zeal to spread the Lord's message in a manner that was especially appealing to London's Black community brought meaning and drive. I have felt the reverberations of this drive myself, years and years later. On particularly gruelling Sundays, even after attending church with my mother, we would drive a short distance to a disused school where my mum's Ghanaian friend, Cynthia, would preach amid stacked assembly chairs to a congregation that rarely breached double figures.

Yet perhaps most significant, amid the stresses and indignities of London in the 1950s, 1960s and 1970s, it wasn't just the promise of free religious expression that filled out these congregations. Black churches, as well as spiritual fulfilment, offered weekly escape and cultural communion. 'In societies that were racist and quite alienating, [Black majority churches] were places where you could be yourself,' says William Ackah. 'They became a home away from home; a place where your culture could flow. And that worked on different levels, whether it was a way to find out about accommodation or to get a job. Those community spaces become quite vital. And that's also because they are places where you're not second-guessing yourself as a Black person.'

There is overlap here with other Black-owned enterprises and endeavours that were also beginning to establish themselves in this period: Afro-Caribbean market stalls, record shops, calypso dances in rented halls. Yet Black majority churches had a legitimacy and increasing sweep that meant they were especially vital for Black Africans and Afro-Caribbeans in diaspora who were growing accustomed, in the mainstream society of the metropole, to being at the fringes of things. Ramdin notes that Black majority churches offered their congregants 'satisfaction of their spiritual and emotional needs'.

This, to my mind, applies collectively as well as personally. There is precedent in the UK for Black majority churches using their organizing power and an engaged community to push for change in areas that extend beyond the bounds of religion. During the 1920s, and with the initial backing of the Methodist Church, Sri Lankan-born Kamal Chunchie established the Coloured Men's Institute as a community centre for Canning Town's disenfranchised Black and Asian settlers. In the 1930s, the pioneering Jamaican-born doctor Harold Moody founded the League of Coloured Peoples, a Para-Church organization created in accordance with his faith and headquartered at the YMCA on Tottenham Court Road, to offer medical advice and attention to a Black population still struggling to access it. The John Loughborough School in Tottenham, a community-run, fee-paying affair founded in 1980 and widely regarded as Britain's first de facto Black private school, was created by Seventh Day Adventists. Here, the influence of Black London's burgeoning religious networks is harnessed to make a tangible, real-world impact. Faith, and the sanctioned collectivism it engenders, becomes a means to balance an unfair system, a way to combat the continued prejudice that caused these institutions to spring up in the first place.

Which brings us to another likely reason for the rise in African and Caribbean churches: seeking comfort amid a country that was increasingly socially and politically intolerant of its Black population. That the establishing of many of these faith groups coincides with a mid-to-late 1960s period that saw the implementation of the Race Relations Act 1965, the emergence of Enoch Powell and a general hardening of attitudes towards Black immigrants, feels significant. Set against this hostility, specifically Black religious spaces offered something to cling to. As Ramdin suggests, within the diaspora at that time, 'the degree of felt deprivation increased the sects' membership'.

One of the flipsides of long-term settlement is an inevitable shift in the complexion of the diaspora. And as the post-*Windrush* Afro-Caribbean community in the UK edged into its third decade in Britain, a generational rift around religion began to emerge. If Black majority churches signified escape through rhapsodic worship – if they offered crumbs of comfort via praise and modest means to gently subvert a racist society – then the new breed of British-born Caribbeans, who had no memories of the pre-*Windrush* myth of an open-armed welcome from the Mother Country, didn't necessarily see that escape as a good thing. Anglican Church, no matter how Black the preacher and congregation, represented the numbing rituals of the establishment (not to mention the strict avoidance of drugs, alcohol and premarital sex).

Ostracized at school, starved of employment opportunities and increasingly entranced by the iconoclastic freedom and poise of Rastafarian culture, plenty in this younger Afro-Caribbean cohort wanted no part in it. 'Young men and women do not', as Ramdin intones in his 1987 book while considering the grim circumstances of Black youth at that time, 'normally turn to religious movements for explanations of their rejection and their deviance'. In 1976 the bookshop owner and Black power activist Tony Soares had put it in even starker terms: 'The older Black folks still feel as if they are in a foreign country, and don't have the *right* to be men. So they go to church, while their children are growing even more alienated from society.'

But then, of course this kind of rift would not be as prevalent in a newer settler community. And so, as Afro-Caribbean sects became a part of the religious establishment in the 1980s and 1990s, a wave of predominantly West African settlers swelled the ranks of majority Black congregations – and altered their texture too. Mid-century, Black African-run churches like the Aladura (founded in 1964) and Celestial Church of Christ (1967) were already fairly well established in London, providing, in some cases, what Ackah describes as an opportunity for the African diaspora 'to get the recognition they weren't getting at Caribbean-controlled churches'.

However, the Black Africans who arrived in London in the 1980s and early 1990s – who were, broadly speaking, people seeking better prospects than those available back home, rather than those here for notionally temporary study – brought a worship with both evangelical intensity and a specifically indigenous sensibility. That wasn't the case at every church, of course. It was around this time, after all, that my family first fully settled in the country and found Trinity: our small, multi-ethnic but, somehow, decidedly British Methodist church in Plumstead, South-East London. And I would say that the relative newness of our status in the country – and, duly, our closer proximity to how we did things in Nigeria – was probably a big part of why we went to church with such habitual regularity. It felt like an unquestioned part of our DNA; another thing that set us apart as Africans. We understood how important school was; we never called an older family friend by their first name without appending it with 'uncle' or 'aunty'; we went to church every Sunday without fail.

You only need to extrapolate this strength of feeling and dutiful attitude – and add in the fact that, between 1991 and 2001, the UK's Black African population grew by 141 per cent – to understand one reason why there was such an explosion in African-initiated, Black majority churches during this time. Or how they came to amass so much wealth and influence. Just as during the West Indian-led boom of the 1960s and early 1970s, the religious sect became a vital way for a new diaspora to organize and establish itself at a time of societal anxiety and upheaval; a rare means for a historically powerless community to accrue some power. Though how the Black African churches would choose to wield that power would bring noise, debate, and a lot of unwanted attention.

I think I was probably in my early twenties, and living in a house-share in New Cross, when I first saw the congregants of an Aladura church on their way to service. It was hard to miss them, in truth: entire families dressed in the pristine white garments that give their denomination its alternate name, swishing through the detritus of a South-East London Sunday morning (the upended chicken shop boxes, the smashed glass, the screaming street drinkers) with nothing but slipper socks on their feet and an air of serene, saintly invincibility.

It took my mother to explain to me, with a degree of cross-denominational scorn, that the lack of shoes signified connection to the Earth, that the white clothes, or *aso-ebi*, represented spiritual cleanliness, and that, despite the fact I had initially assumed they were Muslim, the Aladura are in fact part of Nigeria's Yoruba ethnic group, just like my family. The point is this: they are a head-turning mainstay in this part of the city (where Aladura churches tend to cluster around the New Cross and Old Kent Road areas); a source of anachronistic fascination that has come to almost act as a visual shorthand for both African faith and Black African settlement in London. And it was these feelings that prompted documentary photographer Sophie Green to stop an Aladura worshipper near her Peckham home one day.

'They all looked so beautiful and ethereal in this kind of radiant white dress,' she explains. 'And so I stopped a lady, complimented her and asked if she would mind if I walked with her to church.' From there, Green joined the passing woman for a marathon seven-hour service, before returning to this Aladura church and visiting others in the community many times. It was a slow process of trust-building, as she sought to understand the white garment faith and community and, if they allowed it, create some images together. The end result is 'Congregation': a striking series of portrait photos of congregants from various Southwark Aladura churches, taken by Green over a period of two years. The images, she hopes, portray how the churches 'create a sense of belonging, connection and community for so many African families and individuals'.

They certainly do – capturing a feeling of play, strangeness and the contrast between tradition and modernity that is at the heart of so much of Black African diaspora life in London. 'Congregation' shows these lavishly dressed congregants holding balloons, posing with Afro picks protruding from their hair, and queueing at an ice cream van on a blazingly hot day; it is subtle, sensitively put together and celebratory. But, nonetheless, as an artistic project it seemed to crown a prolonged period of particular media fascination with London's Black African churches. A period that feels particularly entwined with the unimaginable growth and resulting Icarian plight of one church in particular: Kingsway International Christian Centre. Formed in 1992 by Matthew Ashimolowo, a charismatic pastor and born-again Christian from Northern Nigeria, KICC seemed, right from the start, to possess an ambition and business acumen on a different scale to what had come before.

By the early 2000s the church (which, relevantly, is registered as a charity) had an annual turnover of £7 million. In 2009, as the active congregation grew to 8,000 and special conventions at London's Excel Centre drew as many as 94,000 visitors across eight days, Ashimolowo's annual earnings hit £100,000. In the 18 months leading up to April 2008, congregants had tithed and donated £9.5 million. And in the same late-2000s period there was another significant windfall in the shape of a £10.1 million payment from the London Development Agency, in order to acquire KICC's original Stratford headquarters as part of the London 2012 Olympics site.

They are dizzying sums that serve to highlight the intense hold that KICC specifically – and Pentecostal-style Black African churches in general – had on the hearts, minds and wallets of their worshippers in these boom years. However, all KICC and Ashimolowo's successes tended to be accompanied by gathering storm clouds of scandal. As far back as 2005, following a three-year investigation by the Charity Commission, Ashimolowo was removed from KICC's board of trustees and ordered to repay £200,000 after it emerged he used church assets to make a series of lavish personal purchases. Later, in 2017, Ashimolowo was drawn into a City of London fraud investigation into the dealings of former footballer and KICC member Richard Rufus, after he lost £3.9 million of church money (the pastor denied any wrongdoing and involvement with the decision to approve the funds for Rufus).

The almost comically brazen details of these controversies – that, for instance, Ashimolowo used those church assets to buy a £13,000 timeshare in Florida and an £80,000 car – seemed to get to the heart of wider societal anxieties around wealthy, prosperity gospel hucksters. And soon the same fascination that prompted Green to stop that Aladura worshipper one Sunday filtered into the world of tabloid reportage, with both the *Sun* and the *Daily Mail* running late-2010s investigations into the inner workings of Black African churches like KICC, the Dartford-based

Winners' Chapel and Barking's Victorious Pentecostal Assembly (sample breathless headline: 'God Delusion: Mega-rich pastors living in million-pound homes prey on believers with claims of solving deadly diseases').

There was undoubtedly some investigative value in these stories. London's prosperity gospel churches, particularly in this period, had expanded at such a frenzied rate – and offered the city's struggling Black African diaspora such a seductive message – that they were bound to be prone to overreach and what you could very generously term financial mismanagement. The confidence-trickster avarice of figures like the KICC-affiliated American preacher Creflo Dollar (who, as the *Guardian* reported in 2017, once asked worshippers at his church to donate $300 each in order to pay for his new private jet) deserves to be highlighted.

But, again, to assume that this hypocrisy isn't wildly discussed, criticized and darkly mocked within even Black church communities is to misunderstand the multiplicities of both faith and Blackness. And what's striking in the tabloid investigations (beyond the distinct lack of input from Black Brits that might better put these church services in context) is the fretful exoticizing of Black African churches: the sense that, under the veil of concern for worshippers being financially manipulated, these mainstream platforms are merely taking a tour through a world that confirms all sorts of prejudices about the fraudulence of Black preachers, the gullibility of their congregants and the faith-healing mysticism that is rife in their services. In this reading, Black faith and spiritual credulousness are something dark and dangerous, to be exposed, policed and taken in extremely literal, secular terms. Strangely enough, this attitude from White society goes right back to the emergence of those first Black majority churches.

Returning to Brem Wilson and Bethel Chapel, Killingray notes that in 1920 the *Daily Express* sent a reporter to the church to explore this new form of majority Black, Pentecostal worship. The ensuing news story told of 'religious frenzy', 'people [who] writhed in ecstasies of religious emotion' and the sound of people speaking in 'gibberish' tongues. So what are we to make of essentially the same stories about Black churches in London, emerging a century apart? Well, it is hard to look beyond the fact that West African and Afro-Caribbean sects, then and now, represent a sphere of Black power and influence in the metropole that is rare enough to rouse interest in White society. As William Ackah says, 'When you think of how these groups have been able to collectively come together and use their own resources to purchase buildings and generate community assets, in a way it is still probably the most successful Black community model we have.' The independent Pentecostal Afro-Caribbean churches that emerged in the 1990s, like Ruach City Church, had a heavy social focus that encompassed soup kitchens, debt counselling and food banks.

A desire to monitor, or perhaps even blunt, the organizing power that Black faith represents makes sense. Though it's also notable that the intense depth of Black belief and faith – the noise that caused English neighbours near Bethel Road chapel to remark that Brem Wilson 'was of the Devil' – has been a point of interest, and much debate, both within and outside the Black community for centuries.

At its most extreme, Black African diaspora connection to this kind of indigenous spirituality has manifested in modern witchcraft cases. When the discovery of a dismembered torso in the Thames in 2001 prompted multiple investigations into the issue within London's Black community, it again felt like age-old prejudice wrapped in disingenuous concern. But you only have to look at some of the details of modern slavery cases, like the inquiry into the year 2000 murder of Victoria Climbié at the hands of her abusive carers, to know that it is a continued concern among those tasked with safeguarding. 'Poverty, culture and religion are really the key drivers when it comes to trafficking and modern slavery,' says Debbie Ariyo, CEO of Afruca, a safeguarding charity founded following the deaths of Climbié and Damilola Taylor. 'There are people who really will decide that a child is a witch and, based on that, start to abuse them or even to cure them. It doesn't make any sense. But there are people that will tell you they believe it.'

Do extreme examples like this, and the inferences of those perplexed investigations into Black majority churches, point to a people and a culture that are simply more open to faith, superstition and the unexplained? Can the broad rise in religion within London's Black African diaspora actually be attributed to this innate susceptibility to things that are beyond our human comprehension? It is an interesting area to dwell on. In the late nineteenth century, African openness to miracles and limited access to biomedicine was a factor, according to Killingray, in evangelism and divine healing taking root across the continent. The power of prayer or ritual meant something else when it was your only option. What's more, from the Negro spirituals among African American slaves to gospel churches in the Deep South, fervent faith and Black hardship have often gone hand in hand.

Here we find ourselves back at the question of whether Black struggle in London has been a contributing factor when it comes to the eager embrace of religion in the past 50 years or so. And not just in the sense of church offering access to community and practical solutions to the persistent problems of housing, employment and isolation, but also in the specific way that a particular brand of worship – desperate and passionate and cathartic in its garment-rending physicality – could act as an acute balm in the buttoned-up, claustrophobic realm of the metropole. It is a view that has gained some traction over the years.

In his 1973 book *Black Britain*, Chris Mullard draws a link between social deprivation and West Indian sect growth in Britain during the 1960s and 1970s, casting Pentecostal services as a coded form of therapy for the Black community. 'Though there is very little reference made to race and to the sufferings of the Children of God,' he writes, 'both the preacher and the congregation know the ritual, all wrapped in flowery and biblical language, is more concerned with oppression, discrimination and racism than with Christianity.' There is a ready comparison here: between these analogous sermons, which spoke to the Black African and Afro-Caribbean diaspora's experience of a Britain riven by Powellist intolerance, and the prosperity gospel movement that sprang up and came to dominate in an era sandwiched between Thatcherism and austerity. Yet Mullard goes on to highlight the fact that the appeal of Black majority church in this context also lay in its status as an 'insular, all Black . . . energy-providing machine for struggling through another week of hostility'.

Standing among the congregation during that Sunday service at KICC in Walthamstow, I felt these words to be especially relevant. Masked hordes were clapping and dancing; there was fond laughter at Ashimolowo's jokes; those hands stayed raised and aimed towards the pulsing glare of the big screen, as if taking in the power of its light. Even my mum, who arrived with healthy scepticism about this prosperity-focused, Pentecostal branch of Christianity, seemed revived as she grinned and sang along to hymns she knew from her youth. The kinetic exertion of it – an experience caught somewhere between a motivational lecture and a Zumba class – seemed at least half the point. And the same is true at Aladura congregations, where the supersized Yoruba language sermons feature synchronized prayer and dance routines that can resemble an ecclesial endurance sport. It's notable that the same musicians who play on Sundays at London's white garment churches can also be found performing to a celebrating crowd on the hall party circuit. Release and celebration are one and the same. You might assume that a more tolerant age would have lessened the need for the spiritual salve of Black majority church. In fact, it seems the opposite has proved to be true.

But it is the insularity Mullard mentions that has caused some to question whether the current rise in Black African faith, for all its visibility and fundraising power, represents an opportunity missed. In the 1970s and 1980s, much scholarship and commentary wondered whether the startling growth in Black majority congregations could be transferred over to more meaningful areas of society. Mullard speculated that Black faith groups could become 'the nucleus, if not the leadership, of a quasi-political movement'. The religious studies professor Clifford Hill, in a 1973 paper on Britain's West Indian churches, theorized that 'disaffected sect members' could cross over into the burgeoning British Black Power movement. This shift failed to materialize in any significant, centralized way. And, to some people, it highlights the bigger issue at the heart of discussion over Black British Pentecostalism's recent, African-led ascent.

'These churches stand on their own and generate income from the community in a way that is quite remarkable,' says William Ackah. 'That's the positive side of it. But on the other side, there's this frustration that, even though they've got these assets, how come they're not tangibly linking into our community issues? Why haven't there been more education programmes? If knife crime is such an issue, what can be done about it?'

It's a valid point that underscores a collective urge, in some quarters, to see faith groups speak more directly to the problems of the day. Black majority churches have survived a challenging middle age of controversy to emerge seemingly stronger than ever. So now what? Can they adapt and modernize with their congregants in the diaspora? Do they have to? And what does it mean for the future of faith in Black African London if these institutions are unable, or unwilling, to make the shift into enacting social change in a more direct way? For Ackah, a moment in the run-up to the 2015 general election crystallized the issue. As part of his re-election campaign, Conservative party leader David Cameron had gone to a large, Black majority church event: the

Redeemed Christian Church's annual Festival of Life at London's Excel Centre. The senior minister's response to this hugely symbolic visit? He told Cameron he would pray for him. 'On the one hand you've got this massive symbol of your power because the Prime Minister is recognizing that you've got 5,000 members around the country,' says Ackah. 'But then, it's enough for that minister to almost just say, "We're so glad you've come to see us," rather than asking, "OK, what are you actually going to do for our community?"'

Black churches, as even David Cameron will tell you, have grown too big and prosperous to ignore. But are they also too big to make a real difference?

There is not all that much to see yet, in the scantly furnished, green-fronted office building a little way down from the Old Kent Road. But Sheikh Mahdi is nonetheless giving me a guided tour of the new Barakah Educational Cultural Association (or BECA) mosque and Islamic centre. A carpet-tiled upstairs area will become a prayer room and an adjoining space will hold a table tennis area for local kids; the Portakabins outside will be transformed into kitchen space, and a chaotic downstairs area – currently ornamented with an opened selection box of biscuits and a whiteboard bearing equations from a tutor who has been giving additional maths lessons to some of the younger worshippers – will become a classroom.

Faith in African London is, of course, not exclusively Christian. Black Muslims constitute about 10 per cent of the British Muslim population (and this is especially applicable in South London boroughs like Southwark, where a third of the population is Black or minority ethnic). And few organizations or people highlight the potential for religious institutions to be vectors for broader social change like BECA and Mahdi, who happens to be one of its leading imams. Long-limbed, erudite and laconic, Mahdi is originally from Sierra Leone and has been in London since 2005, and with BECA for 14 years. He helped found their main mosque, just off Peckham's Rye Lane and accessed through a shop, in 2010 when they had 20 members and 'no money in our account'. Funds for the rent were raised by donations of 'one pound, five pounds, ten pounds' from those who came to Friday prayers. It wasn't easy. But, as with the Black preachers who established house meetings in the 1950s, Mahdi knew there was a pressing need for a mosque where a predominantly West African cohort of Muslims could go to feel represented, welcomed and – on a fundamental level – understood.

'Obviously, not every South Asian imam speaks the local languages that we have in West Africa,' he says. 'And at some South Asian mosques, they believe that the Friday prayer has to be in Arabic. We do it in English. And, with that, we also give people English lessons, teach them how to integrate, tell them to write down words they don't understand and bring them here to the mosque.' The increasing popularity of BECA's Friday prayers, which now regularly attract more than 200 members, has necessitated the move, via more collective fundraising, to this new building, a sprawled complex of teaching areas, prayer rooms and hireable community space. And it is striking, when listening to Mahdi's grand plans for the mosque's new home, to note that much of what they want to do isn't stringently tied to religion. It is, rather, a series of measures tailored to respond to the specific integrational and social needs of the mosque's Black majority membership.

'Some people are having trouble with their spouses and need someone to talk to,' says Mahdi. 'Or they need somewhere to do an engagement party or wedding. Somewhere to do a naming ceremony for their babies [West African celebrations that are traditionally held seven to ten days after a child's birth] or to bring their teenagers to teach them morals and value.' Throughout 2020's first coronavirus lockdown, for instance, BECA distributed 100 hot meals a day to members unable to easily access food, and later became something of an informal, Covid-age Jobcentre. A place where those who had lost their jobs could deposit CVs that would be distributed within the community to find 'a cleaning job or something to push them; something to make ends meet'. There is a spiritual throughline here. Not just to historic faith-based community organizations like Moody's League of Coloured Peoples, but also to modern initiatives like Noah's Ark: a food bank service established by KICC during the turbulent early waves of the pandemic and kept alive as a permanent endeavour afterwards.

It seems, as life has got progressively harder for the majority of Black Brits – a population who, as the Social Metrics Commission found in 2020, are over twice as likely to live below the poverty line as their White counterparts – that the importance of faith, and its jurisdiction in people's lives, has only grown. As Reverend Israel Olofinjana, an ordained Baptist minister and Black majority church expert, notes, this antidote to marginalization is key to the appeal of these institutions. 'There are variations on prosperity gospel,' he says. 'Yes, there are some prosperity messages that are almost at the expense of poor people. But there is a prosperity that is about empowerment and self-esteem.' This, you'd venture, is another reason for religion's spiking popularity among Black Africans in recent years. In fact, more than that, lots of African-initiated 'reverse mission' sects in London see many of the social issues bedevilling Black families in diaspora as directly linked to the stresses of a secular society. As Leslie Fesenmyer, an assistant professor in social anthropology at the University of Birmingham, puts it in a 2019 exploration of Kenyan Pentecostal churches in London: 'They view urban problems such as poverty and unemployment, familial "breakdown", youth gangs and crime, as spiritual ones, taking them as evidence of people not "knowing" God, and of the city and nation having left God's Kingdom.'

However, the increased primacy of faith within Black African London's communities – the notion that, as far as problems are concerned, all roads lead to the church or mosque – throws up its own knotty questions. By and large, these are determinedly traditional institutions. As pointed out in a 2019 *Time* magazine story by the journalist Kemi Alemoru, some Aladura churches ask female congregants who are on their period to sit outside during service. Their grounding in old-fashioned unchanging values is part of their appeal. But this, you'd imagine, makes them ill-equipped to deal with some of the newer issues facing London's African diaspora. How does a faith group predicated on a specific mode of conservative-leaning, religious observance deal with extreme poverty, ill mental health or issues with addiction? What about – at a time when Black and mixed-heritage Britons remain over-represented within the UK's prisons – the trauma of a family member facing incarceration? Again, it is an issue of power and responsibility. And William Ackah, for one, acknowledges that Black majority churches need to reflect the evolving needs of the communities they serve. 'You'd hope that they'd develop those new skills in a way,' he says. 'That they'd be able to get you access to the lawyer, and not just prayer.'

If nothing else, Black churches and mosques in London sense the need to attract the next generation of worshippers. It is an area that Mahdi, with the recent incidence of violence among Black youth in London fresh in his mind, is especially conscious of: 'Our plan at this centre', he says, 'is to get kids from the road and bring them inside here so they have something to focus on'. This anxiety around the younger generation, and how best to reignite their connection to faith, speaks to how far things have shifted from that initial post-war boom in Black majority churches. In short, a more established diaspora has led to a dilution of religious connection among the generations being born in this country. My own arc of faith – dutiful, privately agnostic church attendance as a child shifting into total disengagement during adulthood – is probably a fairly commonly repeated pattern.

'I think the ties have waned over time,' says Ackah. 'There were horrible things about racism, but one of its benefits, if you will, was that it kept the community tied together and tied to these institutions. Now, those bonds have stretched. And I'd say there are a lot of people who are Black but have no church connection any more.'

Alongside this, just to add to the attendant problems of religious institutions trying to build bridges with a younger community, we have the cautionary tale of SPAC Nation. Founded in 2008, this disruptive, Croydon-based church made headlines thanks to its grandstanding anti-gang message, the weekly 'weapons amnesty' that would see firearms and knives heaped onto a table during service, and the flamboyant charisma of founding British-Nigerian pastor (and cousin of actor John Boyega) Tobi Adegboyega. 'He was obviously a bit of caricature,' says William Ackah. 'He wore these really flash clothes and drove a Rolls-Royce. But they were getting young people off drugs, out of knife crime, and attracting second- and third-generation [African and Afro-Caribbean heritage] youngsters in mass numbers.' In an investigative story for the *Sun* (because, of course, there was one), Adegboyega was reported as saying: 'I realized that to connect with the [younger] generation you have to look like them.' By this logic, Adegboyega was cleverly using the ostentatious trappings of wealth to draw at-risk Black youth back towards the light of the Lord. It seemed a worthy idea.

Until, that is, perhaps predictably, it all came crashing down. SPAC Nation was subject to both a BBC Three documentary and a follow-up *Panorama* episode on financial irregularities. Church members alleged that they had been financially exploited, with various loans taken out in their names. SPAC Nation denied the claims. And beyond the depressing specifics of what actually happened, the fact that another Black majority church had been embroiled in a very familiar scandal feels, to my mind, somewhat telling.

One of the issues that Black African churches have had in recent years is that, as businesses, they are almost too effective. Having initially grown out of a legitimate need for somewhere to worship without fear of racial prejudice or cultural ostracization, these institutions became, almost by accident, one of the more bulletproof industries in Black African London. In the gold rush years of the 1990s and 2000s especially, a precise blend of circumstances – entrepreneurial Africans with precious few other career advancement opportunities, the global might of the Pentecostal industrial complex, a rising tide of Black African migration to the UK and the kind of widespread social deprivation that makes faith all the more vital – made for a potent commercial cocktail.

This is not to say that all of the pastors behind modern Black majority churches are fantastically wealthy. (In fact, among many of the smaller congregations along Old Kent Road, where those involved all have day jobs, the inverse is probably true.) It is more that such a visibly successful, robust business model has inevitably led to a lot of people wanting in on the action. In *Being Built Together*, an exhaustive 2013 survey of Southwark's new Black majority churches, a Black church leader called Rev. William expressed his disquiet at this gold rush.

[These places] have a very different kind of mentality about church. It's more like a business for many of them and, you know, the competitive spirit that they bring to church means that they will not only start a church on your doorstep, they'll start a church on their own doorstep and so on. And so there is this accent on proliferation.

The founding of a new church, in this reading, is something too tempting to resist. And the more a place of worship becomes a durable moneymaking entity

– whether the people in charge of it are conscious of this or not – the harder it is to square it with some broader mission as a societal asset. Commerce and community are destined to be in conflict. But we must switch to the past tense. Because there are signs that the precise conditions that enabled London's golden age of Black faith are altering. And in small but significant ways, the descendants of those who preached in disused schools, rented halls and cramped front rooms are having to fight for space all over again.

In autumn 2017, the London paper the *Evening Standard* (a publication that, full disclosure, I have long worked for) ran an interview with married fitness entrepreneurs Emma Arnold and Sean Hitzelberger. Ostensibly an aspirational business story about how they balanced ownership of their Peckham yoga studio, Yogarise, with life as a young family, the piece began, instead, on an unforeseen issue that had arisen because of the proliferation of Black majority faith groups they shared their building with. 'There were about 20 Western African churches in there,' Hitzelberger was reported as saying. 'There'd be massive ghetto blasters and screaming ... [so] we'd pop by and say, "Excuse me, we have a yoga class in here."'

These quotes elicited a response that was swift and merciless. On Twitter, Kelechi Okafor, a Nigerian heritage actor, dancer and Peckham native, accused Yogarise's founders of having a 'colonialist mentality' and 'insulting [the] communities that existed before your studio'. In a follow-up post on *VICE* (after Arnold and Hitzelberger's original comments had, at their request, been removed from the online version of the story), writer Sam Wolfson noted that 'You can't go round saying, "Yeah, our yoga studio's lovely now since we told all those existing religious communities to be quiet so we could hear our farts during child's pose," and not expect a bit of backlash.'

The righteous adrenaline rush of the social media pile-on was definitely a factor in all this. But something about the Yogarise affair seemed to neatly encapsulate all the problems of gentrification; to briefly corroborate a feeling of social displacement that was easy to feel but hard to spot clear evidence of. It was the tension between overlapping Londons – old and new, Black and White, wealthy and underprivileged – in miniature. Plus another reminder that the othering and suspicion engendered by Thomas Brem Wilson's pioneering church was still a problem. And yet, what few people realized at the time was that it was representative of a specific war being fought by London's Black African churches. Namely, that the winds of socio-economic change blowing through areas like Peckham may not exactly be good news for the Black sects that flourished in a 1990s and 2000s atmosphere of urban deprivation.

'Because areas like South London were quite run-down, it enabled churches to buy these buildings,' says William Ackah. 'But now those areas are gentrifying, we're seeing a different attitude emerging. It's harder for [churches] to get planning permission, they don't want these people coming in and making all their noise, and there's more local resistance to this idea of what happens to the local cinema.'

This attitude shift is borne out by real-life cases. In 2010, the Redeemed Christian Church of God's purchase of a former bingo hall in Camberwell faced robust local opposition, and KICC was effectively stopped from establishing churches in both Crystal Palace and Rainham in Essex, before it opened its 'Prayer City' facility just outside Chatham in Kent. You could say that this opposition, in which bingo halls, cinemas and other fallen cathedrals to working-class British leisure are protected, signifies secular society striking back. In Ackah's view, though, this stymieing of new churches speaks, more generally, to the way 'gentrification erodes and erases Black space'. Most importantly, it points to a hazy future. As he asks, 'Will the next generation hold onto these [church] assets, or will they be sold off and become coffee shops?'

However, if there is another side to the coin then it is this: even if London's Black majority churches are struggling to consolidate their local dominance, their global stature is only growing. Thanks to the practice of church-placing – where vast, generally Pentecostal bodies in African countries implant their institutions in diaspora – and the impact of technology, a Black sect's reach will now extend well beyond the numbers in a congregation thinned and dispersed by both the pandemic and the increased difficulty of finding inner-city space for worship. Redeemed Christian Church of God, which famously planned to plant a place of worship within five minutes' walk of every developing city in the globe, has 177 churches around the world. Tufnell Park's House on the Rock has more than 50 branches, including a Lagos facility featuring a school, hospital and outreach centre. As Ackah says, 'Whereas those early Caribbean churches are probably now just Black British churches with a heavy Caribbean influence, thanks to globalization and technology, the African churches can be global brands with satellites in Ghana, South Africa, Kenya and even the US.'

And it is here that we land, finally, on what might be one of the more central reasons for religion's sustained growth and importance within London's Black African community. It is another reflection of the connectedness of the global diaspora and the general collapsing of the distance between what it is to live on the continent and in the metropole. Or, in other words, faith is another expression of tradition and Black African pride. And if the hundreds and hundreds of new Black majority churches in Southwark signify anything, then it is a replication of the evangelical and Pentecostal boom that has transformed cities like Lagos in recent years.

Naturally, there are, as Wole Soyinka has noted, some mildly unsettling consequences that can come from such religious dominance within a culture and a people. But, at many levels, I can see the positive benefits that come from such a devoted, defining relationship to religion, whether it is the forward-thinking, community-minded Muslim faith of Sheikh Mahdi and BECA, or the battery-charging escapism that comes from three fevered hours in a former bingo hall. Not to mention the networks of assistance – the legal advice, the tip-off about work, the potluck of home-cooked traditional dishes at the end of Sunday service – that are attributed to God but are really expressions of collective Black power and solidarity, accrued after multiple challenging decades of settlement.

I do not remember a time in my life when I had anything like pure, unquestioning faith. But I recognize now, more than ever, that I have benefited immeasurably from the structure, support and values that religion through a specifically African lens has bestowed. For me and so many others, our Black African identity is inextricably linked to faith. They are one and the same. I understand that it has given me more than it has taken away. And I appreciate that, for all its issues and idiosyncrasies, it has long been the only path to sanctuary, success and sanity for those bearing the daily weight of life in diaspora. That it cannot be easily explained is sort of the point.

At the end of the long service at KICC's Land of Wonders, after little disposable, flip-top pots of sweet communion wine had been drunk, final prayers had been muttered and Ashimolowo had disappeared from the screen, my mother and I made our way out through the crowd and onto the street. We traded goodbyes with some other departing congregants. And then, quite unexpectedly, my mum began to let rip. 'So impersonal,' she said distastefully, as crowds hurriedly dispersed to their cars. 'Not even a cup of tea or a biscuit afterwards.' I was confused. Hadn't I just seen her dancing to the band's opening tunes? Wasn't she singing along happily to the hymns? Didn't she laugh and nod approvingly at parts of Ashimolowo's silver-tongued sermon? 'Oh, no, I had fun,' she said, as we removed our masks and crossed the street. 'But you know me. I just love church.'

6

Restaurant

The stomach may, anecdotally at least, be the recommended access point to a lover's heart. But there is no question that it is the best route to African London's soul. Long-term settlement in what the Jamaican poet Una Marson called the city of 'coated people' can loosen a Black Londoner's grasp on their tropical roots; loss of indigenous traditions and the transforming influence of the Western world can induce the sense of being culturally adrift. But, if you are lucky, then food can bring you back ashore. If you are lucky, all it can take is a smell, a taste or the hissing, violent sizzle of onions and palm oil in a hot pan to reconnect you with that missing side of yourself; to bring it all flooding back in the form of a satisfied craving for pounded yam or injera or cow foot soup. If the Black African yearning for that intangible sense of home is written anywhere in London, then it is written here: in the Congolese rumba bars, Ghanaian takeaways and Nigerian suya spots that line high streets like filling stations for a specific sort of cultural nostalgia.

And that was certainly the case for me, as I sat in Pitanga, a modern Nigerian restaurant in West Kensington, and looked on as an Italian-born chef called Nicoletta fried onions and bell peppers for the eggs that would be my lunch. I hadn't even intended to eat here today, in a bright, homey space strewn with wire baskets of fruit and West African knick-knacks. But Nky Iweka, the Nigerian chef who is Pitanga's founder and had agreed to be interviewed about the significance and history of African cuisine in London, had insisted. Iweka, as I quickly learn, is not someone accustomed to taking no for an answer. Raised in Nigeria until she was 15, she grew up in a rural environment (they slaughtered their own pigs and her grandfather cured his own bacon) and initially worked as a management consultant before self-training as a chef.

With soft, rounded features and a beret-style black hat pulled over her hair, she speaks at pace with a faint Nigerian lilt and has the slightly jittery, caffeinated air of someone who has had to keep a food business afloat during the pandemic's obstacle course of ever shifting hazards. To step into her and her business partner and head chef Nicoletta's realm (a fast and furious whirl of running jokes, frequent cigarette breaks and muttered disparagements aimed at the delivery riders who clomp in to pick up takeaway orders) feels a little like entering the world of a long-standing vaudeville double act. 'Remember when I had that shipment of fermented beans sent here?' says Iweka with a smile at one point, during a discussion about acquiring produce.

'Oh, yeah,' says Nicoletta, gratefully accepting the feed line. 'And I asked you if it was a dead body.'

Pitanga, which opened in 2018, is described as 'Nigerian with a twist' and features a vast menu that encompasses classic stews and rice dishes as well as vegan options and African-influenced brunch, was inspired by Iweka's biography and personal appetites rather than any attempt at authenticity. 'We have a take on the Full English breakfast, and people go, "That's not very Nigerian",' she explains. 'And I always say, "Listen, this place is about my nostalgia of Nigeria. And we used to eat sausages and bacon in Nigeria when I was growing up, so that is my experience and it is valid."'

Crucially, it is not just her own sense of nostalgia that she is honouring. When Nicoletta, who has been taught by Iweka to cook Nigerian food, is done making my lunch, she brings over a generous platter and, with it, a piece of my childhood. It is Nigerian scrambled eggs: a heady, tomato-and-Scotch bonnet-swirled mush that comes alongside fluffy, thick planks of Agege, the enriched bread named after a Lagos neighbourhood. After one bite – the almost cakey dough both softening and subverting the fiery, deeply savoury sweetness of the wobbling eggs – I might as well be slumped happily on my mum's corner sofa, listening to the faint sound of her singing church hymns in the kitchen. It is the quintessential Proustian rush. But it is also more than that. Because eating such a decidedly domestic dish in a restaurant context only amplifies the sensation.

And it is this that makes what Iweka is doing – and, more generally, what the other new wave West African diaspora chefs and restaurateurs like her are doing – so vital to the wider understanding of Black African culture in London. The presence of restaurants like Pitanga offer a means for African London's customers and cooks to engage with stories and heritage in a way that, like a Nigerian Full English, can speak eloquently to the happy contradictions that make up modern Black British lives. But with that power comes real responsibility. And an ever growing and ever more prominent African-influenced food scene has also come into contact with disputes over appropriation, authenticity and identity that drive to the heart of what it is to be steeped in a heritage with a new-found cultural currency.

'I get a lot of non-Nigerians coming in here saying they have a friend who talks about the food, or they've heard about it because they follow Nigerian music,' explains Iweka, as more delivery riders appear at the door and Nicoletta foil-wraps another lunchtime order of jollof rice. 'I really think that young Nigerians, young Africans even, are shaping something.' The food that many of us grew up with is having a prolonged, unexpected moment of prominence. It really does feel deeply connected to the soul of modern London's Black African diaspora. But the battle for that soul, over who controls it, who profits from it, and who it serves, has been anything but straightforward.

Michelin's 2018 ceremony, announcing the coming year's restaurant awards for Great Britain and Ireland, did not, on the face of it, have much to mark it as especially unusual. It took place in the vast, blockbusting surrounds of the BFI Imax cinema in London. There were the requisite moments of overlong, scripted patter led by celebrity host Amanda Stretton. Gathered *chefs patrons* – the ones who had been told they were gaining the stars that are Michelin's weighty seal of recommendation – posed for photos with a grinning Gordon Ramsay. It was ever thus, in the glitzy, slightly stilted world of corporatized fine dining.

But for those interested in African cuisine, and specifically West African cuisine, there was a significant moment to look out for. Because, as the UK's accolades were announced, amid an expected first-time star for Basque-influenced live fire spot Brat, and a second star for Clare Smyth's poised, subtle cooking at Core, there was a first star for Ikoyi: a small, singular restaurant in St James, London, named for a ritzy Lagos neighbourhood, created by childhood friends Jeremy Chan and Iré Hassan-Odukale and steeped in the flavours and gastronomic culture of West Africa. Let us say it again: a restaurant using Scotch bonnet pepper, egusi seed, plantain and other staples of the domestic Black African kitchen had been bestowed with one of the culinary world's highest honours. It was a big deal; a huge moment of recognition. As the industry site Eater London wrote, in a story quoted in Nigerian media: '[Ikoyi] is the only starred African restaurant in the UK.'

The accolade was all the more impressive given that this is a cuisine that, even among Africans themselves, has not been traditionally renowned for its obvious crossover appeal. As the Nigerian food writer Yemisi Aribisala writes in her book *Longthroat Memoirs*, 'Nigerian food is often stodgy and soupy. But it is also misunderstood, atrociously photographed, not yet given its due. It's a multifaceted cultural treasure trove full of intriguing stories. It might not be gastronomically illustrious but it is energetic and good-hearted.' Well, here at last was some gastronomic illustriousness. Not just for Nigeria but for all the interlinked food traditions across West Africa and, perhaps, some of the under-appreciated indigenous foodways in other nations across the continent.

What's more, Ikoyi's triumph felt especially gratifying because it seemed to crown a burgeoning movement. Yes, it had been Chan's dishes that had been anointed this time – the smoked jollof rice with sun-yellow splotches of crab custard; a dark puff of malted bread, stuffed with mushrooms spiced with a Northern Nigerian *yaji*; the fried plantain, cross-cut into the shape of a jagged landmass and dramatically finished with a vivid dusting of scarlet raspberry salt – but the success could be viewed as part of a broader breakthrough among Black African restaurants, food businesses and culinary culture in Britain and beyond.

The British-Ghanaian chef Zoe Adjonyoh's residencies as Zoe's Ghana Kitchen; roving London pop-ups like the Nigerian-influenced Chuku's, the Senegalese Little Baobab and the Sierra Leonean- and Liberian-inflected Nim's Din; a 2015 cookbook from Pan-African supper club collective the Groundnut and, yes, Iweka's work at Pitanga – all at once, at the tail end of the 2010s, African cooking seemed to be on the verge of something exciting; a mainstay in the sort of food trend pieces that, naturally, make communities that have long loved those foodstuffs roll their eyes. And so, through this prism of understanding, the sight of Chan on the stage at that Michelin ceremony, talking, a little nervously, about West Africa's undiscovered universe of flavour, wasn't merely about Ikoyi. It was about a culinary moment being cemented; the first sure signal that this long underestimated cuisine was ready to be blasted off into a future of mainstream acclaim.

However, there was a sizeable snag. Because amid all the hoopla and celebration, all the excited write-ups in the Nigerian press, claiming this as a victory for the unsung sophistication and complexity of Black African cuisine, quite an important stipulation had been missed. Ikoyi, in the eyes of its founders, was absolutely not 'a West African restaurant'. True, Chan and Hassan-Odukale – respectively, a Chinese-Canadian chef and Nigerian former insurance executive who had met at sixth-form college in the UK – had initially set out to create an ambitious, elevated Nigerian dining experience. And, yes, Chan's starting point with the food had been to rifle through volumes of literature on indigenous West African ingredients that he had found in the British Library. And, OK, it was true that the Ikoyi menu did feature signature dishes that were versions of definably African classics like efo, suya and banga soup. But, in their view, these young founders had already sensed the possible issues with a version of Ikoyi that sought to straightforwardly reconfigure traditional West African cuisine, and they had evolved their business and idea well beyond that initial spark.

'Some people [from a West African background] took what we were doing really well,' explains Chan, sitting beside Hassan-Odukale in their restaurant, amid the dying embers of a Thursday lunch service. 'Some ate a dish where we'd used a spice and would be like, "This tastes like my grandmother's." And that would be beautiful.' He smiles, taking his time. 'But it was interpreted by a lot of West Africans as a Chinese guy cooking African food and trying to pass it off as authentic, and that is not what we ever said it was. It was all the titles of reviews saying we were this "new Nigerian restaurant", and that absolutely annihilated us because we didn't say that. Everything just got out of control.'

Just to add to the irony, months before the award of that Michelin star they had reimagined the restaurant's offering a little (shifting to a set tasting menu from à la carte in a bid to give diners more context) and even, according to Hassan-Odukale, considered changing the name of the business to fully shake off any misleading associations. Still there were unforeseen issues of interpretation. And not just from perplexed West African diners. 'There were a lot of White people eating at this restaurant saying, "I love my experience of West African food,"' says Chan, with a dismayed look. 'And I was more pissed off with them because, again, I was like, "I'm not educating you on authentic West African food and I never said I was."' This may be somewhat unfair to diners making an honest error. But what Chan had discovered, and what caused him to bridle, was that West African cuisine's lack of mainstream profile meant many were mistaking Ikoyi for a foundational introduction to the region's flavours. 'And then,' he continues, 'customers were saying, "So you've lived in West Africa?" To which I'd be like, "No, I've been to Nigeria for three days, but the food we do here is about being artistic, about produce, about the flavours and originality."' Now he lets out a deep sigh. 'But you can't have anything original. It's always going to be challenged.'

So here we had the oft-cited heralds of a revolution in modern West African cooking, actively trying to distance themselves from that movement. It was less than ideal. We will come to the particulars of the ways that Chan, Hassan-Odukale and the wider industry came to see their business as having been wildly misunderstood. But the entire saga of Ikoyi's first Michelin star is a useful portal into a broader exploration of West African restaurant history in London, and how we weigh a particular cuisine's value. Not to mention a discussion of the way that modernized or adapted food has come to be a vessel for how modern African London has attempted to reconcile both sides of itself.

Within it, there are thorny issues of authenticity, of modernization, and the shifting role that restaurants in particular, and food in general, have played in the lives of London and the UK's Black African settlers. Who, or what, are African restaurants for? Are those ideas fixed? And can you truly claim your restaurant isn't West African when its food plays in that culture's familiar sandbox of tastes, textures and scents? The scramble to ordain Chan and Hassan-Odukale as flagbearers of a moment of culinary crossover tells us as much about West African cuisine's long journey, from humble beginnings and late-flowering boom to its modern yearning for mainstream acceptance, as anything else.

If London's African restaurant story begins anywhere then it is at 62 Camden Road, in an unremarkable four-storey townhouse, currently overlooking a Sainsbury's and untroubled by any sort of commemorative blue plaque. This address, from 1933, was the very first West African Students' Union (or WASU) hostel, established by the trailblazing Nigerian activist Ladipo Solanke and his wife, Opeolu 'Mama WASU' Solanke-Ogunbiyi. Conceived as a meeting place, point of welcome, and overseas residence for African students in Britain, it also featured a small public restaurant.

It's a restaurant that, given there were officially only 26 West African students in the UK at that time, could lay a decent claim to being the very first formal establishment of this kind in the country. Whether it's officially deserving of this accolade or not, the business on 62 Camden Road (succeeded by a bigger, longer-term hostel restaurant at 1 South Villas in nearby Camden Square) was undoubtedly one of the earliest public touchpoints that many of the interwar period's Black African immigrants to Britain would have had with the flavours of home (predating even the International Afro Restaurant that activist Amy Ashwood Garvey opened in her New Oxford Street flat in 1935). And to read Mama WASU's account of setting up this kind of business in 1930s London, as written in an exhaustive memoir she published in 2009, is to get a sense of both the displaced life of Black African Londoners at this time and the acute importance of setting up a restaurant like this. Solanke-Ogunbiyi's description of how she obtained indigenous ingredients in a time long before African supermarkets is worth reading.

Within six weeks we opened the restaurant in the basement with four tables of four chairs each. The restaurant at the basement of the hostel was opened all day for resident students and from 12 noon to non-resident African students to enjoy themselves with African dishes on a cash-and-carry basis. The foodstuffs needed for the African dishes comprised dried fish, dried ewedu, dried okra, dried bitterleaf, apon, ogiri, dried pepper, dried iru, dried melon seed and palm oil, all of which were regularly sent to me by my mother, Mrs Juliana Fuwa Obisanya from Itele-Ijebu. My mother usually packaged these food ingredients and sent them by boat to Tilbury ... She was so happy to do this so that her daughter in 'White man's land' would be able to eat her native food and not forget her own country.

What's striking, beyond the itemized specificity of produce that swiftly rubbishes any notions that West

African food is in any sense simple, is that fostering connection to home is the prime motivator for recreating these dishes. Also notable, deeper into this passage of Solanke-Ogunbiyi's recollections, is the fact that the WASU hostel's restaurant was integral to its wider survival as an entity. Throughout early periods of exorbitant rent, takings for the restaurant were what sustained WASU, a hugely important organization that was a seedbed for the political ideas that would enable African colonies to seek independence – notably, Dr Kwame Nkrumah, Ghana's first president, passed through WASU's doors. Yet, even at this early, embryonic stage, the diasporic Black African restaurant was at least in part about socializing. And, what's more, as Solanke-Ogunbiyi notes, White women guests were not allowed in the WASU restaurant so as not to deny 'the golden opportunities that the elite African ladies (who were then in London) had to meet their elite African male counterparts which culminated in the marriages of many of them either in London or back home in Nigeria'. This was a time when Black Britain was governed by one form of colour bar or another (for instance, refusal of lodgings was commonplace before the cricketer Learie Constantine won a landmark 1943 case against the Imperial Hotel in Russell Square). So it is a fascinating reversal of the order of the age; an insight into the rare sanctity this first WASU restaurant offered. And the food – both a life raft and a means for London's mixed community of Africans and Afro-Caribbeans to affirm their Blackness – was a key part of this sanctity.

But, of course, WASU was still essentially a canteen, operating out of a converted townhouse and relatively humble in its ambition as a business. To locate the first legitimate boom in Black African restaurants in the UK, you need to journey to the period after the Second World War. And, even then, restaurant is perhaps not quite the right word. As Riaz Phillips, the food writer and author of British-Caribbean culinary compendium *Belly Full*, writes in a 2018 exploration of West African food for *VICE*, places like Ridley Road Market and Electric Avenue in Brixton began to feature 'tropical foodstuff' stalls frequented by 'home cooks, but also a burgeoning network of "aunties" and small catering companies that provided traditional foods for weddings, cultural festivals, church gatherings, and other special events'.

It's telling that the auntie network of half a century ago Phillips describes is still just as established and relevant today. In the Black African community, and in many immigrant communities, traditional food tends to be disseminated in an ad hoc, DIY manner that meets need wherever it happens to be (and, it should be said, feeds the African impulse for inveterate entrepreneurialism). Where once it would have been a word-of-mouth introduction to someone with a car boot full of sandwich-bagged Ghanaian kelewele, now it is a Facebook Marketplace advert proffering party-ready servings of the pale orange, spiced Nigerian bean curd cake moin-moin. Personally, I will never forget the time before an upcoming birthday party when my mum sent me to collect some meat pies from a taciturn woman in South-East London, wordlessly accepting a mysterious package like a John le Carré character. The abiding feeling, especially when you add in the West African 'bukas' and 'chop bars' (essentially, Black African pubs with added food) that proliferated in London throughout the 1980s and 1990s, is that the quintessential

African 'restaurant experience' often didn't take place in a restaurant at all.

This approach to food entrepreneurship has parallels in the Afro-Caribbean food scene where, once again, the focus is historically on takeaway operations, catering and market stalls. Partly, Black African food businesses taking this approach were acting pragmatically. From the recent past right up to today, lots of the basic things needed to establish a proper restaurant – investment and amenable commercial landlords among them – are still very much out of reach for those in Britain's Black community. But, in truth, the reason there perhaps wasn't the scramble from West Africans to set up traditional restaurants, replete with lit candles, billowing tablecloths and formal service, was because of cultural stigma attached to them and hospitality in general.

'For us, there's always that disdain about the service industry,' says Adejoké Bakare, the Nigerian heritage chef-founder of Chishuru, an acclaimed contemporary West African restaurant in Brixton. 'It's always, "Oh, no one from a good family does it." In terms of working in a restaurant, and even owning one, it was just always looked down on as if it's for people who are not very well educated. I'm thinking about in Nigeria. But even coming here to London, most people seem to only go into restaurants as a last resort.'

It's important to point out that, as in many things, West African systems of class are coming into play here. Yet these views are still recognizably pervasive within the broader Black African community. Home and home cooking is the alpha and the omega in the Nigerian household especially. The attitude towards restaurants from my mother when I was growing up was very much: why would you go out and pay for something you could have a much better version of in the comfort of your own home?

Yemisi Aribisala, once again in *Longthroat Memoirs*, delves even deeper into the profound, unwavering mistrust some West Africans feel towards restaurants while discussing her mother-in-law's dismayed reaction to the fact that Aribisala planned to accompany her husband out for a meal. Restaurants, according to the mother-in-law, were a place husbands took a 'good-time girl who was being fed for the work she would do after the meal'. And so those wives who accompanied their husbands to these dens of adulterous sinfulness rather than staying home 'were no better than prostitutes'.

With this level of associative negativity to push through, it is little wonder that, in the decades after the days of the WASU hostel, as more Black Africans arrived and inner-city native grocers made it easier for families to recreate the flavours of home in their London kitchens, few budding restaurateurs felt bold enough to launch their own African restaurants. It's another example of cultural tradition latching on to one of the realities of life in diaspora – in this case, the fact that Black socializing often took place in the home due to both socioeconomic circumstances and the hangover of colour bar policies – and creating something new. And, interestingly, the few proper, sit-down African restaurants that did emerge in the 1990s and 2000s tended to be shaped by the available clientele. 'They were solely for bachelors,' says Bakare, with a hearty cackle. 'It was rough and ready. Come and get your stuff and go.'

This archaic idea of Black African – and, given the make-up of London's Black diaspora, we largely mean

West African — restaurants as being a place where the lonesome or unwed could get a particular itch of homesickness scratched very much persists. In this reading, the Black African restaurant is solely about the food and the specific sense memory it induces; and that food is almost always being presented as a watered-down analogue for those unable to access the promised land of proper home-cooked Nigerian eba alongside mucilaginous green okra 'draw' soup, Ghanaian 'red red' beans with a laurel wreath of fried plantain, or the Senegalese sauce-infused rice dish *thieboudienne*.

In fact, this is true of all manner of London immigrant communities, whether that is Northern Chinese international students dipping into a Bloomsbury Uyghur restaurant, or Brazilians heading to the Latin Quarter for breaded pyramids of chicken-filled coxinha croquettes. But it's notable that all notion of a restaurant offering a broader experience is absent. And that, while restaurant ownership is a huge part of other immigrant diasporas in the UK, like the South Asian and Chinese communities, the cultural stigma and other barriers contributed to circumstances that meant we never got the Sierra Leonean or Ghanaian analogue of a bustling curry house. Traditionally, African restaurants were community-facing, almost clandestine enterprises that didn't Westernize their dishes or strain to reach out to a non-African audience. Winning people over or spreading any sort of culinary gospel was rarely the aim.

As with anything, there were exceptions. The WASU-indebted cultural facility the Africa Centre, which began operating out of an address on King Street in Covent Garden in 1964, eventually had a basement restaurant called Calabash. And, with its ranging Pan-African menu of Ethiopian injera, Nigerian egusi and onion-braised Senegalese yassa chicken, it would probably have been an entire generation's gateway to a broad range of African flavours in a restaurant context. Another originator, according to Bakare, was a place that opened in Woolwich, in South-East London, around the turn of the millennium. 'It was called Tasty and it was really bad at one time,' she says, almost admiringly. 'But the guy just kept at it, he got better, and I think he began to see that there was potential in it. And you know how people think, "Oh, somebody is making money from food, I want to do this as well." That's how it grew.' And Tasty, incidentally, has today expanded to become one of the biggest West African food businesses in the country, with more than 20 franchised locations.

Around this time there was also the emergence of 805, a Nigerian restaurant lurking beneath worn maroon awnings on the Old Kent Road. Founded by the Nigerian James family, and also boasting branches in Hendon and Reading, 805 is perhaps as close as it gets to an institution among London's West African restaurants. Each outpost is a slickly run, sprawling mother ship, with low, clubby lighting, African music cranked high and a multigenerational crowd availing themselves of traditional gourds of palm wine, thick, swampy soups, and the signature 'Monica fish', a whole griddled croaker slicked with stridently hot Scotch bonnet marinade. That the James family has even opened branches in West Africa – enacting the culinary equivalent of carrying coals to Newcastle via outposts in Accra in Ghana and Abuja in Nigeria – tells you everything about its status across the diaspora and the weight of its reputation. It is bastion, point of pilgrimage and, fittingly for a culture where food and festivity go hand in hand, land of dim-lit perpetual celebration.

Even so, after they opened the first 805 in 2001, the Jameses still had to work to establish a civilized restaurant culture where one didn't really exist. The clientele in those early days – those looking for fellowship and familiarity in a bottle of Gulder beer and some eforiro spinach soup, bobbing with pungent pieces of stockfish – still tended to be younger, unmarried men, utilizing the space as an extension of the home. 'I used to be the barman, so I was privy to people wanting credit, wanting this, that and the other, and all the arguments that are just a natural thing in Nigerian restaurants,' says 805's director Emmanuel James, whose mother and father founded the brand. 'It was loads of bachelors. A lot of guys in their mid- to late-twenties upwards. And I think it was really a spot for people to hang out as an alternative to a nightclub.'

As per Bakare's view, this was very much the market at that time. And the reason, according to James, why restaurants within the West African community were still something 'people tended to look down on'. The journey towards the 805 of today can be traced back to the fact that James' mother – head chef and driving force behind the launch of the restaurant, despite her husband's initial resistance – had absorbed ideas about professional hospitality from time spent working at the Landmark, a five-star hotel in Marylebone. 'Mum brought a lot of experience from that environment,' says James. 'And one thing my parents did was that they were adamant they weren't going to allow people to smoke. This was way before the smoking ban came into play [in 2007]. But Nigerian restaurants in those days were places where you could smoke and smoke.

So when you came into 805 it was very fresh, very different. That was part of breaking the narrative.'

One of the first things to hit you in 805 is its slickness and scale; it is a white space, sectioned off into quadrants, faintly scented by the smoke of unglimpsed outdoor grills, stalked by stressed-looking young waiters in untucked shirts and almost always filled with big, boisterous groups. That rumours persist of hidden VIP areas with their own superior menus only adds to the allure.

Another key factor in 805's emergence was the stage of settlement that London's Nigerian (and, to an extent, broader Black African) diaspora were at in the early years of the new millennium. 'I think what really happened,' begins James with a smile, 'was that during that time a lot of Nigerians had formalized their status in this country. And that allowed them the freedom to come out. So you had people that maybe wouldn't have been as outgoing, coming out and celebrating.' The notion that this era was boom time for Nigerians gaining a firmer foothold in the UK, through successful applications for either British citizenship or Permanent Residence status, carries some weight. Following the peak in migration instigated by the Nigerian military regimes of the early to mid-1990s, the early 2000s would have represented the point at which lots of Nigerian-born Londoners hit the ten- or five-year thresholds required for both naturalization and indefinite leave-to-remain papers, respectively.

Clearly, this new psychological freedom – the dual citizenship that meant you could shuttle between the UK and Africa as you pleased – triggered a shift in attitude. 'It became a Sunday thing, or a birthday thing where you'd go to church and come out and eat,' says Bakare. 'Almost like how a [White] British family would go for Sunday lunch.' It's true that restaurants like 805 have also risen in tandem with another institution of Black African London life and industriousness: the Black majority church. And the length of service at some of the Pentecostal churches in the area – often stretching into five hours or more – has almost certainly brought in business from weary Black African families desperate to eat after a marathon of praise. It is another sign of the conjoined nature of community hubs in Black African London. And also, perhaps, the way that prolonged settlement – and more deeply embedded roots – can bring about new behaviours.

Joined in later years by counterparts in other parts of London, like Eko, a Nigerian-influenced place in Hackney, Enish, a brash, multi-site affair with branches in Ilford and Lewisham, Gold Coast, a South Norwood Ghanaian spot in a former pub, and Zeret Kitchen in Camberwell, an Ethiopian community staple, these restaurants formed a scattered constellation, where those in the African diaspora could check in with a part of themselves; full-immersion dunk tanks of food, music and people that spoke to a new dawn of cultural pride after a long period of Black African culture operating as something of an underground phenomenon. As Emmanuel James puts it: 'We naturally evolved into becoming a community hub where people could feel at home. Among their own kind, among their own community and really just in a familiar environment.'

What's more, through the signature heft of portions that are designed to enable diners to leave with plenty of leftovers (you have not seen a truly sophisticated doggy bag operation until you've witnessed 805 servers ferrying wobbling towers of plastic tubs back and forth from the kitchen), African restaurateurs and their customers have collaboratively bent the concept of eating out to their will. It is not quite a restaurant in the quintessential European sense; neither is it fully an analogue of a catered domestic event. It is something between the two. Reflective of a customer base who were, and are, Londoners and Africans all at once. However, what is comfort for some can read as inflexibility or a lack of ambition. And as a new generation of Black Africans emerged, and sought to push these restaurants and this misunderstood cuisine off in new, surprising directions, they met a good deal of resistance and a mass of unanticipated controversies.

The woman in Joké Bakare's restaurant didn't understand and she wasn't about to leave until she did. Sitting in the comparatively tiny 25-cover space of Brixton's Chishuru, overlooked by the gleaming metal and concentrated activity of an open kitchen, she held up the menu to the waitress again, gesturing at the words with a perplexed expression. Where is the pounded yam? she asked, once more. The jollof? The pepper soup? How could the people behind this place have the temerity to call themselves a Nigerian restaurant, when these dishes weren't available? Aunty, said the waitress, with a note of pleading desperation in her voice, this is the menu. This is the menu, aunty.

'This woman did not want to leave,' says Bakare with a laugh and a shake of the head, taking up the tale. 'I think we were trying to explain it to her for like 40 minutes, and she was adamant that what we were serving couldn't actually be the menu.' Bakare cackles again. 'She left in the end, but I think if we weren't careful she would have gone to the Nigerian High Commission and had our citizenship revoked.' Bakare, who is warm, mischievous and formidable, can just about see the funny side now. But this incident underscores the constant battle she has had to fight since Chishuru opened, amid the uncertainty of the first year of pandemic, in the late summer of 2020. Named for a Northern Nigerian word that loosely translates as 'to eat silent', Bakare's project is an intensely personal one. Not just because it is the culmination of years of supper clubs and self-training as a hobbyist cook turned professional, but also because her unusual, culture-splicing take on West African cuisine reflects the mixed heritage of her family: a blended amalgam of genes from the Yoruba and Igbo ethnic tribes mixed with a childhood spent in the heavily Muslim North. It is about maintaining links to home and upholding culinary tradition in a way not all that dissimilar from Mama WASU almost a century ago.

Though, crucially, Bakare is casting her net beyond Yoruba-centric, West African restaurant staples like jollof rice, stewed beans and pounded yam, to give airtime to lesser-spotted delicacies like a steamed corn pudding called ekoki and a fonio grain porridge known as gwote. It is an approach that has brought her no little critical acclaim (as well as being featured in the BBC show *Mary Berry: Love to Cook* and the *Observer*, Chishuru was named as one of the best restaurants of 2021 by both The Infatuation and Eater London). But it has also, of course, engendered plenty of responses like that of the woman who refused to accept the menu or leave without giving Bakare and her team a piece of her mind.

'There's still that hesitancy,' she says, sitting at one of Chishuru's vacant tables in a lull before prep for the day's evening service can fully begin. 'People have memories or preconceptions of the food that they don't want to be sullied. So some come in and say, how come you don't serve fufu [fermented cassava flour, beaten into a creamy mash]? How come you don't serve jollof? And then we have to go through this whole process of explaining that we want people to realize there is more [to the food].'

You could say that it is a measure of Bakare's determination and belief in the work of broadening the repertoire of known West African dishes that she has not caved and started playing the hits quite yet. But spend a few minutes in her company – hearing her enthuse about turning plantain into a syrup for Chishuru's cocktails or watching as she blanches dried hibiscus flowers for a new dish she is developing – and you soon sense she sees no alternative but to push, and try to share her passion for a cuisine that is far more varied and nuanced than even other Black Africans perhaps realize.

One thing she is undoubtedly up against is that Black African restaurant goers are not historically renowned for being the easiest to please. 'We are a tough crowd,' laughs Bakare. And that sentiment doesn't solely apply to those from West African countries. Makda Harlow, founder of roving, Eritrean-inspired street food brand and supper club series Lemlem Kitchen, has encountered plenty of East African compatriots who have loudly taken exception to her Mexican-inspired injera 'afro-tacos' or fries dribbled in the creamy Ethiopian chickpea stew, shiro. 'I've got a lot of criticism from my people,' she says, over a forbiddingly huge platter of traditional stews at Adulis, a long-established Eritrean institution in Oval. 'Which I actually love and understand. Some of our families have so much pain and trauma that they want to preserve the culture through food and keep it authentic.' She stops, momentarily, to scoop up another dimpled, tangy shred of injera bread. 'But, I always think, what is authentic?'

This idea is worth dwelling on. The impulse to maintain Black African food traditions, to halt the wheels of change in this area of life, is undoubtedly linked to some of the instability and turmoil that shapes many immigrant experiences. You could say that the alleged toughness of Black African diners is a consequence of that deep-seated cultural stigma around restaurants. But this reputation of spikiness, from both customers and those allegedly serving them, is practically synonymous with African dining. 'People are very, very, very demanding,' agrees 805's Emmanuel James. 'Some can be very aggressive at times but, honestly, they are the most loving bunch of people that you could serve. Because at the end of the day, they may give you stick, but they always smile in the end and you see them coming back.'

You could say, in a sense, that Ikoyi bore the brunt of this tendency even more than Chishuru, Lemlem Kitchen or any others. Because, yes, if it is to be a game of baring the emotional scars of encounters with perplexed restaurant customers, then Chan and Hassan-Odukale will win every time. 'Oh, we had people coming in here and displaying a rudeness that was kind of upsetting,' says Hassan-Odukale, quietly, of that first pre-Michelin star year, following their opening in July 2017, when misunderstanding around their restaurant was perhaps at its peak.

This, according to Ikoyi's founders, was an especially confusing era, when the restaurant was struggling financially, and the people they did manage to get through the door seemed to be either the rapt chefs of other Michelin-level restaurants (including Clare Smyth, Alain Ducasse and Magnus Nilsson) or tablefuls of incensed Nigerians who thought Chan's modernist, painterly interpretations of West African cuisine were a kind of cruel, elaborate prank. 'There would be humiliating comments and people just laughing at the food when it came to the table,' says Chan, his jaw tightening. 'And, look, maybe it was offensive to some people. But if I went to a restaurant and there was a White guy who was serving Chinese food, and I thought it was gimmicky and inauthentic, I would still be gracious and say thank you. I wouldn't be rude.'

It was at that point that Chan – who, in conversation, has both an artist's burning intensity and the analytical tendency you'd expect from someone who studied philosophy at Princeton – made a conscious decision to distance Ikoyi from its African origins; or at least attempt to clarify their project's (admittedly quite complicated) aims. In summer 2018, they introduced a tasting menu and Chan's cooking became more consciously ambiguous, orienting itself more around careful handling of produce and East Asian influences. 'I was literally like, "Fuck this, I'm going to take it to the most extreme level I can."'

Trying to look at this particular debate from as objective a distance as possible, I have some sympathy for both sides. Hassan-Odukale and Chan, of course, did not deserve scorn and ridicule from West African clientele who had arrived at Ikoyi anticipating a version of it that never really existed. Yet, equally, I can see why certain diners were confused to the point of aggravation or disappointment. Among Nigerians, and the wider

Black diaspora in London for that matter, Ikoyi's arrival was a big deal – the promise of familiar West African flavour profiles (rendered by a skilled chef who had put in time in the professional kitchens of Heston Blumenthal's Dinner and René Redzepi's enduringly influential Noma) in a fine-dining environment elevated way beyond even Calabash was exciting. It could be chalked up as another cultural victory for the diaspora alongside a David Adjaye architectural commission or Chris Ofili retrospective. That, in a broad sense, something humble that West Africans were personally invested in was being raised up and praised in the manner of high art was a tantalizing prospect.

Too tantalizing, perhaps. Ikoyi's status as a rare African-influenced blockbuster meant that it came freighted with expectation, but also that it suffered from the lack of an obvious equivalent or reference point.

Social media didn't help either, offering people the irresistible opportunity to form an opinion about Ikoyi's food without actually trying it. And when a 2019 photo of Chan's interpretations of 'moi-moi and fried plantain', looking alien and avant-garde beside those unhelpfully simple, pot-stirring descriptions, went semi-viral on Twitter, it seemed to tap into some deeper frustrations linked to erasure and under-representation. 'It's a Nigerian restaurant that's not for us,' said one dismayed respondent (among some others who, it should be said, were valiantly trying to explain that Ikoyi wasn't attempting to be authentic). The lack of other businesses operating in this creative space was clearly an issue. Or as Chan puts it at one point, after another heavy sigh: 'To be honest, I think we were too early on many things.' Looking at it this way, there is a case to be made that the stresses of Ikoyi's early days were merely the growing pains of a West African restaurant scene only just really moving out of adolescence.

And yet, for me, the bigger issue has always been the hurriedness with which Hassan-Odukale and Chan seemed to reject explicit association with West African culture. Dining in Ikoyi two months before the Michelin announcement, I felt a profound wonder, pride and cultural acceptance; a sense that its stylish little room with its dangling earthenware lampshades and psychedelically flavoursome dishes, at once unusual and familiar, seemed to be melding European and Black African identity in a thrilling, meaningful way. True, not every dish worked, and I have vague memories of there being an unconscionable mark-up on the imported Star beer that one could find in a Peckham off-licence for about £2. But sitting there as a British-Nigerian, surrounded by others making the pilgrimage to see what the fuss was about, I felt it was an important waymarker in the West African diaspora story; the manifestation of a cross-cultural existence many of us lived but rarely saw reflected back.

With all this in mind, to see Ikoyi's founders row back their restaurant's Africanness so frantically throughout 2019 and beyond – mostly through their adamant, constant rebuttals of the charge of being an African restaurant – was personally a little dismaying. Moreover, it made me think of those other excited, curious Black faces I had seen in the dining room at Ikoyi who, whether they liked every dish or not, seemed to be full of the same pride at having their culinary heritage honoured with such care and thoughtfulness.

'We wanted to embrace [the link to West Africa], but it just created too many problems for us,' says Chan, after

I have put this thought process to them. 'It was really bad, and we lost a lot of business and custom.' Hassan-Odukale, who tends to speak sparingly but with a relaxed, soft-toned authority, gets to the nub of it in a business sense. 'Everyone was confused,' he says. 'We couldn't get some customers coming in because they thought it was too African. And then some thought it wasn't African enough, and then the restaurant was just empty.'

'We weren't trying to pull the wool over people's eyes,' says Chan, chipping in. 'And that is what was sad to me. Whenever I had a West African family that were angry at me, that thought I was trying to screw with them, it made me so upset. Because I was actually trying to relate my appreciation of these beautiful ingredients and share something.'

However inadvertently, Ikoyi had touched the live third rail of appropriation in food; a particular point of contention in the 2010s following a number of high-profile flashpoints (including, pertinently, a widely contested 2014 recipe for jollof rice from Jamie Oliver). Though absolutely not his fault, the optics of Chan being thrust forward as the valorized face of West African cuisine were not good. And it was something that other chefs working within this broad genre – and often not getting anything like the attention or adulation Ikoyi was commanding – started to pick up on. As Zoe Adjonyoh put it drily in a 2020 story for *Today*: 'Jeremy Chan of Ikoyi in London is still the only chef celebrated in the mainstream restaurant world for modern African gastronomy, and he is many wonderful things, but not an African.'

Hassan-Odukale and Chan's decision, then, was as much about self-protection as it was about not locking Ikoyi into any particular style. Today, if Chan wants to create a dish that channels the sour tang of a traditional Nigerian banga sauce, he has the good sense to 'conceptually deculturize it' and call it something else. This is, in his words, in the hope of not 'offending people'. But despite the game of disguise and denial that these young restaurateurs have had to play, a close read of one of their post-revamp menus, which might feature an efo stew made from pumpkin and wild leek or pistachio dessert lent a licorice-like fruity bloom by the dried Cameroonian seeds known as Grains of Peace, leaves you in no doubt about Ikoyi's core source of inspiration. 'Maybe it is an African restaurant,' says Chan at one point, with a mischievous smile. 'But it's African in an outsider's sense. So maybe that means that it isn't African.' The point to stress, in all this, is that Ikoyi can of course be neither or both. A restaurant is a business rather than a publicly funded cultural institution. And, despite the understandable misgivings of some observers in the West African diaspora, cuisine cooked, celebrated and adapted by someone outside the food's culture is the bedrock of much of modern gastronomy.

The irony, beyond Chan and Hassan-Odukale's mental contortions, was that Ikoyi's singular, tricky-to-categorize approach begat quite a few imitators. In Mayfair, there was Stork, a Pan-African restaurant with a visually exuberant room and an obliging, Afro-Caribbean-inflected menu. In Marylebone, Akoko brought a detailed, Ikoyi-like experience (and another smoked jollof rice centrepiece) seen through a refined, overtly celebratory African lens. And back down on the Old Kent Road, a short-lived restaurant called Talking Drum proffered maximum hip-wiggling vibes and wild fusion concoctions like plantain gnocchi and suya calamari. Whatever else it had done, Ikoyi had shown prospective West African restaurateurs a future and a business model beyond the signature abundance and simplicity at, say, 805 or Pitanga. Primped, refined Black African dishes were the literal flavour of the month. But, for some, this winning formula also signalled a dismaying homogeneity.

'Lots of the young West African chefs coming out now are doing fine dining,' says Bakare, sounding a note of almost maternal concern. 'It's good to do that. But I think they feel it's the only way they can be welcomed, have a say in the market or make their voices heard. One of the major problems that we have is that we are not confident about our food. We think it's rough and ready and not sophisticated enough. But I think if you know about the food, you know that it's quite nuanced. That it's not just heat or one kind of spice. And if lots of people continue to learn about it then we can take pride in it, and present it as unapologetically West African.'

This idea brings us right back to Ikoyi and what its Michelin star supposedly signified. Because encoded in that debate – and all the many related trend stories that honed in on how likely it was that West African cuisine might finally puncture the mainstream – are interesting questions of Westernization, what the gastronomic world views as worthy of praise, and whether relinquishing a degree of control is just a natural side effect of a food culture's growing popularity. Or, more broadly, how much attention and energy should be devoted to Black African cuisine presented in a context that clearly speaks to non-Africans? Though not without controversy, the natural diversification of, say, French, Sichuan, Mexican, Thai, Spanish and Korean cuisines has enhanced rather than diminished their international status. Ultimately, it is a question of who the modern African restaurant is for. And, truthfully, whether the answer to that should even really matter.

Akwasi Brenya-Mensa still remembers the scent. It was the year of the 2014 World Cup in Brazil, and this Ghanaian-British chef was making his way past a street food stall in Rio Di Janeiro when it hit him. 'I was walking through this market and then, all of a sudden, I could smell palm oil,' he says, grinning. 'You know when your nose can't even compute? I was just, like, "Wow."' The intense, musky familiarity of the palm oil led him to a woman who was making moqueca – a deeply fragrant fish stew, influenced by Brazil's spliced African and European cultures – and other stalls peddling things he instantly recognized as versions of the Ghanaian staples he grew up eating. Suddenly he was alive to 'the techniques and recipes that have travelled' between South American and West African cultures, and the seed of an idea for a food project was planted.

Frequent trips to Brazil and Mexico (via a job as a tour manager in the music industry) gave it water and sunlight. And, after a few years of experimenting with Afro-Latin supper clubs, a trip back to Ghana helped him reframe what he was actually working towards. 'That was the light-bulb moment,' he says. 'I had been going around the world and engaging with people's culture before coming back and doing my own interpretation of their food. But I just realized I could actually do it with my own heritage. So I spent the rest of that year just developing dishes and annoying the hell out of my aunts by asking them questions in the kitchen.'

The result of that moment of connection in Brazil (and all those months aggravating the matriarchal cooks in his family) is a completed restaurant project that puts Brenya-Mensa right at the heart of London's evolving Black African restaurant story and the broader settler narrative of African London. The venture, called Tatale and named for the spiced Ghanaian plantain fritter, is an ambitious but grounded Pan-African establishment where dishes like omo tuo and nkatekwan (a peanut stew alongside mashed rice balls) and fried chicken wings spiced with chichinga (a groundnut-based, suya-style rub) reflect a sensibility that is as rooted in the culinary argot of late-night London as rural Ghana. That it also happens to be in the Africa Centre's revamped new complex in Southwark, London – the very same cultural institution that was home to the Calabash – only makes it feel like a full-circle moment for African gastronomy in the city. It's a detail that brings prestige. And, maybe, a not inconsiderable amount of pressure.

'In terms of the responsibility, it keeps you up some nights,' he adds. 'People do remember the Calabash. They speak fondly of it, and it's renowned within the community. The torch has been passed, and I'm going to be carrying it for a period in the Africa Centre's new building. Which I'm super-excited to shout about. On the one hand I got this because I'm the right person for this job. But on the other it's like, "I can't fuck this up."'

This lurch between confidence and disarming modesty is reflective of time in Brenya-Mensa's company. We meet over a drink in the bar of the ICA gallery in London, bludgeoned a little by loud background music as late afternoon tips into evening. Brenya-Mensa, a freewheeling presence who grew up in Mitcham, South London, wears his hair in bunched braids that protrude beneath a red beanie hat, and partly made his name as a restaurateur with a burger spot he ran in Sheffield for five years. But the spirit of Tatale (which, at the time we talk, is some months away from opening) feels as though it will be drawn from the casual, intensely personal supper club movement that he has been primarily involved in for the last few years.

'I initially did the supper club because I was still working in music, still travelling, and I wanted to do something that wouldn't affect my travel schedule,' he says. 'But, as a model, it allowed me to be more experimental. It was just one meal. The menu was always secret so people didn't get it until the day before. That meant the idea of it was: secret location, secret menu, come if you're curious.' It doesn't feel like an aberration that such a flagship African restaurant would be shepherded by someone with experience in the world of DIY restaurants. Perhaps fittingly for a diaspora food culture that began with entrepreneurial aunties catering weddings, birthday parties and funerals out of their cramped home kitchens, things in the world of West African restaurants seem to be retracting somewhat to this more humble, domestic-centred way of doing things. For every modish, star-chasing launch like Akoko, there are the likes of Future Plate (a collaborative, itinerant dining series that features both African and Afro-Caribbean chefs preparing dishes that knit both cultures together) or Nyamming Series (a similarly pitched tour of the interlinked foodways of Liberia, Sierra Leone and Jamaica). Even Zoe Adjonyoh, who successfully ran her own kitchen residencies in London before relocating to the US, consciously downshifted with Sankofa, a series of West African dinners, hosted in London and New York, that took place in apartment buildings, ran to 12 courses and had no set start time.

As well as echoing the struggle that earlier African food entrepreneurs had to put down professional roots, these forcefully casual, consciously minor key endeavours – not quite restaurants; not merely an informal meal with friends – speak to a frustration with a mainstream industry that often ignores you. As Adjonyoh noted, in a *Food & Wine* interview promoting Sankofa: 'There are African chefs working to do what they love, but it doesn't get the same sort of love or appreciation as the new burger spot opening.'

This notion that Black African restaurants in London are ignored (or, at least, not engaged with in the same way) by Western clientele and Western-centric media feels like the end-of-level boss of this entire conversation. And it brings us back to why Ikoyi, which was seemingly the only kind of West African restaurant that bodies like Michelin and the food world's mainstream felt comfortable engaging with, proved such a lightning rod. When Mama WASU established that first restaurant at 62 Camden Road, it was clear that it was primarily a place for Black Africans needing their version of the same culinary fix I got in Pitanga. But are those traditional, post-church restaurants that line the Old Kent Road for non-Africans? Do they even need to be? 'African culture has become very popular,' begins 805's Emmanuel James. 'And so a lot of non-Nigerians who would previously have turned their noses up at Nigerian food started coming in and being like, "Wow." We have Caribbean people eating our food, non-Africans, Caucasians. Of course we'd love even more sorts of people to come in and connect.' This goes for Joké Bakare too, who has been pleased by the mixed nature of Chishuru's crowd. 'We've had a lot of Americans, middle-class Caucasians, people that have lived or worked in Nigeria,' she says. 'To be honest, when it comes to my own people it has sometimes been harder.'

This, really, is the battle that some contemporary West African restaurants have had to fight in recent years, as the cuisine's rising prominence and popularity have brought fresh challenges. And these moments of friction stem from problems of undiscussed segregation and imbalance, throughout society and across the city, that feel especially pronounced when it comes to food. The writer and photographer Yvonne Maxwell put it best, in a short essay published as part of the Black Food Folks platform:

> As you exit Peckham Rye Station, the sheer number of people that would never cross the invisible partition separating Rye Lane and Blenheim Grove feels remarkable – a partition that separates us from them. These people partake in the everyday segregation that exists in the food world, as they seldom question why their curiosities never seem to steer them to the many West African restaurants and eateries in a predominantly Black area.

It is hard to argue with this reading of the scenario in areas of London like Peckham and Brixton. I personally will never forget a moment involving an acquaintance who worked in food and was enthusing about a Japanese-influenced pop-up that had taken place at a bar that was practically next door to her flat. Oh, wow, I said, excitedly. Had she also been to the really exceptional Afro-Caribbean food residency that was there for the preceding year? She looked at me blankly. She hadn't even heard of it. You try to put moments like this out of your mind, but I think they highlight a truth that creeps at your periphery: that some parts of Black London culture are practically invisible to large swathes of the city. That there is a lack of curiosity that, unconscious as it may be, can't help but read as a symptom of a wider society where only certain things are worthy of the highest forms of acclaim.

This is the bigger, more pervasive and defining issue of Black London that the rise of African restaurants – and especially West African restaurants – seems to speak to. And, crucially, it is this historic indifference that many of these creatives in the culinary world, playing with their sense of identity as well as their understanding of indigenous foods, are pushing against. Black African London's continued restaurant boom matters because of what it tells us about a culture asserting itself on its environment.

In early 2022 Ikoyi was awarded a second Michelin star; in the same year Chishuru was named by *Time Out* as the best restaurant in London; Sketch, Algerian restaurateur Mourad Mazouz's photogenic Mayfair gastrodome, redesigned its flagship Gallery dining room in collaboration with the Nigerian artist Yinka Shonibare and added a spin on jollof rice to the menu. West African cuisine continues to draw praise and move towards the centre of things. But the steady success of restaurants that play the starchy hits for the benefit of an almost exclusively Black customer base show that, in food as in other areas, mainstream approval and integration is not part of the game. Every Black African heritage restaurateur I spoke to was adamant that their restaurants were for everyone. Yet I also felt they were in a happy spot; not feeling the pressure to walk sceptics over the divide or water down what they were doing in order to pander.

There is, I think, a resonant, wider message in that. And it is this conversation, played out in a battle of authentic cassava leaf soups in tiny, family-run Sierra Leonean joints versus suya tacos in slickly appointed restaurants-cum-nightclubs, that is at the joyfully contradictory heart of the diasporic African restaurant story, as it strides into the next phase of its life. Which is to say, as Black settlement makes these dishes almost as commonplace as pub food; executed and enjoyed at many different levels of technique and price point. You may have your own theories about which kind of establishment should come out on top and point to the future; of which way of doing things should prevail. But I am an optimist, inclined to believe that the current breadth of the Black African restaurant world reflects the breadth of the modern Black African community and psyche at large. And that, from the genuinely multicultural crowd of millennials chair-dancing between forkfuls of jollof quinoa at Chuku's and the glamorously dressed friends photographing a Scotch bonnet-dusted ox-cheek bofrot at Akoko to the Gambian father-of-three rolling up a shirtsleeve in anticipation of pounded yam and egusi at Enish, maybe the multiplicity of approaches is precisely the point. These are Africans, after all. It makes sense that even the culinary landscape should feel like a good-natured argument.

7

Classroom

Just like all the other children on the train platform, Ezekiel Abiola had begun to wonder if he would ever actually make it to school. As far as I could tell, his day had started as it almost always did. There was his toddler sister, asleep on a fold-out bed in the middle of the cosy, cluttered living room of the family's Thamesmead home, his mother, Bunmi, scrunching foil around the takeaway fried egg sandwich she'd just made him, and his father, Segun, pulling up outside in the gloomy pre-dawn chill – just back from a night shift, and ready to drive his son to the station so he had ample time to catch his first train of the day. From there, it would be a 30-minute ride from Abbey Wood to Gravesend, plus a brisk 10-minute walk to the single-sex grammar school that Ezekiel, a diminutive, polite 12-year-old with skin buffed to a moisturized, cocoa-butter gleam, has attended for just over three months now. It was all going to plan. Until, all of a sudden, it very much wasn't.

'I think the train's cancelled,' muttered Ezekiel beneath his face mask, as we stood at Abbey Wood Station, at the suburban rim of South-East London, looking up at the flashing arrivals ticker that would decide our fate. On the tannoy system, a train announcer confirmed

as much. And then, as the news made its way along
the uniformed horde of other waiting kids, Ezekiel was
already tapping frenziedly at his phone screen; checking
the Trainline app, sending an update message to his
mum, conducting revised mental arithmetic based
on new train times. As it turned out, we could still
make his school's 08:30 start if we got the slightly later
06:50, changed at Dartford, and got a 07:36 Gravesend
train from there. As we got the new train and made
the connection at Dartford, watching on as yet more
kids, not to mention labourers breakfasting on energy
drinks, joined the trudging crush, something like calm
descended in the carriage. Disaster had been averted.
Ezekiel, like practically every other kid in the carriage,
bowed before his phone, jabbing idly at a puzzle game.

But then, inevitably, another spanner was suddenly
thrown into the works. The power to the train cut out at
Northfleet Station, one stop and a 10-minute drive from
Gravesend; the driver crackled on to the speakers ('I'm
afraid, folks, that due to a person on the line at Gravesend,
we're terminating here'); and, with much groaning and
confusion, the crowd of around 200 school children –
almost all of them Black, and many of them bound for
grammar schools in Chatham, another 20 minutes away
– emptied out onto the platform, just as the sun was
coming up. 'Are you going in? Are you going in?' asked
a couple, catching the mood of panicked delirium as
girls squealed and others cursed. 'Nah, I'm going home,
man,' said another, gleeful but hesitant, gauging the
mood of others who were either heading to the bus
stop or standing with phones clamped to their ears.

Now, you can have a vague, anecdotal sense that
immigrant presence, and especially Black African

presence, has altered the demography of grammar and selective schools in and around London. You may have heard of young people of Ghanaian or Ugandan or Zimbabwean descent embarking on marathon, city-spanning journeys in order to access better education. You may even know that, as an example, a third of all pupils at Townley Grammar girls' school in Bexleyheath, South-East London, are from Black African families.

But I do not know if there is a better representation of this phenomenon – or a more striking way to fully comprehend its scale and strangeness – than the sight of hundreds of Black schoolchildren marooned on the platform at a station in Kent. It is a measure of the literal lengths that ethnic minority British families (again, of all kinds but, in particular, those of South Asian and Black African heritage) are going to in order to bestow their children with the maximum educational and professional advantages. And it is an African diaspora reality that has lurked at the fringes of the public consciousness for some time, detectable only to those that know to look for it. In a 2020 interview with the author and leadership expert Simon Sinek, George the Poet, the award-winning British-Ugandan rapper, podcaster and Cambridge graduate, discussed the significance of journeying from his Neasden estate to Queen Elizabeth's School, a selective grammar school in faraway Barnet that ranks as one of the best schools in the country. 'By the time [I was] 15, I had already gone to school outside the area, which was the final saving grace,' he said. 'I went to high school in the suburbs. It took an hour and a half every morning from like 7 a.m. to travel there. Literally, that's [like being] a physical outcast. I was cast out of my community in the name of education.'

I had accompanied Ezekiel to school that morning (with the consent of his parents) to get a better understanding of the modern manifestation of this trend. That I had encountered such an extreme, seemingly cursed expression of it – which duly evolved from the chaos on the platform into stranded kids and disgruntled commuters alike, shuffling en masse to a nearby bus stop – felt like especially bad luck. Still, let us double back and caveat a little bit. Lots of children travel significant distances to school. Especially in rural areas. And Ezekiel's daily journey – a best-case-scenario 45-minute trip from his front door to school gate – is not too bad, particularly when set against what some other children have to contend with every morning.

However, it's worth pointing out that this isn't merely a case of the closest viable school being inconveniently positioned. Ezekiel's home borough of Greenwich has 35 secondary schools and, as he told me later, most of his friends from primary school went to Woolwich Polytechnic, a modern complex a 15-minute walk from his house with a 'Good' Ofsted rating. No, what's notable is that Ezekiel's family – and all those just like it, all across London – are choosing far-flung selective schools because of their sparkling Ofsted reports, long, venerated histories and private-school-level facilities. In fact, if they live too far away, many of them are figuratively moving Mohammed to the mountain and uprooting their entire lives. As a 2020 *Times* report into rising grammar school popularity noted, while paraphrasing the sentiment of many grammar headteachers, 'immigrant families, who had already moved to Britain, were happier to relocate if their children passed the 11-plus at a school hundreds of miles away'.

These school places, then – secured via months of supplementary tutoring – become a major investment for the entire family; the peg on which an entire life is hung. It is no surprise to learn that the current plan for the Abiolas is to move closer to Gravesend in order to ameliorate Ezekiel's journey to school (and also that of his older sister Hannah, who has a comparatively speedy 30-minute trip to Dartford Grammar School for Girls every morning). It gives you an idea of just how key this academic ecosystem is to so many Black Africans in London. But why put themselves through it? Why alter the whole complexion of your family's life purely in the name of accessing a better Ofsted rating? Why send your children on potentially fraught daily odysseys past a handful of perfectly acceptable schools in order to attend these relics of a deliberately unequal schooling system? Well, as ever, there are a number of justifications.

On the one hand, and perhaps most simply, it is just a case of something being the accepted norm; that there is a tendency, particularly among the aspirational middle class of London's Black African diaspora, to follow the herd. 'I didn't even want Hannah to take the 11-plus but it was my mum and my friends,' says Bunmi Abiola by way of explanation, when we talk much later. 'They were saying, "Oh, no – give her the opportunity. Let her do it." It's almost like people would look down on you if you didn't allow your child to do it.' This sense of pressure is underlined by the fact that, when Ezekiel started his 11-plus tuition in year 4 of primary school, his tutor chided his mother a little for not starting his preparatory lessons a year earlier.

As well as that, there is the basic academic imperative. Department for Education data, which in 2019 showed

Black heritage pupils lagging far behind almost all counterparts in other ethnic groups when it came to attainment, has made for especially grim reading within the Black community in recent years. So, put simply, placing an emphasis on accessing the very best non-independent schools is a way to combat the racial bias and socioeconomic disadvantage that is so inherent in British education. But hovering above all this, I'd say, is a pronounced obsession within Black African culture (and West African culture especially) with academia. From student Fante princes receiving study in eighteenth-century Britain to the post-war independence era's great rush of travelling academics and administrative trainees, education has proved a pivotal part of London's African settler story. It is how Africans have both defined themselves and been defined by others.

And if we take a closer look at the figures concerning ethnic disparities within academic achievement at British schools, it also possibly explains the fact that, somewhat anomalously, in some studies Black Africans tend to outperform Black Caribbeans. In fact, 2019 research within an inner London local authority found that the proportion of Black African pupils achieving five GCSEs was higher than both the national average and that for White British children; a figure attributed within educational researcher Feyisa Demie's accompanying report, at least in part, to 'strong parental support and links with African communities'. This is not to suggest for a moment that education isn't seen as vitally important in plenty of other ethnic minorities and demographics. It is just to note that the numbers bear out the fact that Black Africans are using something – whether it is the grammar school system, tutoring, overriding determination or some combination of all three – to just about buck the grimmest of academic trends. That learning is sacrosanct in an implicitly prejudiced society is something none of us need to be reminded of.

As Bunmi tells me, 'I say to Ezekiel, "Certain people don't want your success. They already think the worst of you." And so that is why I drive him. That's why I tell him, do your work, don't play games."' She pauses for a moment, her voice rising. '"A White boy in the same situation as you will have more opportunities. But you're Black and you're in a White country, so you have to push harder."' It is a wholly understandable speech that I am certain I heard a version of from my own mother when I was growing up. And yet, I think there are questions to be asked. About the physical and psychological pressure that all of this puts on young African heritage kids; about exactly where this zeal to game the system of selective schooling a little comes from; and about what the future holds for it at a time when education itself seems to be just another aspect of life caught in the crossfire of culture war.

These are the factors and considerations invisibly heaped on Ezekiel's slight shoulders, as we wait patiently within the crush of bodies at the bus stop in Northfleet, and fail to quite get on the first, heaving bus into Gravesend. 'This is like survival of the fittest,' he says at one point, almost idly. And it strikes me at the time that he could be speaking about the entire business of life and preparing for adulthood in inhospitable circumstances, rather than merely the brazen older kids who just shoved in front of us. In the end, a much emptier bus hisses to a stop another 20 minutes later. By this point, the day is bright and crisp, and it is almost three hours and a lifetime ago since I arrived at Ezekiel's front door in the darkness.

Having set off extra early, he will, by the time we get there, be almost 30 minutes late for the start of school. But as we arrive in Gravesend at last, and walk through the relatively quiet town centre towards his school, for the first time that day he visibly relaxes and warms up. I hear about the furiously competitive Connect 4 competition he and his classmates are currently running ('We all put our snacks and food in and the winner takes all,' he grins); he tells me about the older Chatham Grammar boys he occasionally encounters who 'think they're gangsters just because they get the train'; and he also admits that he's not actually wildly in favour of the family's plan to move closer to his school. 'If I'm being honest,' he says with a furtive smile, 'I sort of do enjoy the journey.'

Then, a little awkwardly considering the saga we have jointly been involved in, we say goodbye. There is a hesitant wave before he turns, joins a scattered procession of other late arrivals, and shuffles up a sloping hill; a small part of a collective story that spans centuries and touches on exactly what it means to prosper in diaspora. In more ways than one, it is the culmination of a fascinating, difficult journey.

For Dillibe Onyeama, the games field at Eton College was a verdant sanctuary. As one of two Nigerian-born students attending the illustrious private school in 1965, his world was a rolling cavalcade of dehumanizing insults and violent confrontations. There would be ape noises when he walked into rooms. Boys were constantly trying to fight him or blaming his academic difficulties on his race. On one occasion, a fellow pupil asked if his mother wore a bone through her nose. But, when, in his first year, Onyeama was able to play sport, things were different. When he was hoofing the ball forward on the football pitch, running in athletics, scuffling during the chaos of the Eton wall game, or lining up to bowl a violently fast delivery in cricket, there was release, catharsis, and a rare space where his prowess could be packaged in ethnic stereotyping and duly celebrated. 'After being constantly racially abused', as he wrote, 'after having my shortcomings at work attributed to me because I was Black, and having come tacitly to accept that indeed I might be inferior, it was comforting and, indeed, a pleasure when my sporting ability was credited to just that aspect of myself.'

These words, in Onyeama's memoir *A Black Boy at Eton*, are usefully redolent of a book that is, by turns, rage-inducing, funny, unflinchingly honest and hauntingly sad. That Onyeama had to face so much inhuman abuse on his own, and that he found such profound crumbs of comfort in being celebrated by classmates for his 'African' strength and speed, makes you want to reach back in time through the pages and give him a hug. Or, truthfully, maybe at least offer some backup in one of his daily confrontations with highly punchable racists.

However, what's perhaps most striking about the book – first published in 1974 as the far more provocative *A Nigger at Eton* – is that Onyeama is voluntarily there at all. Why did his father, Charles Onyeama, a wealthy judge who ended up working at the International Court of Justice in The Hague, sign him up for Eton when he was born? Why were father and son alike both annoyed when another Nigerian-born boy pipped Dillibe to the title of first Black Etonian? And why, even after four years of relentless, despicable abuse and deep trauma, does the younger Onyeama still sound a note of conflicted pride at having attended 'the world's most famous school'?

In one sense it is another example of the book's uneasy, almost guileless honesty; the way, rather than offer a didactic indictment of a racist time and a racist institution, Onyeama is content to provide us with a conflicting mess of intensely human emotions. No one, least of all him, is let off the hook. But, also, *A Black Boy at Eton* runs deeper than that. Because, really, it is the continuation of a fascination within the West African diaspora with both the Black student as celebrity and the advantages that can be conferred by elite institutions, no matter the cost.

It is a history that goes back over 250 years. In the middle of the eighteenth century, Philip Quaque, a high-born Fante boy from what is now Ghana, was brought to London to receive some education before studying theology at Oxford and going on to become Britain's first ordained African priest in 1765. By the time of the late Victorian era, politically useful figures in the newly established colonies were encouraged to come to the UK to study by abolitionists and Christian missionaries alike. And, come the 1920s, it was a Nigerian law student by the name of Ladipo Solanke who, incensed by the offensive mistruths about West African life that preceded the 1923 Empire Exhibition at Wembley, launched the hugely influential West African Students' Union. These arrivals helped set the texture of Black African settlement in early-twentieth-century London.

Yet it wasn't until the post-war period of intensified migration from the continent that Black African identity in the metropole and studenthood became indivisible. A 1953 column in the international paper *West African Review* tracked gossip amid London's burgeoning Black student population. While, elsewhere, Nigerians who had finished their studies in the UK were hailed like the returning members of a victorious sports team ('They return with golden fleece,' ran the triumphant headline above a photo of six smartly dressed graduates in a 1960 story in the *West African Pilot*). This was the era in which the African student socialite – a kind of stern-gazed intellectual pin-up – fully emerged. What's significant, looking back, is that this image was jointly nurtured to growth by people both within the African community and by the government forces outside it.

As Jordanna Bailkin, historian and author of *The Afterlife of Empire*, puts it, 'There was this moment when the Colonial Office was encouraging tens of thousands of students to the UK, but then making things really difficult for them or not supporting them when they came.' Fundamentally, the Colonial Office's confused charm offensive was about maintaining control and influence in countries leaving the Empire (never mind that the welcoming atmosphere ended up inadvertently incubating a golden age of anti-colonialist politics in London and independence in many African nations).

But if this period marked the birth of the deified student success story, it also signalled the arrival of its inverse: the African academic failure, adrift and possibly destitute in the metropole. 'One of the fictions that the Colonial Office had with these [West African] students was that they were the perfect migrants because they weren't really migrants at all,' says Bailkin. 'That led to a real ethnic siloing where Caribbeans were seen [by the government] as the real migrants and Africans were seen as these often elite students. Until, of course, they become impoverished when they're in Britain or wanted to stay beyond their student visa.'

If we pan out a bit more, to encompass both the Georgian-era arrival of pioneering figures like Quaque and the circumstances that precipitated Ezekiel Abiola's daily journey to Gravesend, this characterization is significant. Despite the fact that some of the oldest African settler communities in Britain have been workers (whether it is Somali seamen in Canning Town or Black miners in Wales), the effectiveness of the government's overseas student strategy – both in how enthusiastically West African students were courted and in the anxieties around migration that they roused – meant the needle had permanently shifted. In the popular imagination, African Londoners and African students were one and the same. In fact, more than that, those in the African diaspora tended to be defined by how well they measured against the collective idea of academic toil, glory and misadventure in the metropole. As an example, Sam Selvon's *The Lonely Londoners*, which, in many ways, is an unofficial census of Black diaspora life in the 1950s, gives us an insight into this categorization, in the character of Captain: 'Captain was Nigerian. His father send him to London to study law, but Captain went stupid when he arrive in the big city. He start to spend money wild on woman and cigarette (he not fussy about drink) and before long the old man stop sending allowance.'

The flawed, former student cut off by their wealthy parents. It is the sort of ancient comic archetype that is so familiar you feel it must have always existed in some form. Though, given that the novel fictionalizes real life events and characters from Selvon's early days in London in the dawn of the *Windrush* era, you imagine that Cap has some basis in truth; that, in keeping with the mordant comic energy of *The Lonely Londoners*, his plight makes a joke of the all too real difficulties that itinerant West African graduates and dropouts faced amid Britain's swirl of fog and myriad temptations. When you know how many Nigerian students were being repatriated during this period owing to severe mental health issues – when you know that there was an overcrowding epidemic in Nigerian asylums for much of the 1950s, or that a study in the same decade by the Nigerian psychiatrist T. Adeoye Lambo suggested up to 25 per cent of Nigerian students in London were mentally ill – then you can discern the currents of sad truth flowing beneath Cap's comic exploits. In fiction as in life, West African students were shown how far they could fall from the haloed celebrity ideal that was still dominating the press. As Bailkin notes: 'These stories [of West African students running into trouble] are often portrayed in the press as stories of individual failure. But I think what's really important to remember is the state apparatus that made those stories [possible].'

It's an important consideration. For all that West Africans in particular – and, I'd argue, Black Africans in general – have self-identified as migrants predominantly motivated by higher education, the influence of authorities in both Britain and African nations cannot be dismissed. To put it another way: which came first, the chicken of postcolonial overseas study propaganda, or the egg of innate academic ambition? Given that both have existed in tandem for so long, it is impossible to really know for certain. And though it is by no means a solely African obsession (for one thing, the interwar period in London was just as notable for its Caribbean and American-born Black intellectuals and agitators like Paul Robeson, Claude McKay, Una Marson and Amy Ashwood Garvey), the promise of a British education seemed to have a unique hold over the psyche of those from former colonies Ghana, Nigeria, Sierra Leone, and other nations across the mother continent.

Moreover, the value and esteem of study in the UK came to be self-fulfilling; an aspirational mark of success that took hold in countries like Nigeria during the boom period of the late 1960s and early 1970s and became something to be passed down through the generations, like a family heirloom. That was certainly the case for Onyeama's father, who first heard about Eton during his own years of study at Oxford in the 1940s. And it was certainly the case in my own family, where the knowledge and positive experience of uncles who had spent their youths at London institutions like Imperial College (and still had the striped college scarves to show for it) certainly speeded the process of deciding to move to this country. Not to mention deciding the kind of schools that my mum and dad – part of the flush, emerging upper middle class springing up in Nigeria around the oil-rich late 1970s – eventually decided to send me and my brothers to.

Well, not all of us. It was my elder brothers who, as was the vogue among Nigerians of means at the time, were sent to reputable private schools as boarders. (It's also relevant that corruption and chronic underfunding within the Nigerian public school system had yielded a parental generation very much accustomed to private schooling.) I went – extremely happily – to a local primary school and a big, state secondary beside a giant supermarket. The line, within family mythology, has always been that I was self-possessed and headstrong enough to insist that I didn't want to go private. But now, as an adult and a parent, I can recognize that, with two children already in fee-paying schools and my late father by the early 1990s spending more time in Nigeria and becoming an increasingly peripheral figure in our lives, there probably wasn't much left in the figurative kitty for my schooling.

Here we land on another feature of the much mythologized, long-running love affair between Black Africans and education. As is often the case, class and race are operating in concert. Because, truthfully, another historic function of education among West African overseas students – particularly within a venerated independent school or university – was its ability to bestow status, power and access to an elite. In eras when Black Londoners were being systematically denied basic humanity, a high-grade course of study (and the non-threatening, temporary stay in the metropole that it implied) acted as something of a protective layer; a cheat code that offered a degree of respectability within wider British society.

Civility and intellect were founding tenets of how African students in twentieth-century London sought to present themselves to the world, while also pushing against the racist mistruths of a colonialist society. In *Black London*, Marc Matera makes the point that the members of WASU, who, with their sharp dress and high-born manners, always strove to project 'a picture of refinement and respectability', saw these middle-class optics as a major part of their anti-colonial work in the city. 'The WASU House and *Wasu* [the students' in-house publication] became related instruments for achieving these goals and demonstrated the fallacy of popular representations of African backwardness.'

Significantly, this student exceptionalism could give rise to division within the Black community: Bailkin points out in her book that 1958's Notting Hill and Nottingham riots were followed by news profiles in the *Daily Mirror* that calculatedly attempted to present Nigerian students as the 'acceptable' face of Black migrant presence in Britain. But the net result of this period, when the trappings of academia in Britain were presented as a means for Black Africans to gain power, social advantages, and something close to acceptance within the White world, was that education and class mingled together to form a potent, symbolic cocktail that would last for generations. For my parents, and those like them, choosing to send your children to private school was a form of 'If you can't beat them, join them' social insurance; a way to step beyond the metaphorical velvet rope and, maybe, transcend race in the spheres of work and society. It does not feel like total coincidence that Kwasi Kwarteng, the British-Ghanaian Conservative MP and one-time Secretary of State for Business, Energy and Industrial Strategy, also happens to be an old Etonian who attended via a scholarship.

However, as Dillibe Onyeama and countless others have found, the ability to pay your way into a

White-dominated space is not the same as being happily accepted into one. The age of the celebrity African student inevitably created something of a distorted picture of what it was really like to be educated, at all levels, in a city like London. And, what's more, while Britain's status as an academic utopia was growing in the hearts and minds of a generation of Black Africans, the Afro-Caribbeans who had been less defined by the softening glow of studenthood were bearing the brunt of a shamefully prejudiced system that was determined to leave them behind.

Now and again, Janet Sherlock will be approached in the street by a grinning relative stranger who just wants to express their gratitude. 'These teenagers will get excited and come rushing up to me,' she says, smiling at the memory. 'And occasionally their parents will be standing next to them just beaming.' A little while ago, it was the parents of England rugby player Maro Itoje, who both insisted on stopping her in Southgate, North London, to offer thanks and prayers. The reason for this celebrity status among other British-Nigerians – the reason children and adults alike practically want to lift her up to shoulder height and start chanting her name in the street – is this: two decades ago, Sherlock started Leaders are Readers, one of the most prominent and impactful, independent-owned tutoring businesses in London.

It was a business sparked into life by personal frustration. Raised in Ibadan, in the south-west of Nigeria, Sherlock had been privately educated, studied English literature at a Nigerian university, and been weaned on postcolonial stories of British education's innate specialness and superiority. 'We were always told that the British education system was the best in the world and that Britain was this supremely advanced nation,' she says. Reports of the glamorous West African students of the 1950s and 1960s had taken root too. 'They were almost like royals,' she adds. 'They'd been abroad, they were polished and respected. Anything that they were and that they gained, we pinned it on the fact that they were educated.'

And so when Sherlock, who had moved to London in the mid-1980s to start a family and train as a solicitor, sent Abimbola, her highly inquisitive daughter, off to reception, she had high hopes. High hopes that were summarily crushed by dull, undemanding phonics books and, more broadly, what she saw as a depressing, one-size-fits-all approach to learning. 'I was so disappointed,' she says. 'Before she could even walk she had been pulling my law textbooks off the shelves and pretending to read them. So I just thought they'd understand that she was eager and that they'd teach her how to read.' To her frustration, they didn't.

There is a wider, thornier debate to be had here about teaching approach and the fixed rigidity of primary school curricula in 1980s Britain; we cannot know the exact motivations of these teachers or why, beyond the realities of comprehensive schooling in that era, they would not brook Sherlock's repeated requests to push Abimbola academically.

To me, however, it feels like what the Sherlocks experienced were the reverberations of an academic culture that had long failed Britain's predominantly Afro-Caribbean Black population. In fact, more than that, a suite of discriminatory policy practices in the

1960s and 1970s – categorizing Black children as uneducable, banding a large proportion of them into classes reserved for so-called 'slow learners', sending them to educationally subnormal (or ESN) schools where they were wildly over-represented – helped to disenfranchise and hold back an entire generation.

Research by the American academic David Kirp has shown that, during this period, West Indian children were three to four times as likely as their White counterparts to be categorized as educationally subnormal. It was the initial catalyst for a cycle of disadvantage that, as noted by the historian Ron Ramdin, meant 'Black youth, as underachievers at school, were unemployed and disillusioned with their prospects in British society'. This was the structurally racist British academic system that no one had told admiring West Africans like Janet Sherlock about. 'I realize now,' she says ruefully, 'that when we were watching television, and they were talking about this brilliant British education, they were probably talking about independent schools.'

But, of course, rather than feel aggrieved, Sherlock decided to find her own solution. Like the Afro-Caribbean parents of previous decades who had founded Black Saturday schools in response to the failings of mainstream education, she took matters into her own hands. She bought a set of less rigid non-curriculum phonics books, taught Abimbola to read in six months, did the same for the children of friends and relatives within her largely Nigerian North London community ('It would be six children all sat at our dining table every Saturday morning,' she says), and turned it into a side business that, after she placed adverts locally, would attract queues of people outside their front door on weekends. Over the course of the next 15 years or so, word spread even further; Sherlock grew Leaders are Readers into a partly franchised business empire comprising, at its height, 900 enrolled students and five separate tutoring centres in and around London.

That Sherlock turned her exasperation with her daughter's schooling into a viable business – while also working as a solicitor – speaks to a diaspora culture often defined by its entrepreneurship and determination ('I think Nigerians are just ambitious people,' she says with a laugh. 'We were doing fairly well, and yet I still felt like I had to be earning more'). It also feels of a piece with a world where, in my experience, it was just accepted that education wouldn't be strictly limited to official school time. 'Lessons' – where some older relative would turn the TV off and run through a mathematics textbook with you – were part of the fabric of my childhood. Before I joined that big comprehensive school by the supermarket, there was a failed 11-plus exam, preceded by weekly tutoring sessions at a big leisure centre where my only real memory is that I was allowed to get a KitKat from the vending machine during break time. The bright-lit tutoring businesses in historically Black parts of London like Peckham, Brixton and Seven Sisters tell their own story about education's continued grip on the modern African imagination.

Again, this focus on study is not unique to the African diaspora. But as demonstrated by the demographic make-up at most Leaders are Readers schools (in their Dartford and Streatham locations, for instance, Sherlock says 70 per cent of students are of Nigerian descent), it has long been an accepted reality for a certain section of London's university-educated Black African families.

Tutoring, grammar institutions, faith-based selective schools in far-flung postcodes: all of these things, fundamentally, are learned methods to combat systemic disadvantage and cobble together something similar to a private education without the outlay. Akala — author, rapper and former attendee of a Black supplementary school — has been among those to highlight the fact that trend-bucking academic performance among African heritage Black pupils has as much to do with class as it does with race and culture. As he said, in a 2018 interview with *VICE*: 'It should be no surprise that immigrant kids whose parents were university-educated back home are doing better in school.'

Ultimately, the additional learning sector in London is Black people helping themselves in lieu of outside assistance from White society at large. These DIY schools are manifestations of a deeper, wholly justified mistrust of the state that touches everything from the embrace of traditional medical remedies and religion to collective finance, or 'pardner' schemes, in response to discriminatory loan policies at mainstream banks.

But the difference between the approaches of Afro-Caribbean-initiated supplementary schools, like the one Akala attended, and the more West African-leaning tutoring businesses in the vein of Leaders are Readers, is worth digging into. Whereas the former often had a Pan-Africanist sensibility — and aimed to introduce Caribbean heritage children to the Black history that was notably absent from the mainstream curriculum — the focus of the latter has traditionally been purely academic. One method is about dismantling a prejudiced system; another is about finding the best ways to navigate it. You could debate what this distinction between

Saturday schools and diasporas signifies for eternity (it feels relevant, for instance, that the more recently arrived Black African community perhaps didn't feel the same imperative to re-forge cultural links broken by enslavement), but it's clear that when it comes to schooling, for many African Londoners it is more about personal advancement than initiating any kind of equitable academic revolution. At the lower end of the class spectrum, this pragmatism is born from the stresses and indignities of life in diaspora. Or, rather, the reality that even education isn't always enough to give you a privileged or especially easy life.

'Of course it is an investment,' says Bunmi Abiola, of the tutoring fees, early morning drives and general sacrifices that have been the bedrock of her children's grammar school educations. Abiola, who is small, plain-speaking and generous with her sputtering, high-pitched laugh, moved to London as a teenager, a small detail that explains why she has a perhaps clearer sense than most of the social adjustments that come with settlement in the UK. 'You know, people come over from Africa and all they can do is care work or cleaning. But back in Nigeria, you wouldn't catch any of us doing menial jobs. I'm 44 this year and I don't have a mortgage [because we rent our house]. Obviously there are reasons for that, but I don't want the same for my children. I don't want them to struggle.' Call it class dysmorphia if you will. Whatever it is, it explains why so many Black Africans see education as a vital way to change the circumstances of lives that they don't feel reflect their true status.

Still, individual successes for Black Africans (and it is hardly surprising to learn that Sherlock's daughter and son are now, respectively, a barrister and a computer scientist) do not necessarily help to shift a broader academic culture weighted against the socioeconomically and ethnically disadvantaged. The pandemic, as well as leading tutoring businesses like Sherlock's to severely downsize, underscored the true scale of the problem. In 2020, even before the effects of successive lockdowns and the benefits of better-resourced remote learning for those at selective schools had been fully felt, a study by the Education Policy Institute found that the attainment gap for Black Caribbean pupils had widened to 4.4 months of schooling (students from other Black backgrounds were effectively three months behind). Later in the same year, another study found that the fixed-term school exclusion rate for Black kids was higher in two-thirds of local authorities in England. For all the academic strides that certain minority groups have made in recent years, the bigger picture tends to be a damning one.

Deep-rooted problems need deep-rooted solutions. And so I find that my mind turns to those Afro-Caribbean-led supplementary schools. I find myself thinking of whether the Black families contorting themselves to reap the rewards of an elite education – whether through paying school fees or throwing money at 11-plus tutors – are having their specific needs met by these institutions and the wider society that supports them. So much of the Black academic story in this country has been about entry, acceptance and the contriving of clever ways to navigate inhospitable environments. But what if, rather than adapting to the rules of this system, the better course of action was to rewrite them?

I can still remember the delirious, ear-splitting shriek. It was the middle of the school day in, I think, the year 2001, and I had peeled away from the sixth form common room to tell my mum the good news: I had just found out I was going to be head boy of the school. 'Folajimi!' she yelled, again and again. 'Wow. Well done, son. Well done.' I remember it as a happy, proud moment (despite the fact I soon realized that, beyond wearing a special pin-badge on my lapel and attending an occasional extra assembly, there really wasn't much to the role).

But it is probably telling that I remember this accolade mostly in relation to my mother's joyful, ecstatic reaction. Despite the modest, decidedly non-prestigious nature of the school I went to (again, it really was a collection of old buildings and Portakabin classrooms next to a very, very big supermarket), I think even back then I sensed that I had reached some sort of pinnacle for what second-generation African acceptance could look like. When my eldest brother was starting at his fee-paying school in the early 1990s, an Irish teacher had seen fit to pull my mother aside and level with her. 'Because he's Black, he'll need to be twice as good and work twice as hard as everyone else,' he said. 'And I only say that because it was the same for us once.' This maxim – of having to outsmart and out-hustle your White counterparts – is one that almost every Black child will have heard in some form. And I think, perhaps more than most, I subconsciously absorbed it and kept it in mind. My academic career and life would have to be conducted as one long rebuke to all the terrible assumptions people made about young Black men. The head boy award – a literal honour badge for my studiousness and favour in the minds of authority figures at school – felt like the ultimate acknowledgement of success by this metric. It was the final form of the Nice African Boy.

But, of course, what this illustrates, on a very mild scale, is the conditional nature of Black entry into coveted White spaces; that – as with the West African students of the 1950s who received favourable treatment from the state so long as they conformed to the bookish stereotype, didn't fall for a White partner and, crucially, made themselves scarce when their visas expired – the greatest privileges of the British education system were contingent on a discreet, non-threatening sort of Blackness. It is an issue that cuts to the core of the uneasy, conflicting Black interactions with school. And, in real life and in literature, it is something that a new generation of Black British kids have been contending with.

The British-Ugandan writer Musa Okwonga's memoir *One of Them* is a case in point. Released almost 50 years after Dillibe Onyeama's book, it is another perspective on what it was like to attend Eton College as a Black pupil (notably at a time when microaggressions had largely replaced overt, violent racism) that is shot through with lyricism, wit and an impressively nuanced look at the way pervasive stereotypes can exert a wearying control in these spaces. 'Not for the first time, I wonder, What was the point?' writes Okwonga, at one juncture, after an old Eton friend has shared a fabricated school days rumour that presents him as an 'angry Black guy'. 'If people thought I was that guy, I may as well have gone and been that guy anyway. Most painfully, I realize that my friend who proudly told me the story believed that it was the kind of thing I would do, and that he, too, did not really know me at all.'

Code-switching is a valuable communicative skill and an integral part of the Black diaspora experience. Yet, here we see how difficult and disorienting it can be within school structures that implicitly align good behaviour with supposedly White traits; how an organization that (as certain selective schools have done) outlaws the bumping of fists in the playground, or sends a pupil home for wearing their hair in a close-fade or dreadlocks, can devalue Black culture and bring children into conflict with themselves. The writer and teacher Derek Oppong, in a 2019 essay reflecting on his time at a selective Catholic school in Enfield called St Ignatius, presents this policing of behaviour as a grim extension of life in the outside world. 'Ignatius to me', he says, 'was a microcosm of wider British society. The willingness to accept Black boys when they are playing the "right" part.'

It is this rigidity of roles that feels most problematic. Looking back at *A Black Boy at Eton*, one of the more shocking, transgressive things about it is Onyeama's candour about the fact that, separate to the heinous prejudice he has to endure, he is thoroughly ill-suited to life at one of the world's most prestigious schools. He is not naturally academic. He is physically violent. He occasionally lashes out and misbehaves just for something to do. In fact, at a time when Black children like him were being sent to ESN schools for far milder infractions, it's clear that – regardless of the ordeal he faced – it was Onyeama's immense wealth and privilege that saved him from a far grimmer fate. That he was allowed to err and make mistakes, as many unexceptional, rich, White children before him were, is fundamentally a good thing.

His story highlights the fact that different kinds of intelligence or creativity – be they artistic, practical or afflicted by any kind of neurodiversity – are not always given the necessary room to flourish within Black African culture's favoured world of discipline and the sanctified fundamentals of knowledge. The strictures of various forms of British academia (not to mention tutoring services) have given the Black African diaspora so much and, in many ways, defined their settlement in the country. But the reluctance of elite schools to adapt is increasingly being questioned by those who have staked so much on attaining the leg-up this kind of education is supposed to offer. 'Now, Hannah is even struggling at her grammar school,' says Abiola, about Ezekiel's 14-year-old sister. 'All they know is results, results, results. And I feel they're not giving her the support she needs.'

This sentiment, I think, speaks to a steady gear shift in how Black Africans are viewing the academic ecosystems they have (both figuratively and literally) invested so much in. Or, at least, there seems to be a new willingness to try to use the clout of increased Black African presence and visibility to try to change these organizations from within; to push them forward and alter their rhythms rather than merely marching to their long-running beat. It is there in the Stormzy scholarship, which sees the British-Ghanaian rapper's special fund offer financial support to multiple Black Cambridge students a year. It is evident in the Black Curriculum, a social enterprise that provides resources and pushes for the permanent inclusion of Black British history at schools. It is even there in the fact that, after distancing themselves from him for years, Eton College, amid the post-George Floyd wave of contrition in 2020, finally issued a formal apology to Onyeama for his treatment while he was at the school. It is slow, steady progress that makes you hope the next generation of Black Africans and Afro-Caribbeans will feel that the schools they send their children to will meet them on a more informed, inclusive and equal footing.

But, of course, the juggernaut of this very African obsession rumbles on. For one thing, 2020 marked a five-year period that has seen grammar school applications grow by almost a quarter. And, while some may have moral misgivings about widening the socioeconomic gaps in the school system, Bunmi Abiola still, despite it all, fantasizes about setting her children off into the academic stratosphere that has captured the Nigerian imagination for centuries. 'If I had money, of course my children would go to private school,' she says. 'Of course. I would send them to Eton or Harrow, let them rub shoulders with the high and mighty. Why not?'

That day may yet come or it may not. It doesn't really matter. What no one can take away is the dream, the hope, and the belief that, in more ways than one, knowledge truly is power.

8

Suburb

Where once the old invocation of a 'Little Lagos' filled
with displaced Nigerians or a 'Mini-Accra' thick with
signs of Ghanaian settlement meant Peckham, or West
Norwood, Brixton or Seven Sisters, now it can mean
something else. Now it is Dartford in Kent, with its
Pentecostal churches, Colindale in Buckinghamshire, with
its Ghanaian *waakye* spots, Thurrock in Essex – where,
between 2001 and 2011, the Black African population
grew by more than 1,000 per cent. Or, for that matter,
it is Erith, where a short walk from the Whitehart, an
'African and continental restaurant' housed in a lavishly
corniced former pub, there are the cash and carries, fabric
shops and event halls ('Weddings, Parties, Birthdays, Etc.')
that are telltale signs of West African life. Black African
London, as a concept and a place, is a shifting, slippery
and ever evolving thing; a fluid parallel city that is as
much a state of mind and vague sense of value systems as
a specific patch of homes, worship houses and businesses.
But one of the more striking facets of this world is that
its future may not actually lie in London at all. Just as
other immigrant groups have done before them, Black
Africans – and especially West Africans – are swapping the
inner-city neighbourhoods that have been synonymous

with Black presence for more than 70 years with outer zones that lie at the very edge of the M25 and beyond.

It is a shift with huge societal ramifications. Yet, as the journalist Hugh Muir noted in a 2016 BBC Radio 4 documentary and accompanying *Guardian* story about the phenomenon, it is also one that few people want to openly acknowledge or discuss. 'Demographers make much of White flight – the movement of White Britons from the inner cities to the suburbs and beyond – interpreting its meaning and consequences,' writes Muir. 'Less talked about is the growing movement of visible minorities into the heartlands of Englishness.'

Businesses like those in Erith, and the new diaspora communities they serve, are examples of Black flight, then. But while there is a clear comparison to be made between Black Africans and Afro-Caribbeans emulating their White (and, notably, South Asian) counterparts in escaping crowded inner-city living for the comparative tranquillity, space and safety of suburbia, it is a mistake to assume that this represents ethnic parity or a neat happy ending. What happens, for instance, when White suburbanites find that their leafy hamlets and semi-detached sanctuaries are being populated by the ethnic minorities they and their ancestors sought to escape? Well, as Muir notes, demographers have found that White residents tend to move even further out, inaugurating a kind of endless game of socioeconomic tag, and pushing the perimeters of both White suburbia and immigrant London out until the city's borders resemble a seeping spillage. Inevitably, this brings its own degree of tension. It is the 'natural order' of things upended – which is to say, that it is a glitch in the matrix of Black disadvantage around housing.

And so, of course, this slight upending of a long-established status quo has led to some inevitable tension. At its mildest, this tension manifests in minor local disputes. For instance, at its opening in 2018, the Whitehart in Erith submitted an application for a late licence (a necessity in a culture where restaurant meals habitually begin very late and stretch to the early hours), only to see it engender local hostility and fears about what it would mean for the neighbourhood. 'Residents have a fear that the area will become known for excessive drinking or possibly worse,' was how the town's borough councillor put it. For Ola Sodunke, the Whitehart's Nigerian-born owner, it was simply a cultural misunderstanding. 'At the weekend, some of my customers only come at midnight and want to stay until three a.m.,' he said, reflecting on the situation to me. 'But I know that, because there is a lot of crime [in the area], they couldn't give us a late licence. I understand.'

It was, ultimately, a storm in a palm wine cup; a fairly commonplace local politics matter that resulted in the proposed 5 a.m. licence being rejected. But, undeniably, it also has some of the hallmarks of an established population exhibiting wariness in the face of conspicuously different newcomers with unusual customs. In more extreme cases, Black African flight to the suburbs can mean daily exposure to prejudice that just isn't as much of a consideration in traditionally multicultural areas. Muttered slurs in the street. Microaggressions at school. The lurking, constant threat of physical violence. This has been the inevitable reality for countless Black families who have decided to move into communities that – with the added backdrop of Brexit and successive financial crises – can feel, from a certain angle, like petri dishes for a specific strain of proudly unrepentant, White English small-mindedness. In his 2018 essay, 'The Sticks', the British-Nigerian writer Aniefiok 'Neef' Ekpoudom describes what it was like to grow up in this kind of atmosphere, after his family moved from Lewisham to the suburban outer London town of Orpington.

'Racism shadowed my steps,' he writes. 'She subtly surfaced in the parks and in the schools, in the summer and in the spring. It was a reminder that regardless of how I dressed or spoke, the sports I played or the friends I kept ... I would find no shelter, no place to call home.' The feeling of racism as an inescapable fact of ethnic minority life in suburbia is one that lingers within the Black community. It is, anecdotally, one of the things that stops many Black Africans and Afro-Caribbeans from making the leap and moving out of city centres to the commuter belt and beyond. And it is, in all honesty, a mindset I recognize, because it comes close to describing the atmosphere I was raised in. The truth is that I am so attuned to Black African suburbia's rapid emergence because I grew up in a nascent, occasionally hostile version of it.

Orpington was a bus ride away from the family home in Crayford; Erith's old brutalist shopping precinct was where I skateboarded as a teenager. I would characterize my childhood as a positive one, broadly speaking, but stray reminders of our minority status – a racist joke; the National Front logo or a swastika carved into the glass of a bus stop – were always hovering just out of view. Of course, one side effect of this intimate knowledge of how things were is that I can better appreciate how dramatically they have changed. Or, in other words,

I can appreciate just how Black African flight to the suburbs has continued, and even accelerated, in spite of all that snarling discouragement.

Ekpoudom notes that, these days, a Black community – one where the 'summer barbecues smell of puff-puff and plantain' – has sprung up in Orpington. And, for my part, return trips back to our old neighbourhood reveal a similar transformation. Banks have become Pentecostal churches. White pensioner couples on our once homogeneously English street have morphed, seemingly overnight, into other Nigerian families. And, yes, former pubs have been turned into jollof-heavy restaurants with an apparently contentious attitude to late-night dining. If the implicit statement coming from those '90s racists was that we were not welcome here – that, whether it was Lagos or Lewisham, we ought to go back where we came from – then it is a message that has been roundly ignored.

But we must be careful here. Visible signs of multiculturalism are not the same thing as open-armed cultural acceptance. In fact, they could act as a catalyst for racism. And, against a charged backdrop of Brexit, the pandemic, culture war and economic difficulty, there is evidence that London's fast-changing suburban spaces are at a tense, crucial inflection point: a tussle between the central migrant idea of either changing your surroundings or being changed by them.

Ultimately, this secondary migration out to the suburbs crystallizes so much of the modern Black story in this country. It is the long, continuing struggle for adequate housing, the established life cycle of immigrant presence, the evolving nature of Black metropolitan identity, and what it means to put down permanent roots in diaspora. As Hugh Muir notes at the end of his documentary, Black flight to suburbia shows us that, in the simplest terms, ethnic minorities 'want what you want'. But what does Black life look like in an area historically defined by Whiteness? And what happens, ultimately, if the denizens of suburbia's leafy lands of plenty don't really want to share?

Before there was Ladbroke Grove, or Woolwich, or Hackney, a significant proportion of Black London could be found beneath the ground, in a disused hostel under Clapham South Tube station. It was 1948 and, having stepped off the docks at Tilbury without lodgings, 242 of the male passengers on the *Empire Windrush* were hurriedly accommodated here: a former air-raid shelter transformed into a mini, subterranean city of sharply dressed Caribbean men, eating strange suet pudding dinners, awaking to the sound of rumbling trains and left to contemplate their uncertain futures in the cold, unglimpsed city above their heads.

As the days ticked by, agitation around what to actually do with these men grew within the Colonial Office. The mayor of the neighbouring borough of Lambeth was asked if he might be able to come up with a solution or, at least, offer this untapped migrant workforce a decent welcome. 40 of them were invited to tea at the Astoria Cinema in nearby Brixton – location of the closest labour exchange. And, as cups were slurped and cakes nibbled, Brixton's Labour MP Marcus Lipton (one of a number of invited politicians) told the men that, as per Ron Ramdin in *The Making of the Black Working Class in Britain*, 'they should regard Brixton as their second home'. Whether this was meant literally or not, the newly arrived Caribbean subjects took it that way. By the time they returned to the air-raid shelter, they reportedly (according to journalist and *Windrush* chronicler Joyce Egginton) spread the news that 'in the unknown and perplexing vastness of England . . . they could be sure of one place'.

This, then, is the accidental birth of Brixton as the long-standing epicentre of Black culture in London. More than 70 years of Caribbean and African presence, affinity and pride is, it turns out, down to an accident of location, the proximity of an employment office and the affecting kindness of a single post-war MP. It is a striking vignette because it highlights both the randomness and relative recency of areas we see as elementally associated with Black life in Britain. But also because it shows the haphazard desperateness of early, post-war Black settlement in London. The only plan for the mid-century era's emerging population of West Indian immigrants and West African overseas students was that there was no plan. Just as those men beneath Clapham South Tube station had been, Britain's Black settlers quickly became a problem to be dealt with. And out of this desperation sprang a housing market (and, relatedly, an employment situation) where bewildered Black arrivants were at the mercy of obstructive colour bars and racist landlords who sensed an opportunity to exploit their plight. One of the early consequences of this was that it quickly became apparent that only certain types of accommodation, and certain neighbourhoods, were available to this new cohort of Black Londoners.

This led to the era of 'No Blacks, No Dogs, No Irish' signs, vindictive Rachman-style slum landlords, and cramped, fetid, subdivided quarters in the deprived parts of London with a more transient, underclass population (generally the west, north-west and south of the city) that made Black presence tolerable. You only need to zoom out a little to see that there was precedent for a more equal spread of Black settlement across London, especially in the interwar period when a Pan-Africanist jazz and countercultural boom led part of Soho to be known as 'the Black Mile'. But it is here, in the post-*Windrush* age, that the abiding notion of metropolitan Blackness – namely, that it is tied to bustling, cheek-by-jowl inner city living, and a degree of crumbling social deprivation – is born. This was the time when, as one of the characters in Sam Selvon's 1963 property-buying farce *The Housing Lark* observes, the only houses available to Black people were 'in all them back streets where the sun don't shine, in some tumbledown old house what only have a year to stand again'.

On top of that, it is notable that, bar a small number of Black dignitaries who had the means to pay their way around the colour bar, housing was a great leveller. As evidenced by 'Telephone Conversation', Wole Soyinka's seminal poem recounting the real-life accommodation struggles he witnessed as a postgraduate student in late 1950s London, an inability to access adequate housing as a Black settler transcended class lines. Even highly educated budding dramatists like Soyinka could be asked, by an apprehensive White landlady, whether they were 'Light or very dark?' Naturally, this desperation played into the hands of landlords ready to capitalize on it. Throughout the 1960s and 1970s, a shortage of viable places to live as a Black Londoner yielded a Black homelessness epidemic that was especially pronounced in the young – by 1974, there were more than 3,000 Black

15–20-year-olds without a fixed address. Ultimately, these converging issues led to even more overcrowding in the few areas that Black people could set up home.

Peter Fryer's *Staying Power* notes that, in the 1970s, West Indian households were three times as likely as White to be living at a density of two or more persons per bedroom. Because this, also, is the dawning of another enduring idea. Specifically, that walls furred with damp, run-down neighbourhoods, and entire multi-generational families squeezed into two-bedroom flats are, rather than the inherited by-product of racist attitudes around housing, an inevitable part of Black immigrant struggle.

On top of this, that London's first Black areas also happened to be the same deprived districts that were home to hard-up, working-class White communities bred resentment, anger and tension. 'This was a classic case,' states Ron Ramdin, analysing the area of Kensal New Town in the 1950s: 'West Indians competing for scarce space and amenities with White tenants who were themselves, for a long time, badly housed. Consequently, physical and social claustrophobia was attributed to the Black newcomer.' Here, the prejudice of landlords exacerbated hostility within the community. Black and White, both victims of the same systems of state ostracism and neglect, were needlessly pitted against one another.

However, that London's post-war Black population tended to be concentrated in a handful of areas (either through direct prejudice or just the feeling of actively wanting to be 'with your own kind') also, it must be acknowledged, forged a vital sense of community and solidarity. Black, generally Afro-Caribbean settlers who were able to buy homes only did so through 'pardner' agreements: the rent-pooling, co-operative saving schemes that were deployed to initiate a chain of ownership (and undoubtedly flourished thanks to the tight-knit nature of Black neighbourhoods). Easy accessibility to businesses that served the community – market stalls, barbers, purveyors of African and Caribbean foodstuffs – also deepened links to these parts of the city.

But perhaps more than that, areas like Brixton, Notting Hill and, a little later, Dalston represented rare zones of Black collective power, fraternity and ownership; in a city where Africans and Caribbeans were often priced out or locked out, these Black hubs offered sanctuary and the familiarity of home. Returning to *The Housing Lark*, which details a motley crew of West Indian friends entering into a doomed house-buying pool in 1960s Brixton, and its description of a character's recent arrival in London from Trinidad, we get a sense of how important London's historically Black spaces were to survival in diaspora:

> adrift in Londontown . . . he make his way down to Brixton with the last two and six he had. Somehow he figure out that that was the safest district to go to, that he bound to meet some fellow countryman who would ease up the situation, give him some shelter and a meal. And as luck would have it, a Jamaican fellar what had a club give him work to clean it out, and say he could sleep in the club for a couple nights until he get a place.

This passage, undoubtedly inspired by real-life stories Selvon had heard, speaks to what somewhere like Brixton has long represented to successive generations of Black settlers: that the question of where to live in

London as a Black immigrant was as much a question of balancing a sense of safety and kinship with the hard realities of racial disadvantage in Britain. By the mid-1980s, almost 40 years after Black Brixton was accidentally born amid tea and cake in a specially hired cinema, this was what Black London looked like: a scattered network of established neighbourhoods and their satellites, characterized by overcrowding and societal neglect, but also a powerful legacy of African and Caribbean collectivism. The ties that bound Black communities to certain areas were strong ones. But if Black diasporas were wedded to any specific streets and areas, then it was very much a marriage of convenience, born from a lack of other realistic options.

It was this contradictory atmosphere that my family – and many other Black African families in the 1980s and 1990s – arrived into. And, while plenty settled in areas where their Blackness wouldn't feel quite as conspicuous, our early years in the UK were marked by a more haphazard, less obvious migratory pattern of settlement as tenants – starting in Wembley, in London's north-west, before a brief stay in Chatham in Kent, followed by longer residence in South-East London and its Kentish outposts. Partly these decisions were simple practicality (Chatham, for instance, was chosen for its proximity to the Canterbury private school my eldest brother went to). But I think, with the caveat that my family's specific experience is hardly a peer-reviewed study, this approach indicates a couple of interesting shifts that would come to play a defining role in the Black African community's takeover of some of London's suburbs.

One is the slightly dysmorphic relationship with class and status that many of the Black Africans who came to

London in this era had. Often well-educated, affluent and upwardly mobile, Black African newcomers would – thanks to a lack of established family links, their arch pragmatism and the way the capital's socioeconomic hierarchies were organized – find themselves either adrift in homogeneously White semi-rural areas or unhappily siloed in a flat in some traditionally multicultural inner-city postcode. Life for this generation of Black African settlers could be an outwardly contradictory one. By the time I was at secondary school, we lived amid a row of forbidding, council-owned pre-fabs near Dartford, alongside a large local Romany Gypsy and White working-class community, but we were also the place where cousins at illustrious fee-paying boarding schools would come to stay during holidays. The implicit message, if there was one, was that it was just a place to live. It did not define us or our situation.

The other factor in this, as hinted at by that mindset, was that this cohort of Black Africans tended to exhibit an eyes-on-the-prize pragmatism when it came to housing. Having not experienced the hatred and indignity of racist landlords in the same way as the post-*Windrush* generation of Caribbeans, many West African settlers in the 1980s and 1990s forged ahead fuelled by a helpful cocktail of bullishness and innocence. In my mother's telling, closeness to good schools and an aversion to high-rise apartments ('When you have three boys you need a garden where they can kick a ball around,' she said, during one conversation on the subject) were the deciding factors for her when she was looking for places to set up home. Even after my brothers were no longer at fee-paying schools, space and comfort was everything.

'That was the priority,' said my mum. 'And we Africans are the same with things like racism. It's there, but you just don't dwell on it.' Ekpoudom, in his account of his early Orpington days, describes a similarly robust attitude from his parents, who tended only to discuss bigotry in terms of the academic motivation it ought to provide. However, as he highlights, 'A high-scoring English essay was no defence from a racial tirade, a successful maths exam no barrier from being labelled a "Black bastard" as I made my way home.'

This is at the heart of it. There is value in this acutely Black African sense of forward momentum, moving wherever the hell you like, and not dwelling on racist incidents. But dignified focus only works up to a point. And as the 1990s and 2000s brought both a resurgence in racist attacks and White nationalist groups vying for political legitimacy, Black and ethnic minority suburbanites found themselves inadvertently positioned on the front line of a new battleground. As a point of comparison, over in Northolt's burgeoning South Asian community, a fevered local campaign opposed the construction of the Dawoodi Bohra mosque on the grounds that it was an 'alien development' that would bring an 'Islamic ghetto' to an otherwise tranquil 'garden suburb'. Closer to home, for me, the British National Party's headquarters – a blue-fronted 'bookshop' on a residential street in Welling that, despite sporadic protests, was operational from 1989 to 1994 – lurked a short bus ride from my school like a constant, quietly threatening reminder; a physical manifestation of the palpable animosity I tried my best to ignore. In fact, the death in 1993 of Stephen Lawrence (whose family attended the same church as mine) felt, when viewed through the prism of that specific space and time, like a tragic inevitability of a multi-ethnic but tensely unintegrated community. It was suburban White entitlement that had curdled into murderous hate. We knew, as young Black men in that area, that we were to be careful and that places like Eltham, where Lawrence was killed, were to be avoided. We knew that, in certain parts of Bexley, Greenwich and other surrounding boroughs, we were effectively under attack. These attitudes and actions do not spring from the ether. So, after the widespread shock and justified institutional reform Lawrence's senseless killing caused, it was not a huge surprise to see the BNP win one in four votes in the nearby North End ward of Bexley in 2000 (despite ultimately losing to Labour).

Now, almost 30 years later, what's especially shocking is that the situation does not seem to have markedly improved. In Bexley, there are still areas that this growing, largely Nigerian community sees as no-go zones. 'By the time I was growing up, it wasn't just the Elthams that we would avoid,' says Mabel Ogundayo, a 30-year-old Bexley borough resident and Labour councillor responsible for the heavily West African Thamesmead ward. 'We couldn't go to Bexleyheath or any of those places, it was very clear. Even after the BNP closed the bookshop.' The late-2000s period that Ogundayo is talking about also coincided with real issues of hate crime and abuse in some Bexley schools, including numerous reports of a proudly prejudiced gang that called themselves RA. 'It stood for Racist Attacks,' she says, with a dark laugh. 'I went to school with people like that.'

The past is a foreign country. Still, the brazen, scarcely believable fact that attitudes and behaviour like this would flourish in the modern age — not that long after I was at school in this exact same area — makes me question the depth of the racial and socioeconomic fissures in suburban towns. And it also makes me think about what I may have forgotten or buried. Because, yes, the more I think about it, the more I remember some of the grimmer details of what it was to be Black African at the very edge of London.

I remember the White girlfriend who apparently got an abusive call to her family phone because we were going out. I remember the squat, aggressive opponent at five-a-side football, calling my brother and me coons and spewing other arcane, racial slurs we didn't even understand. I remember, on at least one occasion, the car that sped up a little as I crossed a road, the driver flashing a malevolent grin to ensure I caught their motive. These are things you cannot easily brush aside. You squash these memories down because you do not want them to define you or hamper your passage through the world; because, really, they are comparatively minuscule incidents in a rich, joyful life full of positives. And to give them your rage or your beaten-down exhaustion would be to let them win.

The Black British capacity for survival and the African tendency to challenge certain orthodoxies, to de-fang racism with determination, are twin superpowers to be admired. But maybe dignified silence and resilience in the face of such pronounced hostility isn't the answer either. Maybe, as social and political history seems to be repeating itself, there is an opportunity to inculcate some positive change. Perhaps, rather than having to acclimatize to White suburban life, the suburbs can gain something powerful from acclimatizing to Blackness.

The screen floods with hazy blue sky and the looming geometry of a vast steel walkway. The rest of Tilbury Docks glimmers dimly in the distance. Towering cranes, distant factories, flues puffing smoke, and the murky, lapping expanse of Thames that once bore the ship that marked the symbolic acceleration (if not, strictly speaking, the actual start) of the modern Black immigrant story in Britain. But today, in this video, the only focus is her: a lone figure, strutting the sunlit catwalk over the water, dressed in shimmering peacock-purple-and-green sequins, trailed by a flapping emerald cape and wielding a blacked-out flag that bears the three cutlasses of Tilbury's home county. Lavish plumage set against the faded backdrop, she is at once poised, playful and solemn; a dutiful one-woman carnival, making her way through the rusted carcass of industrial Britain and London's historic gateway to the world.

And there is something else. As she walks, or gazes contemplatively at the camera from within an abandoned warehouse, voices can be heard. Voices of Black people talking about their experience of living in Essex; about the cans hurled from the windows of speeding cars, the mocking fingers pointed at Afros, sunny days in Leigh-on-Sea ruined by a sudden hail of monkey noises. They are talking about what it is to be other in a county that has long been synonymous with various hues of ridiculed working-class Whiteness.

But, crucially, they are doing so in the way that Black people only tend to when they are talking to each other. Which is to say that the conversations they have are rageful, raw, emotionally open and, despite it all, brutally funny. All while the sequinned figure – who turns out to be Elsa James, the Trinidadian-heritage

visual artist and Southend resident behind the work –
struts, stands and dances to a gentle steel pan soundtrack,
her presence both indicting and reframing a space
freighted with so many highly charged ideas about
immigration, belonging and a changing nation. This is
Black Girl Essex: Here We Come, Look We Here: a 2019
short film by James, exhibited multiple times around
the country, and one of a number of her works that
seek to litigate and explore what Black flight to the
suburbs means for ethnic minorities, suburbia and
Britain at large. It is a sign that these borderland tales
are there to be told. Or as James puts it herself, when
we speak: 'I realized I've got enough bad stories to fill a
whole gallery space. It's quite sad, but it also means that
it's an outlet.'

Tilbury and its surrounding borough, Thurrock, feel
like appropriate vessels for these conversations. Home
to a sixteenth-century fort famously visited by Queen
Elizabeth I and a symbolic hub of immigration and
trade long before the *Windrush* cruised in, Tilbury is
both distinct and representative of a wider trend across
Britain and the world; a once predominantly White
working-class town, fallen a little from former glory and
struggling to define itself in a new, post-globalization
age. Its proximity to London and relatively affordable
housing have made it popular with both Black Africans
getting a first foot on the housing ladder and migrant
workers from 2004's new EU countries like Poland,
Romania and Lithuania.

At the same time, loss of employment in an era
of financial crisis, austerity cuts and an increasingly
mechanized cargo-loading industry led to notorious
deprivation (in 2012, Thurrock finished last in a

national government survey of resident well-being) and a long-established population that felt resentful and dispossessed. Inevitably, these lurching social changes set newcomers and Essex natives in opposition. And – as detailed in the journalist Jack Shenker's exhaustive, post-Brexit exploration of the town, published by the *World Post* in 2017 – it was the Black African settler families that bore the brunt of this resentment.

Pastor Abraham Bamgbose, a Nigerian-born preacher who moved his family to Tilbury in 2004 and established the Black majority Fruitful Land church, shows Shenker the dried remnants of an egg flung at the church's window; he details how his congregants' car windows have been smashed, how his sermon has been disrupted by fake calls to emergency services and how Black worshippers were, in the church's early days, pelted with stones. It is not just in Tilbury, either. In a similarly Brexit-themed Reuters story from 2019, Stella Osunbor, the Nigerian proprietor of a run-down Dagenham pub she had transformed into an African grocer's, describes her door being glued shut by vandals. Elsa James, who grew up in West London but moved to Essex in 2009, remembers walking over a footbridge in Thurrock with her eldest daughter and hearing gleeful n-bombs aimed at them from below. 'She was about ten at the time and thought they had shouted something nice at first,' explains James, in a low voice.

Many of the areas in counties like Essex that have seen influxes of Black Africans are also places with their own histories of deprivation-fuelled far-right activity. Tilbury was, in the 1970s and 1980s, home to the Trojan Skins skinhead group (though whether they were inherently racist is fiercely contested locally), and on moving to

Southend, James notes, the only thing she knew of the seaside town was that it was 'a National Front place'. Though, even with that history, the perfect storm of social decay, economic downturn and Brexit (Tilbury was among the top 1 per cent 'Leave' voting regions in the UK) has undoubtedly exacerbated the atmosphere of ill-feeling and intolerance. That the White resentment in towns like Tilbury – home of the 'left behinds' and proto-Red Wall constituencies beloved of the British press and campaigning politicians – has been so skilfully whipped up and channelled by parties like UKIP hardly helps.

As Shenker notes, deprivation that is actually attributable to larger capitalist forces gets bound up with the presence of visible ethnic minorities who seem, all of a sudden, to be turning pubs and other shuttered high street units into unfamiliar businesses. The change, broadly speaking, is not one that Tilbury's perplexed, disenfranchised residents ever signed up for. This fact, coupled with the sense that White working-class grievance is being specifically ignored – never mind that Black and minority ethnic Brits are still more than twice as likely as their White counterparts to be living in poverty – grows to the point where, just as in the slum London neighbourhoods of the 1950s and 1960s, Black communities are blamed for problems they didn't cause. It is all of this that lands us with the situation that many Black families in suburbia have had to endure in recent decades: a world in which the occasional smashed window, hurled missile or racial slur is simply the price you have to pay for more space, access to better schools and improved living conditions. A world in which the benefits of White society must also bring you into contact with its rage.

Appraising all of that, it is not a surprise to see that, for all the encouraging statistics about the growing multiculturalism of London's suburbs, the migratory drift to places like Essex is still something many Black people resist. Or, at least, something attended by a degree of apprehension and mystified questions from family members. 'When my parents come from London to my house in Essex they still act like they're leaving the country or something,' says James with a laugh. 'They set off early. And they always expect us to come to London for everything.' This, she adds, is tied up with ideas that she and her family have 'sold out' by moving to, first Thurrock, and then Southend. And it is fighting these attitudes that is at the core of *Black Girl Essex* and James's other video and text explorations of what it is to be at the intersection of two seemingly incompatible, frequently misunderstood groups: the Essex girl and the Black woman. It was an artistic breakthrough that James – who, with her blow-out Afro and pronounced cheekbones, still has the poise of a former model – came to view almost as a means of survival.

'I coined the term Black Girl Essex because I just thought, OK, I've got two daughters, and we're not going anywhere,' says James. 'I need to subvert this, I need to make it liberating, and I need to deal with it. Because I can't be ashamed of the geographical part of the UK that I live in.' This notion of shame being attached to Black suburban life is another important factor. Because, for all the discussion of how Black migration sits with suburbia's White incumbents, it is just as valid to ask what it does to Blackness. And whether, ultimately, moving away from places like Peckham or Brixton or Dalston might, as well as exposing you to increased prejudice, also take you away from the pride and cultural connection that proximity to those historically multicultural neighbourhoods represents.

The notion that Essex's Black residents might feel the county was diluting their Blackness was another springboard for James's 2019 film ('It's like you're too Black for the White kids and too White for the Black kids,' says one male interview participant, memorably). I can personally attest to the fact that growing up in a White-dominated area (with, in my case, a mainly White friendship group) can elicit some isolating moments. But, as with a place like Tilbury, which is only a 40-minute train ride from the capital, Black London always felt close at hand and accessible; weekends were a patchwork of odysseys to Jamaican-run barbershops, Ghanaian-led church services and lavish Nigerian hall parties in conspicuously Black parts of South London.

For relatively recent arrivals in the country like us, the concentrated nature of our cultural identity, its inescapable noisiness and attendant litany of family functions, helped open up the world beyond our suburban corner of it. The insularity that can prove defining in London's orbital towns never really got a chance to stick. A trait that came from a tight-knit, church-adjacent community, strict adherence to certain foods and traditions and what feels, to me, like a specifically middle-class West African sense of, well, if not superiority then at least a deep, determined belief that we had a right to be our undiminished selves wherever we pleased. I cannot claim to have always seen the value in this – especially when my mum's shouted Yoruba could be heard in the background as I tried to speak to a school friend on the phone – but I now understand what a protective, important force it was.

This tendency among many Black Africans, James theorizes, probably helps to explain why they have been at the vanguard of the drift to suburban and rural areas. 'I don't think Black flight is happening as much in Caribbean-heritage families,' she says. 'It's predominantly Nigerian. And while I don't want to divide [Black] people, what I really like about West African communities is that progressive, entrepreneurial side. I love it. It's like, "We're going to move there because we can make a good start, and everything else doesn't matter."' Though there are of course many Black Caribbean internal migrants in London's commuter towns, this distinction is reflected in the statistics. And that spirit of entrepreneurialism that's especially pronounced in the Nigerian diaspora has been an important part of Black suburbia's growth – especially when you factor in the Pentecostal church franchises like Fruitful Land that are both successful money-making endeavours and a kind of ready-made community hub for new Black suburbanites. Previous generations of Black Londoners saw a lack of their own businesses as a deterrent. West Africans have looked on and only scented financial opportunity.

As with Fruitful Land, however, these businesses have tended to become a focal point for racism and White resentment; 'exotic' signs of metamorphosis that have been eyed suspiciously in the same way the South Asian community's suburban mosques, temples and gurdwaras once were. That Black African businesses in counties like Essex and Kent often replace closed pubs and bingo halls seems to be at least partly responsible for the ire. 'We've got a greengrocer's now, but it's an Asian greengrocer's,' notes one disgruntled White interviewee in Shenker's piece. 'It actually advertises itself like that.

And the butcher's is for African meat. They don't give you the feeling that you're welcome in there.'

It would be easy to see this as pure xenophobia; a nativist suspicion born from the idea that absolutely everything should centre on and privilege Whiteness. Or, perhaps, to assume that the fractious tensions happening in places like Tilbury are merely the natural growing pains of one community and culture being replaced by another. But both readings are probably overly simplistic. For one thing, to feel disoriented by the sudden appearance of businesses targeted at an unfamiliar community – whether it is a Romanian supermarket or a Brazilian butcher's – is probably more universal than we'd like to admit. London can, at times, feel like multiple distinct cities, rarely interacting and all shouting to be heard over one another. It is when a lack of familiarity with other cultures warps this ignorance into animosity that problems arise. And given the other social divisions that are evident in these flux-state suburbs (differences of faith, of class, and of education), the gap of understanding can feel unbridgeable.

What's more, the implication that Black Africans are actively seeking to completely remould towns in their image – to create their own bubbled, Southall-style 'ethnoburbs', divided from the broader community – feels equally wide of the mark. For one thing, lots of the ambitious Black African parents who view education as a socioeconomic silver bullet also regard the diversity of suburban surroundings as a benefit. In Hugh Muir's *Black Flight*, Susan (a British–Nigerian who moved from East London to Essex when her Pentecostal church planted a satellite branch in Thurrock) explains that this varied environment, coupled with more safety, was a key part of her justification. 'There's something about this area where they aren't exposed to inner-city problems,' she says. 'I don't want my children just to be with people who look like them, eat like them, dress like them, I want them to have a wider spectrum rather than just being isolated. I can go to any workplace now and interact with anybody.'

It shows the idealism and long-term thinking – that 'eyes-on-the-prize' approach again – that are still such a big part of why the suburbs appeal to Black Africans. Undergirding all of this, however, is the persistent lack of communication between the White and Black suburban communities; the lack of easily accessible language to discuss problems of racism and, at times justified, anxieties around displacement. One of the recurring motifs of Shenker's Tilbury piece is White interviewees reluctant to voice their opinion lest they be called racist, coupled with their certainty that they are in no way prejudiced. 'Tilbury's not a racist town any more,' says one, matter-of-factly. Brexit may have been decided by the 2016 referendum, but the culture war it hinted at has only got more pronounced. And the net result in increasingly Black hinterland towns with long, demonstrable histories of prejudice is that it is difficult to get White residents to even admit there is a problem to solve. What's more, it is all the more difficult in an era where 'political correctness' has been skilfully repackaged as 'wokery', poverty among White communities is pointed to as a sign that White privilege doesn't exist, and legitimate anti-racist concerns are cynically bundled up with a liberal elite agenda.

It is a reality that Bexley borough's Mabel Ogundayo came up against when, amid the global calls for racial justice that followed George Floyd's murder in 2020, she went public with a letter to the council's chief executive calling for actionable solutions to the problems of anti-Black racism in the community. These included a forum where Black residents could share experiences of racism and regular meetings with police to discuss inequalities around stop-and-search. 'I had been saying it for years on the council and been told that [racism] wasn't a problem [in the borough] any more,' she explains. 'But obviously, with the George Floyd situation, I had a lot of people reach out to me to ask what the council was doing. The first time I wrote a simple email asking how we would be standing in solidarity with people that have experienced racism. I didn't get a response to that, or a longer email [I sent]. So that was when I posted it online.'

Amid the heightened emotions and pledges of allyship that characterized summer 2020, many responses to Ogundayo's letter were positive. She was praised by other councillors in the neighbouring borough of Greenwich, and it offered Black residents who had their own bottled-up experiences of abuse the opportunity to finally share them. Though, perhaps inevitably, there was some negativity. 'I got a lot of hate mail,' she says solemnly. 'One person threatened to kill me and a few people said I was trying to start a race war.' Less inflammatory but perhaps even more dismaying were rebuttals from elsewhere within the local government. 'What a load of old rubbish,' was the tweeted response of Conservative local councillor John Davey. In follow-up statements, he described the UK 'and Bexley in particular' as 'the most tolerant [places] in the world'.

That these attitudes were so prevalent in the suburbs, even at a time of supposed awakening to anti-racist rhetoric, is not especially surprising. And, to me, having grown up in this atmosphere, they feel symptomatic of a White community struggling to adapt not just to changing neighbourhoods but also to a raised bar of expectation when it comes to race relations in Britain. London's middle-class orbital settlements were initially populated by those fleeing the post-war city's crime, overcrowding and heavily minority ethnic neighbourhoods. The arrival of Black and South Asian families in the 1980s, 1990s and 2000s was predicated on the idea that they were being allowed into areas purposely set up to exclude them. Acceptance, if it came at all, came from White residents who 'didn't see colour' and thought the way to vanquish racism was to deny its existence.

In Shenker's story, Pastor Abraham identifies the fact that people no longer throw eggs or spit at Tilbury's Black community as a sign that things are improving. Yet the fact the threshold for acceptable behaviour is so low tells its own story, and shows why calls for action like Ogundayo's were so hard for some sections of the White suburban community to compute; why a politely worded request for equity and accountability in the face of abuse can be viewed as incitement to race war. Grudging tolerance of Black communities in suburbia was part of the established order for so long. So now that Black Africans at London's fringes want more, now that they want to be respected, celebrated, and have a stake in towns where they have lived for decades, it is proving, in some quarters, to be a problem.

'Things have come a long way from when it used to pretty much be [people saying] they didn't like Black people,' says Ogundayo. 'But I think, as a borough, we are very closed off to change compared to the rest of London.' That's the other thing about suburban areas. The pace of life may be slow. But the pace of lasting attitude change can be slower still. And so, faced with this, it is understandable that some Black suburbanites appear to be running out of patience.

On Orsett Road in Grays, the tidemarks of successive waves of migration are especially stark. Here, in this corner of riverside Essex, the faded livery of Grays Café Pie & Mash marks the arrival of White working classes in the post-war era from the old East End. A brightly lit halal butcher's highlights both South Asian Muslims and a Somali diaspora displaced by the conflict of the 1990s. The green, yellow and red insignia of Signet Afro-Caribbean supermarket, meanwhile, underscores the Black African community that has continued to make this place its own since the 2000s. And before long, these businesses may be joined, in this area if not on this exact road, by an all-new branch of Erith's Whitehart restaurant.

'I'm looking at Grays, Colchester, Stroud and Maidstone,' says Sodunke, the Whitehart's owner, reeling off possible second outposts for his burgeoning restaurant brand. 'I've got two places I'm looking at, at the moment, and one of them is in Chatham, because I found out a lot of people are moving there. It's very close to Gillingham. And I'm looking at Barking as well, because there's no good standard of Nigerian restaurant there.' During the pandemic, he adds, he had diners coming all the way from Croydon, and he even arranged special lockdown deliveries for a customer in

Colchester. There is the basis for an empire out there, if he can only build it.

These ambitious expansion plans show that any reports of Black African suburbia's demise are premature. Wherever there are well-regarded selective schools, planted Pentecostal churches (like the sprawling Chatham complex that has been the headquarters of Kingsway International Christian Centre since 2014) and sturdy transport links, Black African families have continued to cluster. If the street-level incidents of abuse and violence of the past 30 years were designed to drive out or discourage Black African communities then, at macro level at least, they have failed. What's more, a look at available school census figures shows that growth is continuing. In Thurrock, for instance, a 2013/14 survey of the borough's youth found that in the 0–17 age bracket, Black children had actually become far and away the majority ethnic population (12.4 per cent compared to 7.8 per cent among White kids).

On top of this, there are signs Black migration is going even further afield into the White ROSE (the orbital 'Rest Of South-East' commuter towns that geographers identify as the traditional hubs of White flight) and straining the definition of African or Black London. Between 2001 and 2011 the Black and Asian ethnic minority population in Milton Keynes doubled, with the largest gains made among the Black African demographic.

Rewinding back to Black Brixton's accidental birth in 1948, this current moment looks a little like Black communities finally gaining the ability to settle where they'd like rather than simply where they can. In this light, Black settlement in suburbia resembles a way to escape some of the stereotypical limits thrust upon Africans and Afro-Caribbeans by socioeconomic disadvantage, racism and tradition. It is another push against the circumstances and fixed associations of diaspora. As Hugh Muir notes near the end of *Black Flight*, 'I've always found it odd that urban has become a sort of codeword for ethnic minorities . . . where was it ever written that minorities should be synonymous with inner cities and concrete?'

A grotesquely inflated London housing market is, of course, another crucial factor. Coveted boroughs like Peckham and Hackney have effectively become places where house ownership is almost impossible for the Black communities that lived in them before they were desirable. Add in the privatization of social housing and decanting of London residents from regenerated estates after the 2011 riots (a process that has been called the London Clearances), and growing Black presence in London's suburbs can look a little like the latest fallen domino in a chain of displacement. Though, when you factor in the alienating creep of gentrification and legitimate fears about the deprivation and overpricing associated with low-income areas, you could argue that a lot of these families have wilfully displaced themselves.

Crime, and its relationship to inner-city social housing areas, is a factor as well. In the aftermath of the 2011 riots, the then Conservative prime minister David Cameron's voluble war on gang culture and 'sink estates' engendered a policing approach that, as described by Jessica Perera in a 2016 Institute of Race Relations paper, was effectively a 'localized hostile environment'. Here, gentrification, managed decline and intensified policing were the same broom – pushing poor but aspirant Black families out to the fringes of the city to areas they could better identify with.

For some, however, the physical distance from neighbourhoods that are permanently tied to Black Britishness can feel like a kind of grief. 'Sometimes I'll just go to London because I need my Black fix,' says Elsa James. 'It's like I need it for my health. We've been [in Essex] since 1999, which is all of my adult life. And so we're starting to think: is it healthy? Is it good for our health to stay here?' Though Essex has long been her muse as an artist, James and her husband are now considering boomeranging back into Hackney because of its housing stock and cultural diversity. 'Although', she laughs, 'that really nice housing costs a lot of money, so I need to win a few art prizes.'

James reminds us that what outer-London areas sometimes ask of Black residents – namely, that they should get used to a life of suspicion, wariness and ostracism – can feel like too much to bear; too high an emotional bill to pay. Whether Black presence in these traditionally White hinterlands is actually changing attitudes is a question that is more difficult to answer. In local politics, there has been a notable revolutionary sweep in terms of ethnic representation. Ogundayo is one of a number of local politicians and councillors in suburban boroughs that includes Abena Oppong-Asare, the Ghanaian-heritage Labour MP for Erith and Thamesmead, and Bukky Okunade, a British-Nigerian Labour councillor in Tilbury who – symbolically – had been successfully returned to her post at every election since 2006 despite the attempts of multiple BNP candidates. (Okunade did eventually lose her seat in the 2022 local elections.)

However, as Ogundayo notes, the post-Brexit age seems to have yielded a resurgence of some old attitudes in her borough. 'Hate crime went up,' she admits. 'And we still have issues with policing.' What's more, just as in my days of avoiding Eltham, it seems as though there is evidence of area-by-area variance when it comes to intolerance. 'People are quite resistant to change,' she adds. 'But, equally, the more change there is, the more people have to come on board. That is why it's changed so positively in the north of Bexley, in Belvedere where I live. There are now so many Black people and we don't cause any issues, so everyone gets along really well.' She pauses to consider. 'It's just a lack of understanding, to an extent. And so if we did more celebrating of other cultures then maybe some people wouldn't feel the way they do.'

This is an important point. But attempts to celebrate the increased ethnic diversity of London's suburban towns, with carnivals, Black History Month initiatives and more, need to be backed by signs that official bodies are taking issues of racism seriously. Schools, police forces and local councils need to initiate that shift from grudging tolerance to real equality; to calmly make the point that microaggressions on the bus or in the workplace are part of the same racist framework as a gang of kids thinking it's acceptable to hurl rocks at a Black family making their way to church. That ethnic minority communities would want in on the same suburban dream as all sorts of other families should not be all that surprising or controversial.

Again, they want what you want. Much of the story of Black African settlement in London – whether it is late-nineteenth-century seamen, the West African students of the early twentieth century, those who arrived having fled political and economic turmoil in the 1980s and 1990s, or the varied, ambitious groups that have arrived from across the continent more recently – has been about carving out space; about little slivers of the metropole that could be claimed as 'a home from home'. Black flight to the suburbs means that London now glitters with a growing constellation of these spaces. If it is the triumphant endgame of the African diaspora in London, then it is a fittingly ordinary one. But the shift it represents, from a transient population working to earn money for a move back to their country of birth to a thriving community with a sense of belonging and a stake in London and the UK, is a quietly seismic and significant one.

'My friends and I all used to work in the same cab office when I moved here back in 1998, and we would all talk about our plans to go back to Nigeria,' said the Whitehart's Ola Sodunke near the end of our conversation. We were sitting in the white, glitzy interior of his restaurant, a few hours before opening. 'But then we realized that there is no point going back there and doing nothing.' One of his staff made her steady way around the floor with a mop, while Afrobeats puttered away on the stereo at a low volume. 'What we found out was that where you live – that is your home.'

Conclusion

The Next Great Wave

You can talk about the sanctity of two people committing themselves to each other. You can highlight the symbolism of friends and family uniting to toast and support a couple as they embark on an important new chapter of their lives. But at a certain point in the festivities, a traditional Yoruba engagement ceremony just feels like nothing so much as a living, dancing monument to a specific form of Nigerian pride and exuberant celebration; an opportunity to gather, costume yourself in glittering fabrics, and collectively proclaim your cultural identity in its most high-decibel, extravagant guise. Nowhere is that more evident than here, in the tightly proportioned upstairs room of a Bethnal Green community centre, as everyone in the crowd rises to their feet. Camera phones are craned and there is a new charge in the room. The bride is about to make her entrance.

It feels as though we have all been on quite the journey to get here. Those who arrived here 30 minutes late – as my mother and I did – very quickly realized that we were actually very, very early. The consolation prize of the long wait was that we could watch it all whirring to life. We could see the caterers setting up vast, steaming pans of jollof rice and creamy, cling-filmed mounds of pounded yam; hear the repeated snare-hit as the live band's drummer soundchecked; and look on as late-arriving female guests queued up to have their sparkly purple *gele* (or head wraps) tightly tied onto their scalps and fanned out into ornate sculptural arrangements.

We have come along to this ceremony – officially known as the 'engagement', and a symbolic accompaniment to a separate, legally binding Western wedding-proper in the coming weeks – because the bride and groom, Maria Grillo and Henry Oshigbosin, are family friends. Yet it's notable that, even at what is ostensibly a family gathering, and, as my mum points out, a comparatively small one in supersized Yoruba engagement terms, the hustle never stops. There is a mini economy of services being offered: one man charges to take photos in front of an unfurled backdrop, oddly depicting the empty white ballroom of a much grander ceremony. Elsewhere, another is doing a brisk trade converting sterling into dollar bills that will be 'sprayed', or pressed, onto the foreheads of the happy couple and invited guests as they dance.

Then, as the delay hits 90 minutes, the final *geles* are twisted on and guests listlessly pick at snacking plates of cold skewered chicken, the ceremony explodes into life all at once. A roving musician with a traditional 'talking drum' pinned beneath his arm hammers out a bubbling, halting beat and the two *alagas* – hired, dual female MCs who host proceedings, lead prayer and generally feel like the mischievous orchestrators of the whole thing – shout out church-style call and response ('When I say "Jee" you say "zuss"!') and kick-start a frenzied dance-off among the aunties, many of whom return to their tables flapping order-of-service cards to cool themselves.

And then finally, after the families of the couple have been introduced, the *alagas* have – to the audible consternation of my mother and a few others – been repeatedly 'sprayed' with money, Henry and his groomsmen have entered, a formal, printed 'proposal letter' has been passed around, and a symbolic dowry hamper basket of specific arcane items has been inspected, we get to the big moment. The band starts to play, camera phone arms are lifted to find the best vantage point, and Maria and her bridesmaids make their entrance. But in Yoruba tradition, there is no slow, coquettish walk, or organ-driven rendition of the 'Wedding March'. No, at ceremonies like this, you dance up to your seat – a seat that is often a gilded, ersatz throne – and into your new life. And so, met by the flashbulbs of two separate photographers, a crouching videographer and all those raised smartphones, Maria and her friends step from the lift and enter as one wiggling, glittery entity of pure joyful release; five figures in sparkled purple and silver, all twirling, shuffling, spinning, vibing and singing as the band's twanging highlife guitars build and build. It takes, at a generous estimate, maybe five minutes to travel a distance of 10 feet. Even the catering staff have their phones raised. And there is a smile on practically every face that tells you this moment is about more than just two people promising themselves to each other.

It is, essentially, a flurry of fascinating collisions; a modern, social-media-ready interpretation of a tradition that originates from a time when a would-be groom would literally have to travel to his intended's village before proving his worth via symbolic payment and a series of tests. The modern Yoruba engagement ceremony, if it does anything at all, shows us the ways in which African diaspora culture fastidiously honours the past, even as it forges ahead. Even as someone technically born of this world, and with experience of the extroverted, lavish nature of Nigerian events, all I could do was stand back and marvel at the spectacle, and truly drink in the pageantry, the playfulness, and the sense of active custodianship across the generations.

Because that is the other important detail. That the bride and groom — who are both 28 and were raised in Britain — have decided to have this sort of traditional, deeply Nigerian ceremony speaks to a wider trend. Not just in the sense that, before the pandemic especially, there had been a marked uptick in demand for ever more extravagant Yoruba engagement ceremonies in the UK (the more than three million posts on Instagram's #nigerianwedding tell their own story). But also because such a fervent display of cultural pride and fidelity to one's ancestors gestures towards a broader shift in the way a new generation of Africans are thinking about their identity.

Buoyed by the way in which a Black African aesthetic and sensibility has permeated the worlds of film, art, fashion, music and more, this new wave of African Londoners possesses, to my mind, a confident duality that didn't really exist previously. This is not to say that fierce pride in African-influenced Black culture is a modern invention. But through the convulsions of modern African settlement in this country – through struggles with disrupted family units, questions of assimilation and prejudice and stigmatization from both outside and within the wider Black community – it feels as though there has been a significant shift. It feels, just like Maria and her bridesmaids, that something new has come strutting confidently into the light.

In the spring of 1924, long before any London neighbourhood with a preponderance of African supermarkets had been claimed as a diaspora stronghold, a real-life Nigerian village materialized in Wembley Park. One of a number of immersive 'pavilions' spread across a vast, almost 300-acre site, it was part of the landmark British Empire Exhibition: a wildly ambitious, long-running imperialist theme park that cost £25 million to create, was responsible for the construction of the old, iconic Wembley Stadium, initially known as the Empire Stadium, and was conceived to both showcase the resource-rich strength of Britain's dominions and at the same time act as a charm offensive amid growing anti-colonial sentiment.

The Nigerian village – one of three recreated areas where real-life Africans had been shipped in to demonstrate crafts, recreate aspects of their daily life, and generally act like living exhibits – sat within a walled city. And, given that this was an era of intense fascination with African life, it did not take long for this aspect of the Empire Exhibition's so-called 'vast window display' to attract attention that edged, now and then, into distastefulness. A pre-opening write-up in the *Evening News* misappropriated a report by a Nigerian governor to claim that the mock village would recreate a country recently liberated from 'cannibalism, slave-trading, [and] obscure black-magic rites of almost incredible barbarity'. Separately, after the pavilion opened, a *Sunday Express* article used an interpreted interview with one of the female inhabitants of the village as an excuse to engage in sustained innuendo about the sexual habits and appetites of African women.

That the story didn't end there, in an interwar period rife with racist attitudes, is perhaps what makes it most interesting. Impressively, a collective of justifiably outraged West African students – including, again, the West African Students' Union founder Ladipo Solanke – managed to lodge so many well-argued complaints about this harmful press coverage that the village was temporarily closed to the public.

Here then, almost a century ago, is a reminder of an essential truth: for as long as there has been significant Black African presence in London, there has been a pitched battle over the way African life is both represented and misrepresented. In the 1920s it may have been persistent mistruths about cannibalism, primitive beliefs and sexual lasciviousness but, later in the same century, it was an innate association with poverty, famine, disease and scam emails.

But there is, I think, another important consideration in the historic warping of African identity. And it is that some of the inherited falsehoods of colonialism have been so convincing that even Black Africans themselves have become adept at spreading them. Or rather, it is my experience that if the connotations of what it is to be African have become confused – if, as is often cited, Black African children born or predominantly raised in Britain are prone to identity crisis – then some of that confusion has come from within their own community. From the social privileges afforded to those with lighter skin (not to mention the use of bleaching creams across the continent) to the vogue for outfitting children with secondary 'English' names that they are expected to adopt or disregard whenever the situation requires, lots of postcolonial, middle-class African tradition is racked with mixed messages. And that is before we even start on the practice of farming children out to White families so they may better assimilate.

Growing up, I was much more light-skinned than I am now; one of the relatively fair, supposedly White-adjacent chosen ones, with a complexion closer to that of my mother's than my father's. But then, as often happens, as I grew older, my skin got darker. And I can still remember returning to Nigeria in 2015, for the first time in over 20 years, and receiving a quizzical look from a family friend who knew me when I was little, as we visited them at home. '*You got dark*,' she said, in Yoruba, eyeing me up and down and looking gravely disappointed.

I don't say this to indict people for attitudes that are the inevitable by-product of generations of Black subjugation and implicit White superiority. It just feels clear that this dichotomy – the subtle prizing of the gifts that perceived Whiteness and Anglocentric education can confer, allied with that fierce pride in African traditions – is probably what has led many African Londoners like me to be thrown maybe a little out of whack. And then, when you add in previous eras where Africanness was so toxic it forced Black schoolkids to feign Caribbean heritage, you start to understand why a lot of African heritage kids who grew up in Britain speak of feeling they had to pick a side, culturally. That was certainly the case for Sara, a mixed-heritage, British Sudanese entrepreneur and academic who grew up between Sudan and boarding school in the UK.

'Because my mum is half English, I always felt like I had to choose between being the English version of myself and the Sudanese version of myself,' she says. 'My elder siblings made that choice really easily. They were like, "No, we are the Londoners and we'll just go back to Sudan once a year." That's their life, that's their world. Whereas I feel I'm straddling the fence.' This fence-straddling is undoubtedly something a lot of Black Brits, no matter their heritage, will be able to relate to. What's particularly interesting, though, as far as Sara is concerned, is that her strong identification with her Sudanese side led to a history of activism in Sudan during its 2019 revolution and the resultant removal of incumbent dictator Omar al-Bashir. For Sara, who is doe-eyed and striking with a mass of golden curls, this moment of political upheaval was, despite the attendant risks, a hugely rewarding thing to be a part of. 'It was literally the best experience of my life,' she explains. 'There was nothing like it. We have such a history of tribalism [in Sudan], so it was nice to see everybody come together and have one shared message and vision.'

Obviously, not every culturally conflicted second- or third-generation African will stand with their country in quite as dramatic a fashion. But the idea of being politically engaged with what is happening in mother countries feels like another hallmark of how a new generation is defining their African identity. From Nigeria's #EndSars movement, which, in 2020, succeeded in drawing international attention to alleged kidnappings, acts of brutality and extrajudicial killings carried out by Nigeria's notorious, since-disbanded Special Anti-Robbery Squad, to protests in Senegal and Democratic Republic of Congo, all across the continent youth has been leading the way in terms of resistance and finally bringing change in areas long seen as intractably broken or corrupt.

This approach marks a clear attitude shift across the generations. Whereas many of those elders who lived through Africa's economic and political turmoil in previous decades were beaten down by it, there is, as in other cultures, a new appetite for justice – social, economic, sexual – emerging among those Black African children born more recently. Where a protective cynicism is what I tend to remember from the overheard political conversations of my childhood, now youthful idealism is showing the way. 'I feel like it got to the point where the older generation were just tired of the fight,' adds Hannah Ajala, a 28-year-old journalist for the BBC World Service, among other media outlets, who specializes in modern African stories. 'But the times are changing. And it's really remarkable just to see that happening.' It would be naive to assume that the huge problems facing some African nations – of political instability, corruption and basic shortcomings of infrastructure – can be solved overnight. However, the switch from just accepting these issues to actually mobilizing to highlight and fix them is enormously significant.

Naturally, the internet age is a part of this. Not only has social media helped mount protest movements, but it has also collapsed the borders between countries. Where once a

Ghanaian student may have needed to wait for a letter brought by ship or a Zimbabwean refugee may have required an international phone card to check in, now the problems of the home continent are instantly, urgently beamed to the diaspora. But there is another reason why it seems, from a certain distance, as though the concerns of young Black Africans in diaspora and out of it feel much more synchronized and interchangeable. And it cuts to the core of one of the more elemental questions of Black settlement in the UK.

Simply put: Africa is at the forefront of so many African Londoners' minds because lots of them are abandoning the supposed promised land of the West to head back home. For the better part of a decade, there have been regular stories of the repatriates – or repats – who are contravening all the established rules of Black African immigration and returning to make new lives in Freetown or Kinshasa or Nairobi. Ajala, who relocated from London to Lagos in late 2021 and interviewed multiple returnees to their ancestral African nations for an exhibition project with the Migration Museum, confirms that not only is the repat movement real, but it is also being fuelled by a whole range of motivations.

'There was Adwoa, from Ghana, who was tired of the racism she was facing [in the UK],' she says. 'Morris, who moved from London to Sierra Leone to build a resort because there was a stronger market for it here. Issy, who just wanted to feel closer to her roots, and so decided to move to Ghana from the US. Whether it's wanting that safe space, moving for a work opportunity, people leaving corporate jobs to build a farm, or some people finding love, we all have our reasons.'

It is an interesting grenade thrown into the debate around Black settlement and the received wisdom that has long been bound up with it. London and Britain have historically been synonymous with a better life for Black Africans. While generally never wanting their children to lose touch with the African side of themselves, many of the decisions traditionally made by parents – on schooling, on neighbourhood, on social surroundings – were oriented around the idea of setting up a long, prosperous life in the UK. But Ajala and the other repats like her seem to be acknowledging that African life can offer something that an existence in diaspora cannot. 'So many stories from the continent have that really negative gaze that Western media likes to perpetuate,' says Ajala. 'And so a lot of my work has just been in, not romanticizing, but just highlighting the beauty of being in spaces where you are the majority.'

In this, what Ajala's generation is doing is not all that dissimilar to what the students who were appalled by the Empire Exhibition were doing. Which is to say, by actively pushing against the idea that the West is inherently better or more civilized, they are expanding and sharpening our perception of what African identity can mean or look like. I think, for me, returning to Nigeria after so many years almost living in fear of being taken back there, I felt something shift as well. If you have been defined as a minority your whole life, to have that scaffolding fall away – to be lent anonymity by a surrounding whirl of other Black faces – can feel like a kind of rebirth.

Of course, the striking thing about the children of diaspora moving back to the countries of their birth is that it is quite the rug-pull for their parents. 'We're doing in reverse what they did,' says Ajala, with a smile. Though there is a caveat for her, and it again brings us to what may be the most lasting and significant change in how Black African identity is viewed. Though Ajala is very happy in Lagos currently, catching the train up to Ibadan and spending time with her Nigerian-born boyfriend, she still sees a future and connection in the UK. 'I cannot comfortably say that I'm going to retire here and stay here until I'm old,' she says. 'I would love my child to have a similar childhood to me where they are exposed to Nigerian living and British living.'

This is a sentiment I have heard time and time again from a younger generation of Africans who split their time between countries on the continent and in the West. So much of Black settlement in London has been coloured by the decision of staying or going, whether it was the cohort of future leaders who came to stay temporarily in the early twentieth century, or my parents' generation who had looser plans, but essentially wanted to bestow the gifts of Britishness on their children before retiring to some self-built mansion back home. The new mode of behaviour seems less conflicted. Because maybe there is virtue in lives lived in the overlap of two cultures. Maybe you no longer need to pick a side. Maybe the new secret of squaring an African and British identity is to cultivate a way to be both.

It can be fascinating to hear how you might have subtly misread a situation. To be reminded that we all try to fit our own narrative on things. My version of the newly anointed Mrs Maria Oshigbosin's wedding entrance, as I strained to capture video footage alongside everyone else, was of someone completely at ease; a young woman boldly bending tradition to her will, surrounded by adoring friends and family and loving every minute of it. But when we talk, a few weeks after both her symbolic Yoruba engagement and her legally binding white wedding, Oshigbosin serves me with a reminder that appearances can always be slightly deceiving.

'If I'm perfectly honest, [the traditional Yoruba engagement] was a bit more to appease family,' she admits. 'We wanted to keep things quite small with regards to our wedding but, as we know, in Nigerian culture, small is just unheard of. It's literally just, invite your friends, their mums, everyone in life that has ever known you to eat and drink and enjoy, even if you haven't spoken to them in 20 years.' Oshigbosin, who is petite, with hair in long ombré twists, is enjoyably frank company. She sounds as though she is tweaking at the absurdity of the whole enterprise of traditional weddings, rather than venting any anger or resentment (though, again, this could just be how I choose to take it, as one of the freeloading distant acquaintances she's talking about). But the wider context to her stance is that, with both her parents having passed away years before after separate struggles with illness, she had hoped to keep things intimate and manageable. Her ideal scenario was a sizeable white wedding, supplemented by a tiny traditional ceremony held in the family's back garden.

Of course, it soon became apparent that Oshigbosin's grandma and other elders in the family were unhappy with this arrangement, and fretted it was a sign she was 'going away from the culture'. And so, eventually, she relented and gave her wider relatives the day and the traditions that they demanded. 'For them,' she says, 'it was about honouring my parents by doing [the ceremony] in the way that it would have been done should they have been here.' This backdrop, and the unseen inner conflict as Oshigbosin and her bride team made their joyous way into the room, shows there is still a gap between the desires of African London's generations. That, to some degree and in certain spaces, the grown-ups are still very much in charge.

However, that is to be expected. What we are currently seeing is an example of the major intersection between the eras of Black African settlers, as one group hands over to another. And as evidenced by Oshigbosin's broadly positive experience of a traditional Yoruba ceremony (indiscriminate guest list notwithstanding), what's encouraging is that the new generation seem to be bending towards their indigenous culture rather than away from it. 'As much as it was a headache, I'm so glad that we did the traditional ceremony,' she says. 'I felt that hall parties like that might die with the older generation, but now I think they're something that's coming back into fashion.' To her, something as simple as gathering a capacity-straining number of people to eat jollof rice, dance and spray dollar bills is a vital expression of pride. 'There is a beauty to our culture,' she says. 'And so it's about making sure that you pass down the values and traditions that your parents have instilled in you.'

This sense of shielding that flame of tradition, as it passes on to those in the diaspora coming up behind us, has been especially obvious and prevalent in recent years. My own concerted effort to re-engage with Black African culture – through language and food and art and history – coincided, predictably enough, with becoming a father. But the immense good fortune I have had is that this interest and cultural reawakening has occurred in an era where Black British stories, and, specifically, African stories, have a new cache and prevalence. This does not happen, I think, without many of the values and practices that have come to underpin what we think of as the African diaspora experience in the UK. It does not happen without the ballast of faith, the industriousness of Black African entrepreneurs, the enshrining of education and the determination to prosper even within a system historically predicated on maintaining disadvantage among ethnic minorities.

And what's more, from that prosperity and achievement, this new generation have started to adapt and evolve what it means to be Black and of African heritage in the UK. This has meant increased political engagement, more open dialogue about mental health struggles, speaking out about oppression and forging a Black solidarity among those of different ancestry – whether they are West African or South African, Caribbean or Eritrean – that runs contrary to many of the old intra-ethnic tensions of the past.

For so long, a generation of British-raised Black African settlers were defined, both inside and outside their communities, by the supposed limbo of being stuck between cultures. We were too African for the West or too Western for Africa. However, the new triumph of African London seems to me to be an embrace of these multitudes; a glorying in them and a building of something new. More than one older African Londoner I spoke to throughout the course of this book lamented to me, in one way or another, that they felt the younger generation in the city's African diaspora were 'lost'. That they did not know who they are. To me, this seems less like identity crisis and more like people chafing against perceived limitations. It is a new wave, questioning what it really means to be an acceptable and respectable Black African in diaspora. So many of the people I met on my journeys through African London – whether they were prison leavers, shopkeepers, activists, writers or schoolchildren – had a unique perspective on what their identity was. That they can all be right at once, that Black African can also mean suburbanite or activist, hustler or digital nomad, feels to me like one of the more rousing victories of our long, eventful presence in this country.

It would be naive to end on too much of an unambiguously rosy and positive note. For all the supposed great strides made when it comes to awareness of Black British history, the calling out of systemic prejudice within institutions and wider pleas for racial justice, there is undoubtedly still a battle being waged when it comes to how we view these subjects. Disparities are more stark than ever. A concerted effort is being made by the British government and sections of the press to present genuine grievances about discrimination as liberal shrieking over statues and language. On school curriculums and in British institutions, attempts are being made to both discredit the notion of structural inequality and protect the legacy of British Empire from wholesale criticism. That the Conservative politician Kemi Badenoch, one of the chief exponents of accentuating colonialism's positives, is a Lagos-raised British-Nigerian only adds to both the sense of Britain's entrenched African influence and its lack of ideological homogeneity.

Then there is the issue of continued immigration into the UK from African countries, a picture that has only become bleaker since the 1962 Commonwealth Immigrants Act first attempted to stem the flow of Black and Asian migration to Britain. While Brexit was, at one stage, presented as an opportunity for those in former colonies to benefit from a reformed migration system, it has never been harder for those born elsewhere to become resident in African London. In 2019, an All-Party Parliamentary Group report found that applicants from African countries were more than twice as likely to be refused a visa as those from other parts of the world. The closed pathway from the EU has made it much more difficult for, say, a DRC-born naturalized Belgian to make their home in Britain. And Home Secretary Priti Patel's 2022 Nationality and Borders Act – beyond the news-making offshore asylum processing centre in Rwanda – brings in a whole range of strictures tied to entry from countries that the UK government doesn't deem sufficiently co-operative when it comes to deportation.

We shouldn't think that anything has been decisively won, then. Yet we should also take heart from the fact that the sweep of Black African presence across British society can only lead, it is to be hoped, to more accountability, positivity and the continued growth of African culture as a visible, ever-evolving force. Permanence has always been the elephant in the room of Black African settlement in Britain. We have either been characterized by the temporary nature of our stay or defined ourselves as passing through. When I asked my mum, more than 40 years after she moved to the country, if she thinks of herself as here forever, she baulked. 'I still think of myself as just being here for a while before going back to Nigeria,' she said with a laugh. 'It's why I still haven't fixed my curtain rail.'

Well, she is still here. As am I and hundreds of thousands of others. And even those who return to their mother countries still draw positivity from the fact that they are also from London or Manchester or Bristol. Ultimately, the settlers have enmeshed with the hosts; Black African culture, at the end of the day, truly is British culture. And if there are permanent roots and foundations in this country, if African London really does exist, then it manifests in the people. They are the ever shifting and expanding record of its history; an indelible scrawl etched all over the city. They are not going anywhere. And their next chapter is already being written.

Further Reading

These books and articles were vital in helping to expand and enrich my knowledge of Black African diaspora history in London and the UK. I owe all these authors an enormous debt of gratitude. If *Settlers* has set you off on an enjoyable path of discovery, then these are the places to continue that journey.

Adi, Hakim, *West Africans in Britain: 1900–1960, Nationalism, Pan Africanism and Communism* (Lawrence & Wishart Ltd, 1998)

Bailkin, Jordanna, *The Afterlife of Empire* (University of California Press, 2021)

Boakye, Jeffrey, *Black, Listed: Black British Culture Explored* (Dialogue Books, 2019)

Fryer, Peter, *Staying Power: The History of Black People in Britain* (Pluto Press, 2018)

Gates Jr, Henry Louis, *Black London* (The Antioch Review Inc., 1976)

Institute of Race Relations, *Policing Against Black People* (Institute of Race Relations, 1987)

Kilingray, David, *The Diaries of Thomas Brem Wilson, 1865–1929: African Businessman and Pentecostal Pioneer in Britain* (2019)

Matera, Marc, *Black London: The Imperial Metropolis and Decolonization in the Twentieth Century* (University of California Press, 2015)

Mullard, Chris, *Black Britain* (Allen & Unwin, 1973)

Olusoga, David, *Black and British: A Forgotten History* (Pan Macmillan, 2016)

Onyeama, Dillibe, *A Black Boy at Eton* (Penguin Random House, 2022)

Owusu, Derek (ed.), *Safe: 20 Ways to be a Black Man in Britain Today* (Trapeze, 2019)

Ramdin, Ron, *The Making of the Black Working Class in Britain* (Ashgate Publishing Ltd, 1987)

Acknowledgements

The first and perhaps most important thanks has to go to the people who spoke to me for this book. My vision for *Settlers* (and 'vision' was definitely an overly lofty word in its earliest stages) was always that it would be driven by voices and stories that you wouldn't normally hear; that it would be the lives and lineage of ordinary Black African Londoners afforded atypical reverence and scrutiny. Even so, nothing could have really prepared me for how much this work would be shaped by those that were generous enough to give me their time and insight. They are the engine of the pages you have just read. They challenged me, educated me and nudged me into interesting new avenues of research. There would be no book without them.

This especially applies to the experts and academics who, whether through their written words or through interviews, helped sharpen my understanding of this dauntingly huge subject, and often led me to some illuminating recommendation or contact. I'm especially grateful to Jordanna Bailkin, William Ackah, Mama Sylla, Debbie Ariyo and Nky Iweka. They all aided my entry into otherwise inaccessible worlds and deepened my knowledge immensely.

Of course, you absolutely wouldn't be reading this if it wasn't for the team at Bloomsbury, both past and present. I'm especially thankful to Jamie Birkett, who first approached me at an afternoon awards reception in early 2019 – when I was feeling especially out of place and bewildered by my surroundings – and asked me if I had any book ideas. It was that encounter that set this whole thing in motion. And, though Jamie had moved on before *Settlers* was pushed out into the world, his early belief, advice and encouragement was vital. He got it, basically. Long before even I knew exactly what 'it' was. And the same is very much true of Tomasz Hoskins, this book's eventual editor. Thank you so much, Tomasz, for shepherding the book to publication with sensitivity, thoughtfulness and the kind of tactful positivity that this thin-skinned worrier most definitely needed. Above all, you reminded me that writing this book was a fun, achievable thing, right at the moment when it felt like an attritional, wholly impossible homework assignment I had set for myself. Major gratitude is also due to everyone else on Team *Settlers* – from publicity and marketing to editorial squadrons who all helped spread the word about the book and, on the proofreading side, saved me from any number of grievous grammatical clangers. I know that I have been lucky to receive such enthusiasm and attention, straight out of the gate as a writer. That you all put in the work (and were very kind when all the many, many things you needed from me were long overdue) did not go unnoticed.

An enormous hug of appreciation, also, for my agent, Imogen Pelham. It has been so helpful to have a calm, savvy person in my corner throughout all this. You constantly go the extra mile, push at the right times and in the right ways, and are always ready to help me navigate a publishing world that often seems wilfully arcane and confusing. Cheers also to Oliver Holms for the author photos. I've had lots of support and geeing up from friends and colleagues too. Some made encouraging noises when this was just a half-formed idea I would hesitantly disclose in a pub. Others enthusiastically banged the drum for me in that frantic period between reveal and publication. All were appreciated. I'm particularly thankful to Dipo Faloyin and Julian Obubo, for reading draft chapters and offering invaluable feedback and considered notes.

I really have to thank my family too. A scattered network of people who, in true Nigerian fashion, are too numerous to name or reliably count but have all played their part in moulding me and the worldview that fuels this work. To the aunties and uncles that have really been more like additional parents. To my brothers, Folarin and Ray, who have the most cause to quibble with my version of events but, hopefully, will recognise them. To my children, Dylan and Remi. I am so unbelievably proud of you and can't believe I get to be dad to such confident, fiercely independent, intelligent, principled and creative kids. You both wear your Africanness and Britishness (and all the other non-conforming sides of yourselves) with such unabashed pride that it fills me with hope that many of the struggles of the past won't be part of the future.

Then there is my wife, Madeleine. The demands of writing *Settlers* pretty much deprived you of a husband for long stretches of the past year. I morphed, at times, from an engaged, present co-parent into an emotionally fragile, over-caffeinated desk goblin, hemmed in by research texts and biscuit wrappers. It would have been completely understandable for you to have absolutely had enough of me and this all-consuming project of mine. And yet, throughout it all, you were supportive and understanding and talked me down from multiple figurative ledges. You have been creative sounding board, cheerleader, and cackling accomplice through the exhausting absurdities of bringing this thing to life. Words can't really express how much I love and appreciate every bit of you.

This would be the part of an awards show where they cranked up the music to get me off the stage. But the final, and maybe most significant thanks goes to my mother, Kofo Famurewa. Throughout the research of this book she was my constant advisor, fixer and, now and again, high-maintenance plus one. She is the reason I'm an African Londoner. I would not be the person I am or have the perspective that I do if it wasn't for her years of struggle, sacrifice and wise counsel. She did the job of two parents with determination and grace, supporting not just me and my brothers but any number of others in our family; giving and cooking and remembering birthdays with eerie accuracy, even when she had very little and anger or selfishness would have been perfectly reasonable. She blazed a trail in an unfamiliar country yet never let us forget who we were. Thank you for all of it, ma. Sorry for all the long *oyinbo* words. I understand our story that little bit better now and I hope I have done it justice and done us proud.

Index